D1055686

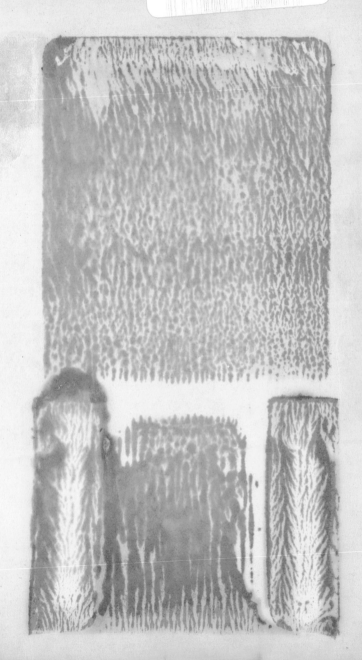

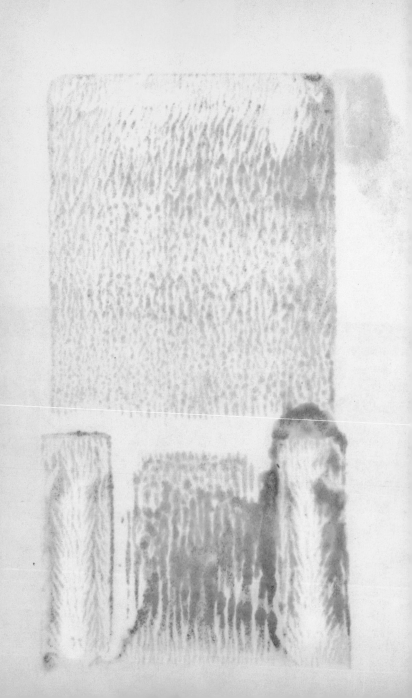

THE SUPREME COURT
AND
AMERICAN ECONOMIC LIFE

CLASH OF ISSUES

. . . But a Constitution is not intended to embody a particular economic theory, whether of paternalism . . . or of laissez faire. *. . .*

> —Mr. Justice Holmes, dissenting in
> *Lochner* v. *New York,* 198 U.S. 45 (1904)

It is urged that the question involved should now receive fresh considerations, among other reasons because of the "economic conditions that have supervened"; but the meaning of the Constitution does not change with the ebb and flow of economic events. . . .

> —Mr. Justice Sutherland, dissenting in *West Coast Hotel Co.* v. *Parrish,* 300 U.S. 379 (1937)

The Supreme Court

and

American Economic Life

Edited with introduction
and notes by

BENJAMIN MUNN ZIEGLER

Amherst College

ROW, PETERSON AND COMPANY

Evanston, Illinois   Elmsford, New York

Table of Contents

v

Federal Action

PART IV: 1932—

Table of Cases

(Boldface page references are to opinions and case abstracts, all others to citations and text references only.)

Introduction

When "the Representatives of the united States of America, in General Congress, Assembled," dissolved "the political bands which [had] connected them with another," they also maintained "that as Free and Independent States, they have full Power to levy War, conclude Peace, contract Alliances, establish Commerce, and to do all other Acts and Things which Independent States may of right do." [1] One of the "Things" they ultimately did was to establish a government, the fundamentals of which were set down in a written constitution and which, by its own terms, was to "be the supreme Law of the Land." [2] Once it is acknowledged and accepted that the Constitution is law, and "supreme Law" at that, there is implied not only that ours was to be a "government of laws, not men" but that, among other things an independent judicial system was necessary to "reduce the broad statements of the Constitution to a form applicable to particular cases; [to] determine the source of powers sought to be exercised by the government and, by construing the relevant provisions, decide how far those powers extend; [and] at all times [to] be prepared to protect individual rights against arbitrary government action." [3] Accordingly, Article III of the Constitution provided that "the judicial Power of the United States, shall be vested in one supreme Court, and in such inferior Courts as the Congress may from time to time ordain and establish," and that "the judicial Power shall extend to all Cases, in Law and Equity, arising under this Constitution, the Laws of the United States, and Treaties made, or which shall be made, under their Authority. . . ."

Despite all this, Alexander Hamilton, writing in *The Federalist*, No. 78, maintained "that the judiciary is beyond comparison the weakest of the three departments . . . [that] from the nature of its functions, it will always be the least dangerous to the political rights of the Constitution, because it will be least in a capacity to annoy or injure them." Pointing out that the "Executive not only dispenses the honors, but holds the sword of the community [while] the legislative not only commands the purse, but prescribes the rules by which the

[1] The Declaration of Independence.
[2] Constitution of the United States, Art. VI, cl. 2.
[3] Mason and Beaney, *American Constitutional Law* (New York: Prentice-Hall, Inc., 1954), p. 9.

1

duties and rights of every citizen are to be regulated . . . the judiciary, on the contrary has no influence over either the sword or the
purse; no direction either of the strength or of the wealth of the
society; and can take no active resolution whatever," he concluded
that "it may be truly said to have neither *Force nor Will* but merely
judgment; and must ultimately depend upon the aid of the executive
arm even for the efficacy of its judgment." Small wonder, then, that
President Jackson thirty years after was reputed to have said of a
decision of the Supreme Court, "John Marshall has made his decision,
now let him enforce it." And, again, on another occasion, in his Veto
of the Bank Bill, July 10, 1832, ". . . The opinion of the Supreme
Court . . . ought not to control the coordinate authorities of this
Government. The Congress, the Executive, and the Court must each
for itself be guided by its own opinion of the Constitution. . . . The
authority of the Supreme Court must not, therefore, be permitted to
control the Congress, or the Executive, when acting in their legislative capacities but to have only such influence as the force of their
reasoning may declare." [4]

While Jackson's statement sets up for us as clearly as can be done
a basic factor of our governmental system, namely, the doctrine of
separation of powers, it also raises another of vital importance and
significance—that of judicial review. For even granting the equal power
of the "coordinate authorities" (and here we may even include the
doctrine of federalism and accept the states as a coordinate authority
as well) the question still remains as to who is to determine whether
these authorities have been acting in their legal capacities, and what
consequences will flow if they have not. These and similar questions
were, in a measure, anticipated by the Founding Fathers. Again *The
Federalist*, No. 78, sets forth the problem: "Some perplexity respecting the rights of the courts to pronounce legislative acts void, because
contrary to the Constitution, has arisen from an imagination that the
doctrine would imply a superiority of the judiciary to the legislative
power . . . [for] it is urged that the authority which can declare the
acts of another void, must necessarily be superior to the one whose
acts may be declared void." But to Hamilton, this was a "red herring"
of the 1787 variety, for there was no clearer principle than the one
which states that "no legislative act contrary to the Constitution can
be valid . . . [and] that the Courts were designed to be an intermediate body between the people and the legislature . . . [so that]
the representatives of the people could [not] substitute their will to
that of the constituents." And this to him did not "by any means
suppose a superiority of the judicial to the legislative power . . .
[rather] it supposes that the power of the people is superior to both;
and that where the will of the legislature, declared in its statutes,
stands in opposition to that of the people, declared in the Constitu-

tion, the judges ought to be governed by the latter rather than the former . . . they ought to regulate their decisions by fundamental laws, rather than by those which are not fundamental." How and why the Justices of the Court are better able to reflect the thoughts and feelings of the American people than are their duly elected representatives Hamilton does not make clear, but that there is a further interplay between the judicial power and the political forces cannot be denied for amendments, new legislation, and public opinion can still be invoked albeit through processes that seem somewhat cumbersome.

But to the statement of Hamilton in *The Federalist* can be added much further historical evidence. This power of the Courts "to pronounce legislative acts void" was explicitly discussed and accepted in at least seven state ratifying conventions. The first Congress wrote judicial review of state measures into Section 25 of the Judiciary Act of 1789. And the congressional debates on the Repeal Act of 1802 leave no doubt that judicial review of national legislation was generally accepted and contemplated as part of our scheme of government. Yet every era has had its conflicts with this doctrine and the more difficult the era the greater the conflict. Lincoln, for example, in his First Inaugural Address, March 4, 1861 said: "I do not forget the position assumed by some that constitutional questions are to be decided by the Supreme Court . . . [but] at the same time, the candid citizen must confess that if the policy of the Government upon vital questions affecting the whole people is to be irrevocably fixed by decisions of the Supreme Court, the instant they are made in ordinary litigation between parties in personal actions the people will have ceased to be their own rulers, having to that extent practically resigned their Government into the hands of that eminent tribunal." [5] And in more recent days the attempt by President Roosevelt to "pack" the Supreme Court because, among other things, "in the uncertain state of the law, it is not difficult for the ingenious to devise novel reasons for attacking the validity of new legislation or its application . . . [and] while these questions are laboriously brought to issue and debated through a series of courts, the government must stand aside [despite the fact] that Congress enacted the law, that the Executive has signed it and that the Administrative machinery is waiting to function" [6] is still another reminder that the conflict is a continuing one.

What keeps the battle alive and makes it almost appear new to each generation? That courts are vital to our democratic system based on the "rule of law" is too obvious to warrant further comment. For that matter so are legislative bodies and an executive necessary to maintain our "representative government." The real problem, it would seem, concerns itself rather with the fact that the Constitution seldom pro-

[5] Vol. 6 Richardson, *supra*, 5, 9–10 (1897).
[6] President Roosevelt's Court Message, Washington, Feb. 5, 1937.

vides obvious answers to the important and significant problems of the day. Moreover, precedent (*stare decisis*), while useful as a general guide, must sometimes yield to the pressure of events. In fact it can be argued that if the Constitution were always fully explicit, we would need no Supreme Court: it is not a matter requiring court adjudication to understand that there shall be two houses in the Congress or that the term of office for senators shall be six years. The crux, then, seems to be this: Is the accommodation of modern needs to ancient traditions, is reconciliation of stability and change, essentially a judicial or a political function? And while, in reality, we in the United States do not cling exclusively to one or the other, in practice the effect of the influence of the former over the latter is much more pronounced than the other way around.

That gifted young European observer of American life, Alexis de Tocqueville, saw this challenge as early as 1835 when he characterized the judge in our system as "one brought into the political [or economic, or social] arena independently of his own will. He only judges the law because he is obliged to judge a case; the political [or economic, or social] question he is called upon to resolve is connected with the interest of the parties and he (the judge) cannot refuse to decide it without abdicating the duties of his post." [7] And by the same token, as Mr. Justice Jackson observed when the Court was asked to "interpret" the constitutional restraint upon an establishment of religion: "It is idle to pretend that this task is one for which we can find in the Constitution one word to help us as judges to decide where the secular ends and the sectarian begins in education. Nor can we find guidance in any other legal source." [8] But the fact remains that it is precisely in such cases (and these include problems of economic, social, and political values as well) that the Court is expected to give a decision, or else it would, as de Tocqueville has suggested, abdicate its duties. Where are to be found the criteria for judgment? Where are the values by which to apply a document written in 1789 with its standards and mores to the dynamic society of yesterday or the nuclear society of today? And this becomes even a greater matter of concern when we remember as Frankfurter did when he was *Professor* Frankfurter: "That the courts are especially fitted to be the ultimate arbiters of policy is an intelligent and tenable doctrine. But let them and us face the fact that five Justices of the Supreme Court *are* conscious molders of policy instead of the impersonal vehicles of revealed truth." [9]

---

[7] Alexis de Tocqueville, *Democracy in America*, text by Henry Reeves; revised by Francis Bowen; further corrected by Phillips Bradley (New York: Alfred A. Knopf, Inc., 1945), p. 1.

[8] *McCullum* v. *Board of Education*, 333 U.S. 203, 237–38 (1948).

[9] Felix Frankfurter, *Law and Politics*, ed. by Archibald MacLeish and E. F. Prichard (New York: Harcourt, Brace and Company, 1939), p. 26.

Given this situation we must accept as fact that judges do err from time to time; and that once in a great while they even err grievously. And perhaps these errors tend to magnify the problem because, as Lord Bryce has observed, we Americans tend to confuse constitutionality with desirability and usefulness and hence are apt to assume that where a court majority has held a law unconstitutional it was by definition socially or economically or politically undesirable and, conversely, that where a law has been held valid and constitutional it is therefore by definition socially or economically or politically desirable and useful and necessary. In the final analysis perhaps Holmes's admonition that "the life of the law has not been logic: it has been experience," [10] can serve us well.

The cases in this collection of readings concentrate on *economic* problems though, of course, these are not so distinct as not to have, at times, political and/or social overtones. But they do express the attitude of the Court as to fundamental changes in our social and economic structure as they have emerged and developed from the very beginning. While the cases presented are put into separate sections to indicate limits of time which for obvious reasons are important in understanding these changes, it must be borne in mind that eras seldom emerge or close with neat lines, and that the United States did not change overnight when, for example, the 14th Amendment was passed. The hope also is that enough cases are presented to demonstrate one very important idea: namely, that the protection of property has been a constant concern of the Supreme Court, and that the Court has used a great variety of arguments to protect property. It must be understood that the Court has never had to defend the principle of property itself: no agency of government—state or federal—has contrived schemes to nationalize or collectivize, abolish or expropriate, private property. Rather, it has been, from the beginning, a question of state and federal intervention to *regulate* property in the name of some rough conception of the common good or the general welfare, or in behalf of some majority interest. And this regulation has involved certain restrictions on freedom of contract, on the absolute right of every man to do what he wants with his own.

If one does not find the cases included herein exciting because of their contribution, or lack thereof, to what we euphemistically call the "American way of life," many of them are great works of legal literature in and of themselves and perhaps can be appreciated on that score alone. But from whatever viewpoint they are approached (and there are many possible viewpoints) it should be obvious that there is much in what Charles Warren wrote: "The history of the United States has been written not merely in the halls of Congress, in the Executive offices, and on the battlefield, but *to a great extent*

[10] Oliver Wendell Holmes, *The Common Law* (Boston: Little, Brown & Company, 1881), p. 1.

in the chambers of the Supreme Court of the United States." [11]
And if there be some need for humor to balance our thoughts as we
tackle the seriousness of the problems with which this book is concerned, we can do no better than to quote the Lord Chancellor in
Iolanthe:

> *The Law is the embodiment*
> *Of everything that's excellent.*
> *It has no kind of fault or flaw,*
> *And I, my Lords, embody the Law.*[12]

and ponder whether it is really so.

[11] Charles Warren, *The Supreme Court in United States History* (2 vols.;
Boston: Little, Brown & Company, 1937), Vol. 1, p. 1.
[12] Gilbert and Sullivan, *Iolanthe*, Act 1.

Part I: The Supreme Court
and Judicial Review

Part II: The Supreme Court

and Judicial Review

MARBURY v. MADISON

1 Cranch 137, 2 L.Ed. 60 (1803)

So much has been written about the instant case that it is difficult if not impossible, to begin with a dimension that is at once new or startling. Yet it is a fact, and it cannot be avoided, that no real understanding of the subject matter of this book, or any other that affects our "American way of life" can begin without it. On its face there would appear little reason for the case to become the cause célèbre of American jurisprudence that it is. In its simplest terms it involved an original suit before the Supreme Court for an order to show cause why a writ of mandamus should not be granted requiring James Madison, Secretary of State under President Thomas Jefferson, to deliver a commission as justice of the peace to William Marbury (and three others as well). Stated this way the case is indeed pedestrian. Mandamus ("a high prerogative writ, usually issuing out of the highest court of general jurisdiction in a state, directed to any natural person, corporation, or inferior court of judicature within its jurisdiction, requiring them to do some particular thing therein specified and which appertains to their office or duty") was an accepted and ancient legal practice of long standing which "American" courts had carried over from their English heritage and long practiced. For that matter the office for which Marbury sought his commision was indeed a small one in the District of Columbia, and while all courts are vital to a society governed by "law" it cannot be conceived by any stretch of the imagination that chaos or anarchy would have resulted without it. Nor again, with all due respect to the persons involved, were they (aside from Marbury there were also Dennis Ramsay, Robert Hooe, and William Harper) of such legal talent, learning, and brilliance that their absence would darken what otherwise would be a brilliant judiciary—indeed if it were not for the case itself Marbury, like so many of his contemporaries, would have lived and passed on without even a footnote in the historical development of our country. Furthermore, Section 13 of the Judiciary Act of 1789 which granted power to the Supreme Court to issue writs of mandamus "in cases warranted by the principles and usages of law . . ." had actually been enforced by the Supreme Court as early as 1794—and by a Court which contained as justices three ex-members of the Philadelphia Convention. What, then, gives this case its position as an outstanding landmark in American constitutional development? What, then, permits a great student (Charles Warren) of the Court to say "it is difficult to imagine what the history of the country would have been" without it? To assert that as a result of this case the Court has been permitted to participate in the control and direction of the course of American economic and social development is, while true, to state a conclusion

9

which—because it is true and so relevant to all the pages that follow —needs more than the statement itself. The case, like all other cases, cannot be read in a vacuum. It becomes intelligible only if the circumstances from which it arose are read into it—or at least kept in mind while reading it.

Defeated in the election of 1800, the Federalists seemed to turn their attention to the judiciary which to many of them was "as good to the party as an election." Accordingly in the few months remaining before Jefferson and his Anti-Federalists took over, the Circuit Court Act of 1801 and the Organic Act of the District of Columbia, also of 1801, were passed. Both of these increased the number of judicial officeholders, the offices for which were to be filled by the Administration of President Adams—an Administration already repudiated at the polls. It was under these circumstances that Marbury was appointed ("midnight [outgoing] appointments") to his post as justice of the peace in the District of Columbia. To this must be added the fact, which in its own way heightens the drama, that President Adams had also appointed John Marshall, his then Secretary of State, as Chief Justice, and his holding of the two positions simultaneously must have created such a work load that Marbury failed to receive the formal commission of his appointment to office. When on March 4, 1801, Jefferson took over as President and ordered his Secretary of State, James Madison, not to deliver the commissions, the stage was set for the next act to begin—and this time in the legal arena. Marshall, to be sure, was not as trained in the law as was Story (Marshall only went to the William and Mary Law School for less than six weeks, during which period war and love both took much of his time), but he certainly knew enough about the law to realize that as a purely legal problem he could have simply decided the case, as he ultimately did anyway, on the basis of jurisdiction and no more. But this was not enough. For Marshall saw in the case an opportunity to do things which needed doing and which to him were of the utmost importance: to read to his cousin and political foe, Jefferson, a lecture on political power and its relationship to order in a society; to establish a connecting link between the judicial function and the policy-making function; to evaluate the democratic dualism of the will of the people and the rule of law; to breathe life and meaning into Article III of the Constitution by emphasizing the theory and practice of judicial independence; and to accept and restate (see The Federalist, No. 78) the idea of judicial review as an inherent power of the courts. The cumulative effect of all this was indeed overwhelming for it charted a direct course for the growth of the doctrine of judicial supremacy by which laws of either the state or nation may be declared unconstitutional if the Court sees fit, even when the case is not an open and shut one, and that such a decision by the Court is binding on other branches of the government. Small wonder then that Jefferson and the Anti-Federalists were beside themselves, calling it *"a high-handed exertion of Judiciary power," "the most daring attack which the annals of Federalism have yet exhibited," "a purely political move on the part of the Federalist Party . . . to scare off their opponents . . . ," and the like. Small wonder also that it marks the beginning of any real study concerning America and the American way of life.*

The following opinion* of the court was delivered by the CHIEF JUSTICE [MARSHALL]. . . .

The first object of inquiry is—Has the applicant a right to the commission he demands? . . . [The court finds that as Marbury's appointment was complete he has a right to the commission.]

2. This brings us to the second inquiry; which is: If he has a right, and that right has been violated, do the laws of this country afford him a remedy? . . . [The court finds that they do.]

3. It remains to be inquired whether he is entitled to the remedy for which he applies? This depends on 1st. The nature of the writ applied for; and 2d. The power of this court.

1st. The nature of the writ. . . . This, then, is a plain case for a *mandamus*, either to deliver the commission, or a copy of it from the record; and it only remains to be inquired, whether it can issue from this court.

The act to establish the judicial courts of the United States authorizes the supreme court "to issue writs of *mandamus*, in cases warranted by the principles and usages of law, to any courts appointed, or persons holding office, under the authority of the United States." . . . The constitution vests the whole judicial power of the United States in one supreme court, and such inferior courts as congress shall, from time to time, ordain and establish. This power is expressly extended to all cases arising under the laws of the United States; and consequently, in some form, may be exercised over the present case; because the right claimed is given by a law of the United States.

In the distribution of this power, it is declared, that "the supreme court shall have original jurisdiction, in all cases affecting ambassadors, other public ministers and consuls, and those in which a state shall be a party. In all other cases, the supreme court shall have appellate jurisdiction." . . . If it had been intended to leave it in the discretion of the legislature, to apportion the judicial power between the supreme and inferior courts, according to the will of that body, it would certainly have been useless to have proceeded further than to have defined the judicial power, and the tribunals in which it should be vested. The subsequent part of the section is mere surplusage—is

* Editor's Note.—In order to preserve the flavor and tone of the cases in their original form they are reproduced in this book verbatim: but wherever some portions of any case have been omitted for the sake of simplicity, these are indicated by the use of ellipses; and wherever some words have been interpolated for the sake of clarity, these are indicated by the use of brackets.

entirely without meaning, if such is to be the construction. If congress remains at liberty to give this court appellate jurisdiction, where the constitution has declared their jurisdiction shall be original; and original jurisdiction where the constitution has declared it shall be appellate; the distribution of jurisdiction, made in the constitution, is form without substance. . . . To enable this court, then, to issue a *mandamus*, it must be shown to be an exercise of appellate jurisdiction, or to be necessary to enable them to exercise appellate jurisdiction. . . . It is the essential criterion of appellate jurisdiction, that it revises and corrects the proceedings in a cause already instituted, and does not create that cause. Although, therefore, a *mandamus* may be directed to courts, yet to issue such a writ to an officer, for the delivery of a paper, is, in effect, the same as to sustain an original action for that paper, and therefore, seems not to belong to appellate, but to original jurisdiction. Neither is it necessary in such a case as this, to enable the court to exercise its appellate jurisdiction. The authority, therefore, given to the supreme court, by the act establishing the judicial courts of the United States, to issue writs of *mandamus* to public officers, appears not to be warranted by the constitution; and it becomes necessary to inquire whether a jurisdiction so conferred can be exercised.

The question, whether an act, repugnant to the constitution, can become the law of the land, is a question deeply interesting to the United States: but, happily, not of an intricacy proportioned to its interest. It seems only necessary to recognize certain principles, supposed to have been long and well established, to decide it. That the people have an original right to establish, for their future government, such principles as, in their opinion, shall most conduce to their own happiness, is the basis on which the whole American fabric has been erected. The exercise of this original right is a very great exertion; nor can it, nor ought it, to be frequently repeated. The principles, therefore, so established, are deemed fundamental: and as the authority from which they proceed is supreme, and can seldom act, they are designed to be permanent.

This original and supreme will organizes the government, and assigns to different departments their respective powers. It may either stop here, or establish certain limits not to be transcended by those departments. The government of the United States is of the latter description. The powers of the legislature are defined and limited; and that those limits may not be mistaken, or forgotten, the constitution is written. To what purpose are powers limited, and to what purpose is that limitation committed to writing, if these limits may, at any time, be passed by those intended to be restrained? The distinction between a government with limited and unlimited powers is abolished, if those limits do not confine the persons on whom they are imposed, and if acts prohibited and acts allowed, are of equal obligation. It is a proposition too plain to be contested, that the constitution controls any legislative act repugnant to it; or that the legislature may alter the constitution by an ordinary act.

Between these alternatives, there is no middle ground. The constitution is either a superior paramount law, unchangeable by ordinary means, or it is on a level with ordinary legislative acts; and, like other acts, is alterable when the legislature shall please to alter it. If the former part of the alternative be true, then a legislative act, contrary to the constitution, is not law; if the latter part be true, then written constitutions are absurd attempts, on the part of the people, to limit a power, in its own nature, illimitable.

Certainly, all those who have framed written constitutions contemplate them as forming the fundamental and paramount law of the nation, and consequently, the theory of every such government must be, that an act of the legislature, repugnant to the constitution, is void. This theory is essentially attached to a written constitution, and is, consequently, to be considered, by this court, as one of the fundamental principles of our society. It is not, therefore, to be lost sight of, in the further consideration of this subject.

If an act of the legislature, repugnant to the constitution, is void, does it, notwithstanding its invalidity, bind the courts, and oblige them to give it effect? Or, in other words, though it be not law, does it constitute a rule as operative as if it was a law? This would be to overthrow, in fact, what was established in theory; and would seem, at first view, an absurdity too gross to be insisted on. It shall, however, receive a more attentive consideration.

It is, emphatically, the province and duty of the judicial department, to say what the law is. Those who apply the rule to particular cases, must of necessity expound and interpret that rule. If two laws conflict with each other, the courts must decide on the operation of each. So, if a law be in opposition to the constitution; if both the law and the constitution apply to a particular case, so that the court must either decide that case, conformably to the law, disregarding the constitution; or conformably to the constitution, disregarding the law; the court must determine which of these conflicting rules governs the case: this is of the very essence of judicial duty. If then, the courts are to regard the constitution, and the constitution is superior to any ordinary act of the legislature, the constitution, and not such ordinary act, must govern the case to which they both apply.

Those, then, who controvert the principle, that the constitution is to be considered, in court, as a paramount law, are reduced to the necessity of maintaining that courts must close their eyes on the constitution, and see only the law. This doctrine would subvert the very foundation of all written constitutions. It would declare that an act which, according to the principles and theory of our government, is entirely void, is yet, in practice, completely obligatory. It would declare, that if the legislature shall do what is expressly forbidden, such act, notwithstanding the express prohibition, is in reality effectual. It would be giving to the legislature a practical and real omnipotence, with the same breath which professes to restrict their powers within narrow limits. It is prescribing limits, and declaring that those limits may be passed at pleasure. That it thus reduces to nothing, what we have deemed the greatest improvement on political institutions, a written constitution, would, of itself, be sufficient, in America, where written constitutions have been viewed with so much reverence, for rejecting the construction. But the peculiar expressions of the constitution of the United States furnish additional arguments in favor of its rejection. The judicial power of the United States is extended to all cases arising under the constitution. Could it be the intention of those who gave this power, to say, that in using it, the constitution should not be looked into? That a case arising under the constitution should be decided, without examining the instrument under which it arises? This is too extravagant to be maintained. In some cases, then, the constitution must be looked into by the judges. And if they can open it at all, what part of it are they forbidden to read or to obey?

There are many other parts of the constitution which serve to illustrate this subject. It is declared, that "no tax or duty shall be laid on articles exported from any state." Suppose, a duty on the export of cotton, of tobacco, or of flour; and a suit instituted to recover it. Ought judgment to be rendered in such a case? ought the judges to close their eyes on the constitution, and only see the law?

The constitution declares "that no bill of attainder or *ex post facto* law shall be passed." If, however, such a bill should be passed, and a person should be prosecuted under it; must the court condemn to death those victims whom the constitution endeavors to preserve?

"No person," says the constitution, "shall be convicted of treason, unless on the testimony of two witnesses to the same overt act, or on confession in open court." Here, the language of the constitution is addressed especially to the courts. It prescribes, directly for them, a rule of evidence not to be departed from. If the legislature should change that rule, and declare one witness, or a confession out of court, sufficient for conviction, must the constitutional principle yield to the legislative act?

From these, and many other selections which might be made, it is apparent, that the framers of the constitution contemplated that instrument as a rule for the government of courts, as well as of the legislature. Why otherwise does it direct the judges to take an oath to support it? This oath certainly applies, in an especial manner, to their conduct in their official character. How immoral to impose it on them, if they were to be used as the instruments, and the knowing instruments, for violating what they swear to support!

The oath of office, too, imposed by the legislature, is completely demonstrative of the legislative opinion on this subject. It is in these words: "I do solemnly swear, that I will administer justice, without respect to persons, and do equal right to the poor and to the rich; and that I will faithfully and impartially discharge all the duties incumbent on me as ———, according to the best of my abilities and understanding, agreeable to the constitution and laws of the United States." Why does a judge swear to discharge his duties agreeably to the constitution of the United States, if that constitution forms no rule for his government? if it is closed upon him, and cannot be inspected by him? If such be the real state of things, this is worse than solemn mockery. To prescribe, or to take this oath, becomes equally a crime.

It is also not entirely unworthy of observation, that in declaring what shall be the supreme law of the land, the constitution itself is first mentioned; and not the laws of the United States, generally, but those only which shall be made in pursuance of the constitution, have that rank.

Thus, the particular phraseology of the constitution of the United States confirms and strengthens the principle, supposed to be essential to all written constitutions, that a law repugnant to the constitution is void; and that courts, as well as other departments, are bound by that instrument.

The rule must be discharged.

EAKIN v. RAUB

12 Sergeant and Rawle 330 (Pa.) (1825)

There can, of course, be little doubt but that Chief Justice Marshall, through the opportunities he opened for the judiciary in MARBURY v. MADISON *by, as one recent writer put it, "his courage, convictions, and intellectual vigor . . . raised the Supreme Court to a position of equality with the President and Congress." Nowhere in that decision, it should be recognized, does Marshall buttress his arguments by citing judicial authority. Rather he relies "on general intention" of the framers of the Constitution and a form of logic peculiarly his own, which means only "that judges are expert specialists in knowing or finding the law." The result is that it brings the courts into the political processes of government by having them, through this expertness, act as the final determinants of what legislative bodies have thought necessary, wise, and correct for the body politic. That this may be a desirable result is one thing. But whether it is an inevitable result is a far different thing. And the case below, though coming from a State Supreme Court and not the Supreme Court of the United States, addresses itself to that value. The facts of this case (an action of ejectment brought by Eakin*

*to which the defendant, Raub, pleaded the Statute of Limitations
as amended—an amendment which would have barred Eakin's
action at once unless he could show that a special clause protecting
persons living abroad was carried into the amendment) have been
for all practical purposes consigned to oblivion. Even the majority
decision written by Chief Justice Tilghman, holding that the saving
clause was retained, has been completely forgotten. Its real importance
lies in the dissenting opinion below, for it is generally recognized as
the most effective answer to Marshall's argument, in MARBURY v.
MADISON, supporting judicial review.*

GIBSON, J. . . .

I am aware that a right [in the judiciary] to declare all unconstitutional acts void . . . is generally held as a professional dogma;
but, I apprehend, rather as a matter of faith than of reason. I admit
that I once embraced the same doctrine, but without examination,
and I shall therefore state the arguments that impelled me to
abandon it, with great respect for those by whom it is still maintained.
But I may premise, that it is not a little remarkable, that although
the right in question has all along been claimed by the judiciary,
no judge has ventured to discuss it, except Chief Justice Marshall,
and if the argument of a jurist so distinguished for the strength of
his ratiocinative powers be found inconclusive, it may fairly be set
down to the weakness of the position which he attempts to defend. . . .

I begin, then, by observing that in this country, the powers of
the judiciary are divisible into those that are POLITICAL and those
that are purely CIVIL. Every power by which one organ of the
government is enabled to control another, or to exert an influence
over its acts, is a political power. . . . [The judiciary's] civil, are
its *ordinary* and *appropriate* powers; being part of its essence, and
existing independently of any supposed grant in the constitution.
But where the government exists by virtue of a *written* constitution,
the judiciary does not necessarily derive from that circumstance,
any other than its ordinary and appropriate powers. Our judiciary is
constructed on the principles of the common law, which enters so
essentially into the composition of our social institutions as to be
inseparable from them, and to be, in fact, the basis of the whole
scheme of our civil and political liberty. In adopting any organ or
instrument of the common law, we take it with just such powers and
capacities as were incident to it at the common law, except where
these are expressly, or by necessary implication, abridged or enlarged
in the act of adoption; and, that such act is a written instrument,
cannot vary its consequences or construction. . . . Now, what are
the powers of the judiciary at the common law? They are those that
necessarily arise out of its immediate business; and they are therefore commensurate only with the judicial execution of the municipal

law, or, in other words, with the administration of distributive justice, without extending to anything of a political cast whatever. . . . With us, although the legislature be the depository of only so much of the sovereignty as the people have thought fit to impart, it is nevertheless sovereign within the limit of its powers, and may relatively claim the same pre-eminence here that it may claim elsewhere. It will be conceded, then, that the ordinary and essential powers of the judiciary do not extend to the annulling of an act of the legislature. . . .

The constitution of *Pennsylvania* contains no express grant of political powers to the judiciary. But, to establish a grant by implication, the constitution is said to be a law of superior obligation; and, consequently, that if it were to come into collision with an act of the legislature, the latter would have to give way. This is conceded. But it is a fallacy, to suppose that they can come into collision *before the judiciary.* What is a constitution? It is an act of extraordinary legislation, by which the people establish the structure and mechanism of their government; and in which they prescribe fundamental rules to regulate the motion of the several parts. What is a statute? It is an act of ordinary legislation, by the appropriate organ of the government; the provisions of which are to be executed by the executive or judiciary, or by officers subordinate to them. The constitution, then, contains no practical rules for the administration of *distributive justice*, with which alone the judiciary has to do; these being furnished in acts of ordinary legislation, by that organ of the government, which, in this respect, is exclusively the representative of the people; and it is generally true, that the provisions of a constitution are to be carried into effect immediately by the legislature, and only mediately, if at all, by the judiciary. . . .

The constitution and the right of the legislature to pass the act, may be in collision. But is that a legitimate subject for judicial determination? If it be, the judiciary must be a peculiar organ, to revise the proceedings of the legislature, and to correct its mistakes; and in what part of the constitution are we to look for this proud pre-eminence? Viewing the matter in the opposite direction, what would be thought of an act of assembly in which it should be declared that the supreme court had, in a particular case, put a wrong construction on the constitution of the United States, and that the judgment should therefore be reversed? It would doubtless be thought a usurpation of judicial power. But it is by no means clear, that to declare a law void which has been enacted according to the forms prescribed in the constitution, is not a usurpation of legislative power. . . .

But it has been said to be emphatically the business of the judiciary, to ascertain and pronounce what the law is; and that this necessarily involves a consideration of the constitution. It does so: but how far? If the judiciary will inquire into anything besides the form of enactment, where shall it stop? There must be some point of limitation to such an inquiry; for no one will pretend that a judge would be justifiable in calling for the election returns, or scrutinizing the qualifications of those who composed the legislature. . . .

. . . In theory, all the organs of the government are of equal capacity; or, if not equal, each must be supposed to have superior capacity only for those things which peculiarly belong to it; and, as legislation peculiarly involves the consideration of those limitations which are put on the law-making power, and the interpretation of the laws when made, involves only the construction of the laws themselves, it follows that the construction of the constitution in this particular belongs to the legislature, which ought therefore to be taken to have superior capacity to judge of the constitutionality of its own acts. But suppose all to be of equal capacity in every respect, why should one exercise a controlling power over the rest? That the judiciary is of superior rank, has never been pretended, although it has been said to be co-ordinate. It is not easy, however, to comprehend how the power which gives law to all the rest, can be of no more than equal rank with one which receives it, and is answerable to the former for the observance of its statutes. Legislation is essentially an act of sovereign power. . . . It may be said, the power of the legislature, also, is limited by prescribed rules. It is so. But it is, nevertheless, the power of the people, and sovereign as far as it extends. It cannot be said, that the judiciary is co-ordinate merely because it is established by the constitution. . . . Inequality of rank arises not from the manner in which the organ has been constituted, but from its essence and the nature of its functions; and the legislative organ is superior to every other, inasmuch as the power to will and to command, is essentially superior to the power to act and to obey. . . .

Everyone knows how seldom men think exactly alike on ordinary subjects; and a government constructed on the principle of assent by all its parts, would be inadequate to the most simple operations. The notion of a complication of counter checks has been carried to an extent in theory, of which the framers of the constitution never dreamt. When the entire sovereignty was separated into its elementary parts, and distributed to the appropriate branches, all things incident to the exercise of its powers were committed to each branch exclusively. The negative which each part of the legislature may exercise, in regard to the acts of the other, was thought sufficient to prevent material infractions of the restraints which were put on the power of the whole; for, had it been intended to interpose the judiciary as an additional barrier, the matter would surely not have been left in doubt. The judges would not have been left to stand on the insecure and ever shifting ground of public opinion as to constructive powers; they would have been placed on the impregnable ground of an express grant. They would not have been compelled to resort to the debates in the convention, or the opinion that was generally entertained at the time. A constitution, or a statute, is supposed to contain the whole will of the body from which it emanated; and I would just as soon resort to the debates in the legislature for the construction of an act of assembly, as to the debates in the convention for the construction of the constitution.

The power is said to be restricted to cases that are free from doubt or difficulty. But the abstract existence of a power cannot depend on the clearness or obscurity of the case in which it is to be exercised; for that is a consideration that cannot present itself, before the question of the existence of the power shall have been determined; and, if its existence be conceded, no considerations of policy arising from the obscurity of the particular case, ought to influence the exercise of it. . . .

To say, therefore, that the power is to be exercised but in perfectly clear cases, is to betray a doubt of the propriety of exercising it at all. Were the same caution used in judging of the existence of the power that is inculcated as to the exercise of it, the profession would perhaps arrive at a different conclusion. The grant of a power so extraordinary ought to appear so plain, that he who should run might read. . . .

What I have in view in this inquiry, is the supposed right of the judiciary to interfere, in cases where the constitution is to be carried into effect through the instrumentality of the legislature, and where that organ must necessarily first decide on the constitutionality of its own act. The oath to support the constitution is not peculiar to the judges, but is taken indiscriminately by every officer of the government, and is designed rather as a test of the political principles of the man, than to bind the officer in the discharge of his duty: otherwise it is difficult to determine what operation it is to have in the case of a recorder of deeds, for instance, who, in the execution of his office, has nothing to do with the constitution. But granting it to relate to the official conduct of the judge, as well as every other officer, and not to his political principles, still it must be understood in reference to supporting the constitution, *only as far as that may be involved in his official duty*; and, consequently, if his official duty does not comprehend an inquiry into the authority of the legislature, neither does his oath. . . .

But do not the judges do a positive act in violation of the constitution, when they give effect to an unconstitutional law? Not if the law has been passed according to the forms established in the constitution. The fallacy of the question is, in supposing that the judiciary adopts the acts of the legislature as its own; whereas the enactment of a law and the interpretation of it are not concurrent acts, and as the judiciary is not required to concur in the enactment, neither is it in the breach of the constitution which may be the consequence of the enactment. The fault is imputable to the legislature, and on it the responsibility exclusively rests. . . .

But it has been said, that this construction would deprive the citizen of the advantages which are peculiar to a written constitution, by at once declaring the power of the legislature in practice to be illimitable. . . . But there is no magic or inherent power in parchment and ink, to command respect and protect principles from violation. In the business of government a recurrence to first principles answers the end of an observation at sea with a view to correct the dead reckoning; and for this purpose, a written constitution is an instrument of inestimable value. It is of inestimable value, also, in rendering its first principles familiar to the mass of people; for, after all, there is no effectual guard against legislative usurpation but public opinion, the force of which, in this country is inconceivably great. . . . Once let public opinion be so corrupt as to sanction every misconstruction of the constitution and abuse of power which the temptation of the moment may dictate, and the party which may happen to be predominant, will laugh at the puny efforts of a dependent power to arrest it in its course.

For these reasons, I am of opinion that it rests with the people, in whom full and absolute sovereign power resides, to correct abuses in legislation, by instructing their representatives to repeal the obnoxious act. What is wanting to plenary power in the government, is reserved by the people for their own immediate use; and to redress an infringement of their rights in this respect, would seem to be an accessory of the power thus reserved. It might, perhaps, have been better to vest the power in the judiciary; as it might be expected that its habits of deliberation, and the aid derived from the arguments of counsel, would more frequently lead to accurate conclusions. On the other hand, the judiciary is not infallible; and an error by it would admit of no remedy but a more distinct expression of the public will, through the extraordinary medium of a convention; whereas, an error by the legislature admits of a remedy by an exertion of the same will, in the ordinary exercise of right of suffrage,—a mode better calculated to attain the end, without popular excitement. It may be said, the people would probably not notice an error of their representatives. But they would as probably do so, as notice an error of the judiciary; and, besides, it is a postulate in the theory of our government, and the very basis of the superstructure, that the people are wise, virtuous, and competent to manage their own affairs; and if they are not so, in fact, still every question of this sort must be determined according to the principles of the constitution, as it came from the hands of the framers, and the existence of a defect which was not foreseen, would not justify those who administer the government, in applying a corrective in practice, which can be provided only by convention. . . .

But in regard to an act of [a state] assembly, which is found to be in collision with the constitution, laws, or treaties of the *United States*, I take the duty of the judiciary to be exactly the reverse. By becoming parties to the federal constitution, the states have agreed to several limitations of their individual sovereignty, to enforce which, it was thought to be absolutely necessary to prevent them from giving effect to laws in violation of those limitations, through the instrumentality of their own judges. Accordingly, it is declared in the sixth article and second section of the federal constitution, that "This constitution, and the laws of the *United States* which shall be made in pursuance thereof, and all treaties made, or which shall be made under the authority of the *United States,* shall be the *supreme* law of the land; and the *judges* in every *state* shall be BOUND thereby: any thing in the *laws* or *constitution* of any *state* to the contrary notwithstanding."

This is an express grant of a political power, and it is conclusive to show that no law of inferior obligation, as every state law must necessarily be, can be executed at the expense of the constitution, laws, or treaties of the *United States.* It may be said, these are to furnish a rule only when there is no state provision on the subject. But, in that view, they could with no propriety be called supreme; for supremacy is a relative term, and cannot be predicted of a thing which exists separately and alone: and this law, which is called supreme, would change its character and become subordinate as soon as it should be found in conflict with a state law. But the judges are to be bound by the federal constitution and laws, notwithstanding any thing in the constitution or laws of the particular state *to the contrary.* If, then, a state were to declare the laws of the *United States* not to be obligatory on her judges, such an act would unquestionably be void; for it will not be pretended, that any member of the union can dispense with the obligation of the federal constitution: and, if it cannot be done directly, and by a general declaratory law, neither can it indirectly, and by by-laws dispensing with it in particular cases. . . .

ASHWANDER v. T.V.A.

297 U.S. 288, 80 L.Ed. 688 (1936)

Together with FLETCHER v. PECK, *6 Cranch 87 (1810), the first clear-cut decision predicated on the assumption that the power of the Court to declare laws void applies to state legislation as well, the Courts, and particularly the Supreme Court, became a vital institution in the American governmental process. Indeed all that follows is a succession of concrete, specific, and realistic (the hope is that they are also important) instances (albeit limited to economic problems) of judicial governance and how American growth and development were shaped, guided, influenced, and directed by it.*

And because such participation and governance do not operate in a vacuum but rather on people, on property, and on interests, there is involved at the same time, as one recent writer has put it, "the necessity to avoid, if possible, head-on collisions with the dominant political forces of the moment; the undesirability of claiming too much too soon; the great advantage of taking the long view, especially when others take the short; the usefulness of diverting criticism from weakness to strength; the importance of identifying judicial claims to authority with the claims of the Constitution." This is, obviously, a formidable task. Nor has the Court been unaware of it. It is not enough to assert glibly as did Mr. Chief Justice Marshall that "judicial power, as contradistinguished from the power of the laws, has no existence. Courts are the mere instruments of the law, and can will nothing." (Cf. also Mr. Justice Roberts in the Butler case, p. 184.) Nor is it enough to say as Mr. Justice Stone said, "For the removal of unwise laws from the statute books appeal lies not to the courts but to the ballot and to the processes of democratic government. . . . Courts are not the only agency of government that must be assumed to have the capacity to govern." To walk the tightrope the Supreme Court has frequently called attention to the "gravity and delicacy" of its place and its function in its exercise of judicial review, and has over the years asserted self-imposed principles to guide them in their governance. Though the substantive issues in the case below challenge the validity of the Tennessee Valley Authority to commit the government of the United States to a permanent commercial utility business, its real value here is that it sets forth these accumulated self-imposed restraints and "ground rules" which the Court uses in its "delicate and difficult" function of judicial review. Only that part of the opinion is reproduced here which deals with these considerations.

Excerpt from the concurring opinion of MR. JUSTICE BRANDEIS in which JUSTICES STONE, ROBERTS, and CARDOZO joined:

"Considerations of propriety, as well as long-established practice, demand that we refrain from passing upon the constitutionality of an act of Congress unless obliged to do so in the proper performance of our judicial function, when the question is raised by a party whose interests entitle him to raise it." (*Blair* v. *United States*, 250 U.S. 273, 279)

The Court has frequently called attention to the "great gravity and delicacy" of its function in passing upon the validity of an act of Congress; and has restricted exercise of this function by rigid insistence that the jurisdiction of federal courts is limited to actual cases and controversies; and that they have no power to give advisory opinions. On this ground it has in recent years ordered the dismissal of several suits challenging the constitutionality of important acts of Congress. . . .

The Court developed, for its own governance in the cases confessedly within its jurisdiction, a series of rules under which it has avoided passing upon a large part of all the constitutional questions pressed upon it for decision. They are:

1. The Court will not pass upon the constitutionality of legislation in a friendly, nonadversary, proceeding, declining because to decide such questions "is legitimate only in the last resort, and as a necessity in the determination of real, earnest, and vital controversy between individuals. It never was the thought that, by means of a friendly suit, a party beaten in the legislature could transfer to the courts an inquiry as to the constitutionality of the legislative act." . . .

2. The Court will not "anticipate a question of constitutional law in advance of the necessity of deciding it." . . . "It is not the habit of the court to decide questions of a constitutional nature unless absolutely necessary to a decision of the case." . . .

3. The Court will not "formulate a rule of constitutional law broader than is required by the precise facts to which it is to be applied." . . .

4. The Court will not pass upon a constitutional question although properly presented by the record, if there is also present some other ground upon which the case may be disposed of. This rule has found most varied application. Thus, if a case can be decided on either of two grounds, one involving a constitutional question, the other a question of statutory construction or general law, the Court will decide only the latter. . . . Appeals from the highest court of a state challenging its decision of a question under the federal Constitution are frequently dismissed because the judgment can be sustained on an independent state ground. . . .

5. The Court will not pass upon the validity of a statute upon complaint of one who fails to show that he is injured by its operation. . . . Among the many applications of this rule, none is more striking than the denial of the right of challenge to one who lacks a personal or property right. Thus, the challenge by a public official interested only in the performance of his official duty will not be entertained. . . . In *Fairchild* v. *Hughes*, 258 U.S. 126, the Court affirmed the dismissal of a suit brought by a citizen who sought to have the Nineteenth Amendment declared unconstitutional. In *Massachusetts* v. *Mellon*, 262 U.S. 447, the challenge of the federal Maternity Act was not entertained although made by the commonwealth on behalf of all its citizens.

6. The Court will not pass upon the constitutionality of a statute at the instance of one who has availed himself of its benefits. . . .

7. "When the validity of an act of Congress is drawn in question, and even if a serious doubt of constitutionality is raised, it is a cardinal principle that this Court will first ascertain whether a construction of the statute is fairly possible by which the question may be avoided." . . .

Part II: 1789-1867

DARTMOUTH COLLEGE v. WOODWARD

4 Wheaton 518, 4 L.Ed. 629 (1819)

*Daniel Webster was only thirty-six when he argued this case
before the Supreme Court, yet his final sentence, "It is, sirs, a
small college, yet there are those who love it" is about the only
thing that most people remember about the case itself. That this
should be so is not at all surprising. Indeed the "college case," as
it was called at the time, aroused little if any attention from either
the legal profession or the general public. Few could see in the case
the constitutional seeds that were to nourish our future economic
development. And how could they? The case was dealt with as one
involving "the advancement of literature" and such terms as "literary
institution" and "literature in general" are sprinkled generously
throughout the opinion. Dartmouth College, whose motto is: "The
Voice of one crying in the Wilderness," was established in 1769
by a royal charter which provided, among other things, for a self-
perpetuating board of trustees to govern and manage it. Shortly after
the American Revolution, as the clientele changed from Indians to
another type completely, the College became enmeshed in New
Hampshire politics. The result was an Act passed in 1816 by which
the College was to be converted into a state university by placing
it under a Board of Overseers appointed by the state governor. The
old trustees, now ousted, brought suit to recover the college charter,
seal, and records, thus challenging directly the power of the state
legislature to enact such legislation. Though in the state court such
a challenge was on common law grounds, in the Supreme Court of
the United States the arguments were confined to a consideration
of the constitutional question alone—whether the state law was
an impairment of the obligation of contract under Article I, Section
10. There is no doubt that, from one point of view at least, the
case came at a most opportune time. Business corporations, canal,
road, and insurance companies were all seeking capital, and capital in
turn was seeking fields for investment if only it could be sure that
its investments would be secure and protected from partisan politics,
popular passions, or state legislatures reeking with fraud or capricious-
ness. From another point of view, the case afforded Marshall and
his Court another opportunity to reaffirm and restate, with greater
vigor and certitude because of the facts of this case, statements and
principles announced in FLETCHER V. PECK in 1810 (see 6 Cranch
87); and in NEW JERSEY V. WILSON in 1812 (see 7 Cranch 164).
But what is, for our purposes, perhaps most important of all, is
the fact that the cumulative result of these cases (together with
STURGES V. CROWNINSHIELD, 4 Wheaton 122) made the contract
clause the most powerful instrument for the safeguarding of vested*

private property rights which capitalists thought so vital to the economic development of our country. Indeed one writer (B. F. Wright, "The Contract Clause of the Constitution") points out that up to 1889 the contract clause had been considered in about 40 per cent of all the cases coming before the Supreme Court which involved the validity of state legislation; and that during this period the same clause was the constitutional doctrine on which the Supreme Court based its decisions invalidating seventy-five cases—just about half of all the cases it declared unconstitutional which involved state legislation. Nor is 1889 to be looked upon as an arbitrary date, for it was at that time that "substantive" due process under the Fourteenth Amendment came into its own.

The opinion of the Court was delivered by MR. CHIEF JUSTICE MARSHALL: . . .

It can require no argument to prove, that the circumstances of this case constitute a contract. An application is made to the crown for a charter to incorporate a religious and literary institution. In the application, it is stated that large contributions have been made for the object, which will be conferred on the corporation, as soon as it shall be created. The charter is granted, and on its faith the property is conveyed. Surely in this transaction every ingredient of a complete and legitimate contract is to be found.

The points for consideration are,

1. Is this contract protected by the Constitution of the United States?

2. Is it impaired by the [legislative] acts under which the defendant holds?

1. On the first point it has been argued, that the word "contract," in its broadest sense, would comprehend the political relations between the government and its citizens, would extend to offices held within a State for State purposes, and to many of those laws concerning civil institutions, which must change with circumstances, and be modified by ordinary legislation; which deeply concern the public, and which, to preserve good government, the public judgment must control. That even marriage is a contract, and its obligations are affected by the laws respecting divorces. That the clause in the Constitution, if construed in its greatest latitude, would prohibit these laws. Taken in its broad unlimited sense, the clause would be unprofitable and vexatious interference with the internal concerns of a State, would unnecessarily and unwisely embarrass its legislation, and render immutable those civil institutions, which are established for purposes of internal government, and which, to subserve those purposes, ought to vary with varying circumstances. That as the framers of the Constitution could never have intended to insert in that instrument a provision so unnecessary, so mischievous, and so

repugnant to its general spirit, the term "contract" must be understood in a more limited sense. That it must be understood as intended to guard against a power of at least doubtful utility, the abuse of which had been extensively felt; and to restrain the legislature in future from violating the right to property. That anterior to the formation of the Constitution, a course of legislation had prevailed in many, if not in all, of the States, which weakened the confidence of man in man, and embarrassed all transactions between individuals by dispensing with a faithful performance of engagements. To correct this mischief, by restraining the power which produced it, the State legislatures were forbidden "to pass any law impairing the obligation of contracts," that is, of contracts respecting property, under which some individual could claim a right to something beneficial to himself; and that since the clause in the Constitution must in construction receive some limitation, it may be confined, and ought to be confined, to cases of this description; to cases within the mischief it was intended to remedy.

The general correctness of these observations cannot be controverted. That the framers of the Constitution did not intend to restrain the States in the regulation of their civil institutions, adopted for internal government, and that the instrument they have given us, is not to be so construed, may be admitted. The provision of the Constitution never has been understood to embrace other contracts, than those which respect property, or some object of value, and confer rights which may be asserted in a court of justice. It never has been understood to restrict the general right of the legislature to legislate on the subject of divorces. Those acts enable some tribunal, not to impair a marriage contract, but to liberate one of the parties because it has been broken by the other. When any State legislature shall pass an act annulling all marriage contracts, or allowing either party to annul it without the consent of the other, it will be time enough to inquire, whether such an act be constitutional. . . .

This is plainly a contract to which the donors, the trustees, and the crown (to whose rights and obligations New Hampshire succeeds) were the original parties. It is a contract made on a valuable consideration. It is a contract for the security and disposition of property. It is a contract on the faith of which real and personal estate has been conveyed to the corporation. It is then a contract within the letter of the Constitution, and within its spirit also, unless the fact that the property is invested by the donors in trustees, for the promotion of religion and education, for the benefit of persons who are perpetually changing, though the objects remain the same, shall create a particular exception taking this case out of the prohibition contained in the Constitution.

It is more than possible that the preservation of rights of this description was not particularly in the view of the framers of the

Constitution, when the clause under consideration was introduced into that instrument. It is probable that interferences of more frequent recurrence, to which the temptation was stronger, and of which the mischief was more extensive, constituted the great motive for imposing this restriction on the State legislatures. But although a particular and a rare case may not, in itself, be of sufficient magnitude to induce a rule, yet it must be governed by the rule, when established, unless some plain and strong reason for excluding it can be given. It is not enough to say, that this particular case was not in the mind of the Convention when the article was framed, nor of the American people when it was adopted. It is necessary to go further, and to say that, had this particular case been suggested, the language would have been so varied as to exclude it, or it would have been made a special exception. The case being within the words of the rule, must be within its operation likewise, unless there be something in the literal construction so obviously absurd or mischievous, or repugnant to the general spirit of the instrument, as to justify those who expound the Constitution in making it an exception. . . .

The opinion of the Court, after mature deliberation, is, that this is a contract, the obligation of which cannot be impaired, without violating the Constitution of the United States. This opinion appears to us to be equally supported by reason, and by the former decisions of this Court.

2. We next proceed to the inquiry, whether its obligation has been impaired by those acts of the legislature of New Hampshire, to which the special verdict refers.

From the review of this charter, which has been taken, it appears, that the whole power of governing the college, of appointing and removing tutors, of fixing their salaries, of directing the course of study to be pursued by the students, and of filling up vacancies created in their own body, was vested in the trustees. On the part of the crown it was expressly stipulated, that this corporation, thus constituted, should continue forever; and that the number of trustees should forever consist of twelve, and no more. By this contract the crown was bound, and could have made no violent alteration in its essential terms, without impairing its obligation.

By the revolution, the duties, as well as the powers, of government devolved on the people of New Hampshire. It is admitted, that among the latter was comprehended the transcendent power of parliament, as well as that of the executive department. It is too clear to require the support of argument, that all contracts, and rights, respecting property, remained unchanged by the revolution. The obligations then, which were created by the charter to Dartmouth College, were the same in the new, that they had been in the old government. The power of the government was also the same. A repeal of this charter at any time prior to the adoption of the present Constitution of the United States, would have been an extraordinary and unprecedented act of power, but one which could have been contested only by the restrictions upon the legislature, to be found in the constitution of the State. But the Constitution of the United States has imposed this additional limitation, that the legislature of a State shall pass no act "impairing the obligation of contracts."

It has been already stated, that the act "to amend the charter, and enlarge and improve the corporation of Dartmouth College," increases the number of trustees to twenty-one, gives the appointment of the additional members to the executive of the State, and creates a board of overseers, to consist of twenty-five persons, of whom twenty-one are also appointed by the executive of New Hampshire, who have power to inspect and control the most important acts of the trustees.

On the effect of this law [of 1816], two opinions cannot be entertained. Between acting directly, and acting through the agency of trustees and overseers, no essential difference is perceived. The whole power of governing the college is transferred from trustees appointed according to the will of the founder, expressed in the charter to the executive of New Hampshire. The management and application of the funds of this eleemosynary institution, which are payed by the donors in the hands of trustees named in the charter, and empowered to perpetuate themselves, are placed by this act under the control of the government of the State. The will of the State is substituted for the will of the donors, in every essential operation of the college. This is not an immaterial change. The founders of the college contracted not merely for the perpetual application of the funds which they gave to the object for which those funds were given; they contracted, also, to secure that application by the constitution of the corporation. They contracted for a system which should, as far as human foresight can provide, retain forever the government of the literary institution they had formed, in the hands of persons approved by themselves. This system is totally changed. The charter of 1769 exists no longer. It is reorganized; and reorganized in such a manner as to convert a literary institution, moulded according to the will of its founders, and placed under the control of private literary men, into a machine entirely subservient to the will of government. This may be for the advantage of this college in particular, and may be for the advantage of literature in general; but it is not according to the will of the donors, and is subversive of that contract on the faith of which their property was given. . . .

It results from this opinion, that the acts of the legislature of New Hampshire, which are stated in the special verdict found in this cause, are repugnant to the Constitution of the United States; and that the judgment on this special verdict ought to have been for the plaintiffs. The judgment of the State Court must, therefore, be reversed.

[JUSTICES WASHINGTON and STORY concurred in separate opinions. MR. JUSTICE DUVALL dissented without discussion.]

GIBBONS v. OGDEN

9 Wheaton 1, 6 L.Ed. 23 (1824)

That GIBBONS v. OGDEN *is one of the truly great landmarks in American constitutional development cannot be denied. It was, of course, the first case before the Supreme Court of the United States concerning the "commerce clause." But its greatness goes beyond that, for obviously there were other "firsts" before the Court which have now been assigned to oblivion. Its greatness rests on the fact that (1) it recognized the past ("the power over commerce . . . was one of the primary objects for which the people of America adopted their government"); (2) it was cognizant of its vitality even in 1824 in the development of America as a business and commercial power ("it describes the commercial intercourse between nations, and parts of nations, in all its branches"); (3) it set the stage for its result to weave its way and profoundly affect our whole future history as a nation ("commerce, as the word is used in the Constitution, is a unit, every part of which is indicated by the term"); (4) and finally, it helped to create the many future cases before the courts which involved not only commerce and state rights, but potential class distinctions as well for ("comprehensive as the word is . . . it does not [apply] to those [actions] which are completely within a particular state, which do not affect other states, and with which it is not necessary to interfere, for the purpose of executing some of the general powers of the government").*

Robert R. Livingston and Robert Fulton had been granted, through several acts of the New York Legislature, the right for the exclusive navigation of all the waters within the jurisdiction of that state, with boats moved by fire or steam, for a term of years which had not yet expired. This right had, by assignment, been received by Aaron Ogden. Gibbons operated two steamboats between New York and Elizabethtown, New Jersey; these boats had been duly enrolled and licensed under an Act of Congress (1 Stats. at Large, 305 cl. 8, passed 18th February 1793) entitled "an act for enrolling and licensing ships and vessels to be employed in the coasting trade and fisheries, and for regulating same." Claiming that this operation of Gibbons was a violation of the exclusive privilege conferred by the New York Legislature and now in the hands of Ogden, Ogden filed

*his bill in the Court of Chancery of New York praying an injunction
to restrain Gibbons from his activities. The injunction was granted
and was affirmed on appeal by Chancellor Kent, who maintained
that the Acts of the New York Legislature were not repugnant to
the Constitution and/or the laws of the United States. The case was
then brought to the Supreme Court by appeal.*

MARSHALL, CH. J., delivered the opinion of the court. . . .

The appellant contends, that this decree is erroneous, because
the laws which purport to give the exclusive privilege it sustains, are
repugnant to the constitution and the laws of the United States.

They are said to be repugnant—1st. To that clause in the constitution which authorizes congress to regulate commerce. 2d. To
that which authorizes congress to promote the progress of science
and useful arts.

The state of New York maintains the constitutionality of these
laws; and their legislature, their council of revision, and their judges,
have repeatedly concurred in this opinion. It is supported by great
names—by names which have all the titles to consideration that
virtue, intelligence and office can bestow. No tribunal can approach
the decision of this question without feeling a just and real respect
for that opinion which is sustained by such authority; but it is the
province of this court, while it respects, not to bow to it implicitly;
and the judges must exercise, in the examination of the subject,
that understanding which Providence has bestowed upon them,
with that independence which the people of the United States expect from this department of the government.

As preliminary to the very able discussions of the constitution,
which we have heard from the bar, and as having some influence
on its construction, reference has been made to the political situation
of these states, anterior to its formation. It has been said, that they
were sovereign, were completely independent, and were connected
with each other only by a league. This is true. But when these allied
sovereigns converted their league into a government, when they
converted their congress of ambassadors, deputed to deliberate on
their common concerns, and to recommend measures of general
utility, into a legislature, empowered to enact laws on the most
interesting subjects, the whole character in which the states appear,
underwent a change, the extent of which must be determined by
a fair consideration of the instrument by which that change was
effected.

This instrument contains an enumeration of powers expressly
granted by the people to their government. It has been said, that
these powers ought to be construed strictly. But why ought they to
be so construed? Is there one sentence in the constitution which
gives countenance to this rule? In the last of the enumerated powers,
that which grants, expressly, the means for carrying all others into

execution, congress is authorized "to make all laws which shall be necessary and proper" for the purpose. But this limitation on the means which may be used, is not extended to the powers which are conferred; nor is there one sentence in the constitution, which has been pointed out by the gentlemen of the bar, or which we have been able to discern, that prescribes this rule. We do not, therefore, think ourselves justified in adopting it. What do gentlemen mean, by a strict construction? If they contend only against that enlarged construction, which would extend words beyond their natural and obvious import, we might question the application of the term, but should not controvert the principle. If they contend for that narrow construction which, in support of some theory not to be found in the constitution, would deny to the government those powers which the words of the grant, as usually understood, import, and which are consistent with the general views and objects of the instrument—for that narrow construction, which would cripple the government, and render it unequal to the objects for which it is declared to be instituted, and to which the powers given, as fairly understood, render it competent—then we cannot perceive the propriety of this strict construction, nor adopt it as the rule by which the constitution is to be expounded. As men whose intentions require no concealment, generally employ the words which most directly and aptly express the ideas they intend to convey, the enlightened patriots who framed our constitution, and the people who adopted it, must be understood to have employed words in their natural sense, and to have intended what they have said. If, from the imperfection of human language, there should be serious doubts respecting the extent of any given power, it is a well settled rule, that the objects for which it was given, especially, when those objects are expressed in the instrument itself, should have great influence in the construction. We know of no reason for excluding this rule from the present case. The grant does not convey power which might be beneficial to the granter, if retained by himself, or which can enure solely to the benefit of the grantee; but is an investment of power for the general advantage; in the hands of agents selected for that purpose; which power can never be exercised by the people themselves, but must be placed in the hands of agents, or lie dormant. We know of no rule for construing the extent of such powers, other than is given by the language of the instrument which confers them, taken in connection with the purposes for which they were conferred.

The words are: "congress shall have power to regulate commerce with foreign nations, and among the several states, and with the Indian tribes." The subject to be regulated is commerce; and our constitution being, as was aptly said at the bar, one of enumeration, and not of definition, to ascertain the extent of the power, it becomes necessary to settle the meaning of the word. The counsel for the appellee would limit it to traffic, to buying and selling, or the interchange of commodities, and do not admit that it comprehends navigation. This would restrict a general term, applicable to many objects, to one of its significations. Commerce, undoubtedly, is traffic, but it is something more—it is intercourse. It describes the commercial intercourse between nations, and parts of nations, in all its branches, and is regulated by prescribing rules for carrying on that intercourse. The mind can scarcely conceive a system for regulating commerce between nations which shall exclude all laws concerning navigation, which shall be silent on the admission of the vessels of the one nation into the ports of the other, and be confined to prescribing rules for the conduct of individuals, in the actual employment of buying and selling or of barter.

If commerce does not include navigation, the government of the Union has no direct power over that subject, and can make no law prescribing what shall constitute American vessels, or requiring that they shall be navigated by American seamen. Yet this power has been exercised with the consent of all, and has been understood by all to be a commercial regulation. All America understands, and has uniformly understood, the word "commerce," to comprehend navigation. It was so understood, and must have been so understood, when the constitution was framed. The power over commerce, including navigation, was one of the primary objects for which the people of America adopted their government, and must have been contemplated in forming it. The convention must have used the word in that sense, because all have understood it in that sense; and the attempt to restrict it comes too late. . . .

The word used in the constitution, then, comprehends, and has been always understood to comprehend, navigation within its meaning; and a power to regulate navigation, is as expressly granted, as if that term had been added to the word "commerce."

To what commerce does this power extend? The constitution informs us, to commerce "with foreign nations, and among the several states, and with the Indian tribes." It has, we believe, been universally admitted, that these words comprehend every species of commercial intercourse between the United States and foreign nations. No sort of trade can be carried on between this country and any other, to which this power does not extend. It has been truly said, that commerce, as the word is used in the constitution, is a unit, every part of which is indicated by the term.

If this be the admitted meaning of the word, in its application to foreign nations, it must carry the same meaning throughout the sentence, and remain a unit, unless there be some plain intelligible cause which alters it. The subject to which the power is next applied, is to commerce, "among the several states." The word "among" means intermingled with. A thing which is among others, is intermingled with them. Commerce among the states, cannot stop at the external boundary line of each state, but may be introduced into the interior. It is not intended to say, that these words comprehend that commerce, which is completely internal, which is carried on between man and man in a state, or between different parts of the same state, and which does not extend to or affect other states. Such a power would be inconvenient, and is certainly unnecessary. Comprehensive as the word "among" is, it may very properly be restricted to that commerce which concerns more states than one. . . . The completely internal commerce of a state, then, may be considered as reserved for the state itself.

But, in regulating commerce with foreign nations, the power of congress does not stop at the jurisdictional lines of the several states. It would be a very useless power, if it could not pass those lines. The commerce of the United States with foreign nations is that of the whole United States; every district has a right to participate in it. The deep streams which penetrate our country in every direction pass through the interior of almost every state in the Union, and furnish the means of exercising this right. If congress has the power to regulate it, that power must be exercised whenever the subject exists. If it exists within the states, if a foreign voyage may commence or terminate at a port within a state, then the power of congress may be exercised within a state.

This principle, is, if possible, still more clear, when applied to commerce "among the several states." They either join each other, in which case they are separated by a mathematical line, or they are remote from each other, in which case other states lie between them. What is commerce "among" them; and how is it to be conducted? Can a trading expedition between two adjoining states, commence and terminate outside of each? And if the trading intercourse be between two states remote from each other, must it not commence in one, terminate in the other, and probably pass through a third? Commerce among the states must, of necessity, be commerce with the states. In the regulation of trade with the Indian tribes, the action of the law, especially, when the constitution was made, was chiefly within a state. The power of congress, then, whatever it may be, must be exercised within the territorial jurisdiction of the several states. . . .

We are now arrived at the inquiry—what is this power? It is the power to regulate; that is, to prescribe the rule by which commerce is to be governed. This power, like all others vested in congress, is complete in itself, may be exercised to its utmost extent, and acknowledges no limitations, other than are prescribed in the constitution. These are expressed in plain terms, and do not affect the questions which arise in this case, or which have been discussed at the bar. If, as has always been understood, the sovereignty of congress, though limited to specified objects, is plenary as to those objects, the power over commerce with foreign nations, and among the several states, is vested in congress as absolutely as it would be in a single government, having in its constitution the same restrictions on the exercise of the power as are found in the constitution of the United States. The wisdom and the discretion of congress, their identity with the people, and the influence which their constituents possess at elections, are, in this, as in many other instances, as that, for example, of declaring war, the sole restraints on which they have relied, to secure them from its abuse. They are the restraints on which the people must often rely solely, in all representative governments. The power of congress, then, comprehends navigation, within the limits of every state in the Union; so far as that navigation may be, in any manner, connected with "commerce with foreign nations, or among the several states, or with the Indian tribes." It may, of consequence, pass the jurisdictional line of New York, and act upon the very waters to which the prohibition now under consideration applies. But it has been urged, with great earnestness, that although the power of congress to regulate commerce with foreign nations, and among the several states, be co-extensive with the subject itself, and have no other limits than are prescribed in the constitution, yet the states may severally exercise the same power, within their respective jurisdictions. In support of this argument, it is said, that they possessed it as an inseparable attribute of sovereignty, before the formation of the constitution, and still retain it, except so far as they have surrendered it by that instrument; that this principle results from the nature of the government, and is secured by the tenth amendment; that an affirmative grant of power is not exclusive, unless in its own nature it be such that the continued exercise of it by the former possessor is inconsistent with the grant, and that this is not of that description. The appellant, conceding these postulates, except the last, contends, that full power to regulate a particular subject, implies the whole power, and leaves no residuum; that a grant of the whole is incompatible with the existence of a right in another to any part of it. Both parties have appealed to the constitution, to legislative acts, and judicial decisions; and have drawn arguments from all these sources, to support and illustrate the propositions they respectively maintain. . . .

In discussing the question, whether this power [of regulating commerce] is still in the states, in the case under consideration, we may dismiss from it the inquiry, whether it is surrendered by the mere grant of congress, or is retained until congress shall exercise the power. We may dismiss that inquiry, because it has been exercised, and the regulations which congress deemed it proper to make, are now in full operation. The sole question is, can a state regulate commerce with foreign nations and among the states while congress is regulating it? . . .

In our complex system, presenting the rare and difficult scheme of one general government, whose action extends over the whole, but which possesses only certain enumerated powers; and of numerous state governments, which retain and exercise all powers not delegated to the Union, contests respecting power must arise. Were it even otherwise, the measures taken by the respective governments to execute their acknowledged powers, would often be of the same description, and might, sometimes, interfere. This, however, does not prove that the one is exercising, or has a right to exercise, the powers of the other. . . .

The act passed in 1803 (2 U.S. Stat. 205), prohibiting the importation of slaves into any state which shall itself prohibit their importation, implies, it is said, an admission that the states possessed the power to exclude or admit them; from which it is inferred, that they possess the same power with respect to other articles. If this inference were correct, if this power was exercised, not under any particular clause in the constitution, but in virtue of a general right over the subject of commerce, to exist as long as the constitution itself, it might now be exercised. Any state might now import African slaves into its own territory. But it is obvious, that the power of the states over this subject, previous to the year 1808, constitutes an exception to the power of congress to regulate commerce, and the exception is expressed in such words, as to manifest clearly the intention to continue the pre-existing right of the states to admit or exclude, for a limited period. The words are, "the migration or importation of such persons as any of the states, now existing, shall think proper to admit, shall not be prohibited by the congress, prior to the year 1808." The whole object of the exception is, to preserve the power of those states which might be disposed to exercise it; and its language seems to the court to convey this idea unequivocally. The possession of this particular power, then, during the time limited in the constitution, cannot be admitted to prove the possession of any other similar power.

It has been said that the act of August 7, 1789, acknowledges a concurrent power in the states to regulate the conduct of pilots, and hence is inferred an admission of their concurrent right with congress to regulate commerce with foreign nations, and amongst the states. But this inference is not, we think, justified by the fact. Although congress cannot enable a state to legislate, congress may adopt the provisions of a state on any subject. When the government of the Union was brought into existence, it found a system for the regulation of its pilots in full force in every state. The act which has been mentioned, adopts this system, and gives it the same validity as if its provisions had been specially made by congress. But the act, it may be said, is prospective also, and the adoption of laws to be made in future, presupposes the right in the maker to legislate on the subject. . . . But the adoption of the state system being temporary, being only "until further legislative provision shall be made by congress," shows, conclusively, an opinion, that congress could control the whole subject, and might adopt the system of the states, or provide one of its own. . . .

These acts were cited at the bar for the purpose of showing an opinion in congress, that the states possess, concurrently with the legislature of the Union, the power to regulate commerce with foreign nations and among the states. Upon reviewing them, we think, they do not establish the proposition they were intended to prove. They show the opinion, that the states retain powers enabling them to pass the laws to which allusion has been made, not that those laws proceed from the particular power which has been delegated to congress.

It has been contended by the counsel for the appellant, that, as the word "to regulate" implies in its nature, full power over the thing to be regulated, it excludes, necessarily, the action of all others that would perform the same operation on the same thing. That regulation is designed for the entire result, applying to those parts which remain as they were, as well as to those which are altered. It produces a uniform whole, which is as much disturbed and deranged by changing what the regulating power designs to leave untouched, as that on which it has operated. There is great force in this argument, and the court is not satisfied that it has been refuted.

Since, however, in exercising the power of regulating their own purely internal affairs, whether of trading or police, the states may sometimes enact laws, the validity of which depends on their interfering with, and being contrary to, an act of congress passed in pursuance of the constitution, the court will enter upon the inquiry, whether the laws of New York, as expounded by the highest tribunal of that state, have, in their application to this case, come into collision with an act of congress, and deprived a citizen of a right to which that act entitles him. Should this collision exist, it will be immaterial, whether those laws were passed in virtue of a concurrent power "to regulate commerce with foreign nations and among the several states," or, in virtue of a power to regulate their domestic trade and police. In one case and the other, the acts of New York must yield to the law of congress, and the decision sustaining the privilege they confer, against a right given by a law of the Union, must be erroneous. . . .

But if the license be a permit to carry on the coasting trade, the respondent denies that these boats were engaged in that trade, or that the decree under consideration has restrained them from prosecuting it. The boats of the appellant were, we are told, employed in the transportation of passengers; and this is no part of that commerce which congress may regulate.

If, as our whole course of legislation on this subject shows, the power of congress has been universally understood in America, to comprehend navigation, it is a very persuasive, if not a conclusive, argument, to prove that the construction is correct; and, if it be correct, no clear distinction is perceived between the power to regulate vessels employed in transporting men for hire, and property for hire. The subject is transferred to congress, and no exception to the grant can be admitted, which is not proved by the words, or the nature of the thing. A coasting vessel employed in the transportation of passengers, is as much a portion of the American marine, as one employed in the transportation of a cargo; and no reason is perceived, why such vessel should be withdrawn from the regulating power of that government, which has been thought best fitted for the purpose generally. . . .

. . . The questions, then, whether the conveyance of passengers be a part of the coasting trade, and whether a vessel can be protected in that occupation by a coasting license, are not, and cannot be, raised in this case. The real and sole question seems to be, whether a steam machine, in actual use, deprives a vessel of the privileges conferred by a license.

In considering this question, the first idea which presents itself is, that the laws of congress for the regulation of commerce, do not look to the principle by which vessels are moved. That subject is left entirely to individual discretion; and in that vast and complex system of legislative enactment concerning it, which embraces everything which the legislature thought it necessary to notice, there is not, we believe, one word respecting the peculiar principle by which vessels are propelled through the water, except what may be found in a single act, granting a particular privilege to steamboats. With this exception, every act, either prescribing duties, or granting privileges, applies to every vessel, whether navigated by the instrumentality of wind or fire, or sails or machinery. The whole weight of proof, then, is thrown upon him who would introduce a distinction to which the words of the law give no countenance. If a real difference could be admitted to exist between vessels carrying passengers and others, it has already been observed, that there is no fact in this case which can bring up that question. And if the occupation of steamboats be a matter of such general notoriety, that the court may be presumed to know it, although not specially informed by the record, then we deny that the transportation of passengers is their exclusive occupation. It is a matter of general history, that, in our western waters, their principal employment is the transportation of merchandise; and all know, that in the waters of the Atlantic they are frequently so employed.

But all inquiry into this subject seems to the court to be put completely at rest, by the act already mentioned, entitled, "an act for the enrolling and licensing of steamboats." This act authorizes a steamboat employed, or intended to be employed, only in a river or bay of the United States, owned wholly or in part by an alien, resident within the United States, to be enrolled and licensed as if the same belonged to a citizen of the United States. This act demonstrates the opinion of congress, that steamboats may be enrolled and licensed, in common with vessels using sails. They are, of course, entitled to the same privileges, and can no more be restrained from navigating waters, and entering ports which are free to such vessels, than if they were wafted on their voyage by the winds, instead of being propelled by the agency of fire. The one element may be as legitimately used as the other, for every commercial purpose authorized by the laws of the Union; and the act of a state inhibiting the use of either, to any vessel having a license under the act of congress, comes, we think, in direct collision with that act.

As this decides the cause, it is unnecessary to enter in an examination of that part of the constitution which empowers congress to promote the progress of science and the useful arts.

Reversed and annulled. . . .

[Mr. Justice Johnson delivered a concurring opinion.]

BROWN v. MARYLAND

12 Wheaton 419, 6 L.Ed. 678 (1827)

It is difficult to determine in advance what essential characteristics are needed to mark a case so "great" that any study of the topic with which it is involved would of necessity also include it. It might, of course, be the subject matter itself; or it might be that it brings some new dimension to an already important subject; or it might be that counsel in the case sit, in later life, on the very Court they tried (successfully or unsuccessfully) to convince to their point of view; or it might be that what the Court said in passing about the case (dicta) becomes more vital than the holding in the case itself; or it might be that certain parts of the decision in the case are used as a point of departure for other and later decisions, thus either limiting or expanding the holding in the case itself; or it might be because the Court seems to be going out of its way to declare an act constitutional because of the Court's own economic predilections. In the light of many of these considerations, the case below, whose facts are sufficiently set forth in the opinion itself, merits thought, evaluation, and consideration. Certainly on its face it concerns the all-important problem of interstate commerce and state taxation. It adds some new dimensions in that it discusses in particular terms just where federal control over commerce ends so that state control may begin, thus making the decision acceptable to the business interests on both the national and local level. It creates a fundamental decision in American constitutional law; yet as one writer puts it, it [the principle of constitutional law] "started life . . . [with] a dictum unnecessary to the decision of the case, a rule regarded by its author [Marshall] as premature, a doctrine weakened by a telltale 'perhaps' in its middle." It says, and again parenthetically, (in a dictum) that it "supposes" the principles set forth will apply also, and "equally" at that, to goods coming from a "sister state," thus permitting future Courts to draw vital distinctions between different kinds of importations (see, for example, Wood-

RUFF V. PARHAM, 1869, 8 *Wallace* 123). *It marks the first time that Roger B. Taney, appearing for the State of Maryland, which is in itself a clue that cannot be ignored, argued a case on the commerce clause before the Supreme Court. And finally, its cumulative effect in being discussed by Marshall from the dual point of view of commerce (Art. I, Sec. 8) and the import and export clause (Art. I, Sec. 10, Cl. 2) helped again to expand and expound Hamiltonian mercantilism, and to defend vested business interests.*

MR. CHIEF JUSTICE MARSHALL delivered the opinion of the court:

This is a writ of error to a judgment rendered in the Court of Appeals of Maryland, affirming a judgment of the City Court of Baltimore, on an indictment found in that court against the plaintiffs in error, for violating an act of the legislature of Maryland. The indictment was founded on the second section of that act, which is in these words: "And be it enacted, that all importers of foreign articles or commodities, of dry goods, wares, or merchandise, by bale or package, . . . and other persons selling the same by wholesale, bale or package, hogshead, barrel, or tierce, shall, before they are authorized to sell, take out a license, as by the original act is directed, for which they shall pay fifty dollars; and in case of neglect or refusal to take out such license, shall be subject to the same penalties and forfeitures as are prescribed by the original act to which this is a supplement." The indictment charges the plaintiffs in error with having imported and sold one package of foreign dry goods without having license to do so. A judgment was rendered against them on demurrer for the penalty which the act prescribes for the offense; and that judgment is now before this court.

The cause depends entirely on the question, whether the legislature of a state can constitutionally require the importer of foreign articles to take out a license from the state, before he shall be permitted to sell a bale or package so imported.

It has been truly said, that the presumption is in favor of every legislative act, and that the whole burthen of proof lies on him who denies its constitutionality. The plaintiffs in error take the burthen upon themselves, and insist that the act under consideration is repugnant to two provisions in the constitution of the United States:

1. To that which declares that "no state shall, without the consent of Congress, lay any imposts, or duties on imports or exports, except what may be absolutely necessary for executing its inspection laws."

2. To that which declares that Congress shall have power "to regulate commerce with foreign nations, and among the several states, and with the Indian tribes."

1. The first inquiry is into the extent of the prohibition upon states "to lay any imposts or duties on imports or exports." The counsel for the state of Maryland would confine this prohibition to the

laws imposing duties on the act of importation or exportation. The counsel for the plaintiffs in error give them a much wider scope.

In performing the delicate and important duty of constructing clauses in the constitution of our country, which involve conflicting powers of the government of the Union, and of the respective states, it is proper to take a view of the literal meaning of the words to be expounded, of their connection with other words and of the general objects to be accomplished by the prohibitory clause, or by the grant of power. . . .

. . . What, then, are "imports"? The lexicons inform us, they are "things imported." If we appeal to usage for the meaning of the word, we shall receive the same answer. They are the articles themselves which are brought into the country. "A duty on imports," then, is not merely a duty on the act of importation, but it is a duty on the thing imported. It is not, taken in its literal sense, confined to a duty levied while the article is entering the country, but extends to a duty levied after it has entered the country. The succeeding words of the sentence which limit the prohibition, show the extent in which it was understood. The limitation is, "except what may be absolutely necessary for executing its inspection laws." Now, the inspection laws, so far as they act upon articles for exportation, are generally executed on land, before the article is put on board the vessel; so far as they act upon importations, they are generally executed upon articles which are landed. The tax or duty of inspection, then, is a tax which is frequently, if not always, paid for service performed on land, while the article is in the bosom of the country. Yet this tax is an exception to the prohibition on the states to lay duties on imports or exports. The exception was made because the tax would otherwise have been within the prohibition. . . .

If we quit this narrow view of the subject, and passing from the literal interpretation of the words, look to the objects of the prohibition, we find no reason for withdrawing the act under consideration from its operation.

From the vast inequality between the different states of the confederacy, as to commercial advantages, few subjects were viewed with deeper interest, or excited more irritation, than the manner in which the several states exercised, or seemed disposed to exercise, the power of laying duties on imports. From motives which were deemed sufficient by the statesmen of that day, the general power of taxation, indispensably necessary as it was, and jealous as the states were of any encroachment on it, was so far abridged as to forbid them to touch imports or exports, with the single exception which has been noticed. Why are they restrained from imposing these duties? Plainly because, in the general opinion, the interest of all would be best promoted by placing that whole subject under the control of Congress. Whether the prohibition to "lay imposts, or duties on imports or exports," proceeded from an apprehension that the power might be so exercised as to disturb that equality among the states which was generally advantageous, or that harmony between them which it was desirable to preserve, or to maintain unimpaired our commercial connections with foreign nations, or to confer this source of revenue on the government of the Union, or whatever other motive might have induced the prohibition, it is plain that the object would be as completely defeated by a power to tax the article in the hands of the importer the instant it was landed as by a power to tax it while entering the port. . . . No goods would be imported if none could be sold. . . . It is obvious that the same power which imposes a light duty can impose a very heavy one, one which amounts to a prohibition. Questions of power do not depend on the degree to which it may be exercised. If it may be exercised at all, it must be exercised at the will of those in whose hands it is placed. . . .

. . . Conceding, to the full extent which is required, that every state would, in its legislation on this subject, provide judiciously for its own interest, it cannot be conceded that each would respect the interest of others. A duty on imports is a tax on the article, which is paid by the consumer. The great importing states would thus levy a tax on the non-importing states, which would not be less a tax because their interest would afford ample security against its ever being so heavy as to expel commerce from their ports.

This would necessarily produce countervailing measures on the part of those states whose situation was less favorable to importation. For this, among other reasons, the whole power of laying duties on imports was, with a single and slight exception, taken from the states. . . .

The counsel for the state of Maryland insist, with great reason, that if the words of the prohibition be taken in their utmost latitude, they will abridge the power of taxation, which all admit to be essential to the states, to an extent which has never yet been suspected, and will deprive them of resources which are necessary to supply revenue, and which they have heretofore been admitted to possess. These words must therefore be construed with some limitation; and, if this be admitted, they insist, that entering the country is the point of time when the prohibition ceases, and the power of the state to tax commences. . . .

. . . The power, and the restriction on it, though quite distinguishable when they do not approach each other, may yet, like the intervening colors between white and black, approach so nearly as to perplex the understanding, as colors perplex the vision in marking the distinction between them. Yet the distinction exists, and must be marked as the cases arise.

. . . The object of importation is sale; it constitutes the motive for paying the duties; and if the United States possess the power of conferring the right to sell, as the consideration for which the duty is paid, every principle of fair dealing requires that they should be understood to confer it. The practice of the most commercial nations conforms to this idea. Duties, according to that practice, are charged on those articles only which are intended for sale or consumption in the country. Thus, sea stores, goods imported and re-exported in the same vessel, goods landed and carried over land for the purpose of being re-exported from some other port, goods forced in by stress of weather, and landed, but not for sale, are exempted from the payment of duties. The whole course of legislation on the subject shows that, in the opinion of the legislature, the right to sell is connected with the payment of the duties.

The counsel for the defendant in error have endeavored to illustrate their proposition, that the constitutional prohibition ceases the instant the goods enter the country, by an array of the consequences which they suppose must follow the denial of it. If the importer acquires the right to sell by the payment of duties, he may, they say, exert that right when, where, and as he pleases, and the state cannot regulate it. He may sell by retail, at auction, or as an itinerant peddler. He may introduce articles, as gunpowder, which endangers a city, into the midst of its population; he may introduce articles which endanger the public health, and the power of self-preservation is denied. An importer may bring in goods, as plate, for his own use, and thus retain much valuable property exempt from taxation.

These objections to the principle, if well founded, would certainly be entitled to serious consideration. But we think they will be found, on examination, not to belong necessarily to the principle, and, consequently, not to prove that it may not be resorted to with safety, as a criterion by which to measure the extent of the prohibition.

This indictment is against the importer, for selling a package of dry goods in the form in which it was imported, without a license. This state of things is changed if he sells them, or otherwise mixes them with the general property of the state, by breaking up his packages, and traveling with them as an itinerant peddler. In the first case, the tax intercepts the import, as an import, in its way to become incorporated with the general mass of property and denies it the privilege of becoming so incorporated until it shall have contributed to the revenue of the state. It denies to the importer the right of using the privilege which he has purchased from the United States, until he shall have also purchased it from the state. In the last cases, the tax finds the article already incorporated with the mass of property by the act of the importer. He has used the privilege he had purchased, and has himself mixed them up with the common mass, and the law may treat them as it finds them. . . .

But if it should be proved that a duty on the article itself would be repugnant to the constitution, it is still argued that this is not a tax upon the article, but on the person. The state, it is said, may tax occupations, and this is nothing more.

It is impossible to conceal from ourselves that this is varying the form, without varying the substance. It is treating a prohibition which is general, as if it were confined to a particular mode of doing the forbidden thing. All must perceive that a tax on the sale of an article, imported only for sale, is a tax on the article itself. It is true, the state may tax occupations generally, but this tax must be paid by those who employ the individual, or is a tax on his business. The lawyer, the physician, or the mechanic, must either charge more on the article in which he deals, or the thing itself is taxed through his person. This the state has a right to do, because no constitutional prohibition extends to it. So, a tax on the occupation of an importer is, in like manner, a tax on importation. It must add to the price of the article, and be paid by the consumer, or by the importer himself, in like manner as a direct duty on the article itself would be made. This the state has not a right to do, because it is prohibited by the constitution. . . .

2. Is it also repugnant to that clause in the constitution which empowers "Congress to regulate commerce with foreign nations, and among the several states, and with the Indian tribes"? . . .

. . . Sale is the object of importation, and is an essential ingredient of that intercourse, of which importation constitutes a part. It is as essential an ingredient, as indispensable to the existence of the entire thing, then, as importation itself. It must be considered as a component part of the power to regulate commerce. Congress has a right, not only to authorize importation, but to authorize the importer to sell.

If this be admitted—and we think it cannot be denied—what can be the meaning of an act of Congress which authorizes importation, and offers the privilege for sale at a fixed price to every person who chooses to become a purchaser? How is it to be construed, if an intent to deal honestly and fairly, an intent as wise as it is moral, is to enter into the construction? What can be the use of the contract? What does the importer purchase, if he does not purchase the privilege to sell? . . .

If the principles we have stated be correct, the result to which they conduct us cannot be mistaken. Any penalty inflicted on the importer for selling the article in his character of importer, must be in opposition to the act of Congress which authorizes importation. Any charge on the introduction and incorporation of the articles into and with the mass of property in the country, must be hostile to the power given to Congress to regulate commerce, since an essential part of that regulation, and principal object of it, is to prescribe the regular means for accomplishing that introduction and incorporation. . . .

. . . It results, necessarily, from this principle, that the taxing power of the states must have some limits. It cannot reach and restrain the action of the national government within its proper sphere. It cannot reach the administration of justice in the courts of the Union, or the collection of the taxes of the United States, or restrain the operation of any law which Congress may constitutionally pass. It cannot interfere with any regulation of commerce. If the states may tax all persons and property found on their territory, what shall restrain them from taxing goods in their transit through the state from one port to another, for the purpose of re-exportation? The laws of trade authorize this operation, and general convenience requires it. Or what should restrain a state from taxing any article passing through it from one state to another, for the purpose of traffic? or from taxing the transportation of articles passing from the state itself to another state, for commercial purposes? These cases are all within the sovereign power of taxation, but would obviously derange the measures of Congress to regulate commerce, and affect materially the purpose for which that power was given. . . .

It may be proper to add, that we suppose the principles laid down in this case, to apply equally to importations from a sister state. We do not mean to give any opinion on a tax discriminating between foreign and domestic articles.

We think there is error in the judgment of the Court of Appeals of the State of Maryland, in affirming the judgment of the Baltimore City Court, because the act of the legislature of Maryland, imposing the penalty for which the said judgment is rendered, is repugnant to the constitution of the United States, and, consequently, void. The judgment is to be reversed, and the cause remanded to that court, with instructions to enter judgment in favor of the appellants.

[The dissenting opinion of MR. JUSTICE THOMPSON is omitted.]

BARRON v. BALTIMORE

7 Peters 243, 8 L.Ed. 672 (1833)

By 1833 the Supreme Court had come a long way since the days of Mr. Chief Justice Jay who for a period of six months had held the office of Chief Justice and Secretary of State of the United States; who ran for the election of Governor of New York State while still on the bench; and who for over a year had been both Chief Justice and Ambassador to England. If any one person can be held directly responsible for the growth and importance of the Court, that person must be John Marshall. That he dominated the Court cannot be denied. Harriet Martineau, a good observer of America in these formative days, though certainly no Tocqueville, wrote in 1835: "I have watched the assemblage while the Chief Justice was delivering a judgment, the three Judges on either hand gazing at him more like learners than associates. . . ." Moreover, Marshall and his Court had, to say the least, given the impression that they were operating under a *basic philosophy whose value was of the utmost importance and vitality in the growth of the United States: the supremacy of the nation. And in its formulation as well as in its articulation and its realization he had, in a manner of speaking, taken on all comers. Its inculcation was achieved and maintained against political party opposition, against Presidents, against countervailing philosophies of States' Rights, Federalism, Nullification and the like. And because he held his office and his position of dominance for over thirty years he had ample opportunity to express his doctrine in all kinds of cases of various degrees of magnitude. That he as a person and the institution he dominated should have, from time to time during this period, been the center of political, sectional, and economic attack was inevitable— indeed our worry would have been greater had his accomplishments been free from attack or opposing pressures and forces. Now by 1833, Marshall, and hence his Court, was nearing the end. The Chief Justice could have taken comfort, if he needed it, from the fact that the Court seemed relatively free from serious criticism and antagonism; that it had withstood the assaults on it with its function and power increased rather than impaired; and that one of his truly great antagonists, President Jackson ("Marshall has made his decision, now let him enforce it"), had joined his forces of national supremacy and authority by taking strong, positive action in the Nullification conflict. And as though fate wanted to be sure that Marshall would at least set the pattern on all major constitutional questions, the Supreme Court was now presented with the last of the series of vital questions: the applicability of the Bill of Rights, and more particularly of the first eight amendments, to the states. In the case below, the City of Baltimore, exercising its corporate authority over the harbor, streets, and health of Baltimore, began an extensive project of street improvement. In the completion of such project it was found necessary to divert from their accustomed and natural course certain streams of water. The result was that deposits of sand and gravel were formed at the head of the plaintiff's wharves, making them so shallow that it prevented access thereto by vessels. The plaintiff brought an action against the City of Baltimore to recover damages and was awarded the sum of $4500. On appeal to the Maryland Court of Appeals this judgment was reversed without remanding the case to the lower court for further trial. Barron now brings the case to the Supreme Court of the United States on a writ of error. In its own way there are many interesting twists involved here. It is somewhat startling to see Marshall's last opinion on this branch of the law seemingly limit the operation of the Constitution against state action—a reversal, in its way, from the extension he had so long fought for and established. And again, it is somewhat startling to recall that the very opponents of Marshall's extension theory into state activity, thought him wrong in not applying the Bill of Rights to state action—something we had to wait for until the alternate route of the due process* *clause and the equal protection of the laws clause of the 14th amendment came into their own. It is likewise startling to see Marshall open the door to this kind of state action against property, insisting that since the "amendments contain no expression indicating an intention to apply them to state goverments . . . [the] Court cannot so apply them," when this limitation had never been set forth by him in dealing with the body of the Constitution itself. May it be—and this is only a surmise—that this was a small price he and his Court were willing to pay lest the "civil liberties" problems that might come to the fore in the same way, open a veritable Pandora's box of values that might jeopardize the foundations of our economic growth on which our greatness, as he and other Hamiltonians saw it, depended?*

MARSHALL, CH. J., delivered the opinion of the court. . . .

The plaintiff in error contends, that it [the judgment of the Court of Appeals] comes within that clause in the fifth amendment to the constitution, which inhibits the taking of private property for public use, without just compensation. He insists, that this amendment being in favor of the liberty of the citizen, ought to be so construed as to restrain the legislative power of a state, as well as that of the United States. If this proposition be untrue, the court can take no jurisdiction of the cause.

The question thus presented is, we think, of great importance, but not of much difficulty. The constitution was ordained and established by the people of the United States for themselves, for their own government, and not for the government of the individual states. Each state established a constitution for itself, and in that constitution, provided such limitations and restrictions on the powers of its particular government, as its judgment dictated. The people of the United States framed such a government for the United States as they supposed best adapted to their situation and best calculated to promote their interests. The powers they conferred on this government were to be exercised by itself; and the limitations on power, if expressed in general terms, are naturally, and, we think, necessarily applicable to the government created by the instrument. They are limitations of power granted in the instrument itself; not of distinct governments, framed by different persons and for different purposes.

If these propositions be correct, the fifth amendment must be understood as restraining the power of the general government, not as applicable to the states. In their several constitutions, they have imposed such restrictions on their respective governments, as their own wisdom suggested; such as they deemed most proper for themselves. It is a subject on which they judge exclusively, and with which others interfere no further than they are supposed to have a common interest. . . . If the original constitution, in the ninth and tenth sections of the first article, draws this plain and marked line of discrimination between the limitations it imposes on the powers of the general government, and on those of the states; if, in every inhibition intended to act on state power, words are employed which directly express that intent,—some strong reason must be assigned for departing from this safe and judicious course, in framing the amendments, before that departure can be assumed. We search in vain for that reason.

Had the people of the several states, or any of them, required changes in their constitutions; had they required additional safe-guards to liberty from the apprehended encroachments of their particular governments; the remedy was in their own hands, and would have been applied by themselves. A convention could have been assembled by the discontented state, and the required improvements could have been made by itself. The unwieldy and cumbrous machinery of procuring a recommendation from two thirds of congress, and the assent of three fourths of their sister states, could never have occurred to any human being, as a mode of doing that which might be effected by the state itself. Had the framers of these amendments intended them to be limitations on the powers of the state governments, they would have imitated the framers of the original constitution, and have expressed that intention. Had congress engaged in the extraordinary occupation of improving the constitutions of the several states, by affording the people additional protection from the exercise of power by their own governments, in matters which concerned themselves alone, they would have declared this purpose in plain and intelligible language.

But it is universally understood, it is a part of the history of the day, that the great revolution which established the constitution of the United States was not effected without immense opposition. Serious fears were extensively entertained, that those powers which the patriot statesmen, who then watched over the interests of our country, deemed essential to union, and to the attainment of those invaluable objects for which union was sought, might be exercised in a manner dangerous to liberty. In almost every convention by which the constitution was adopted, amendments to guard against the abuse of power were recommended. These amendments demanded security against the apprehended encroachments of the general government— not against those of the local governments. In compliance with a sentiment thus generally expressed, to quiet fears thus extensively entertained, amendments were proposed by the required majority in congress, and adopted by the states. These amendments contain no expression indicating an intention to apply them to the state governments. This court cannot so apply them.

We are of opinion, that the provision in the fifth amendment to the constitution, declaring that private property shall not be taken for public use without just compensation, is intended solely as a limitation on the exercise of power by the government of the United States, and is not applicable to the legislation of the states. We are, therefore, of opinion, that there is no repugnancy between the several acts of the general assembly of Maryland, given in evidence by the defendants at the trial of this cause, in the court of that state, and the constitution of the United States. This court, therefore, has no jurisdiction of the cause; and it is dismissed. . . .

Dismissed, for want of jurisdiction.

CHARLES RIVER BRIDGE v. WARREN BRIDGE

11 Peters 420, 9 L.Ed. 773 (1837)

If ever a case can be said to raise issues vital to the growth of American life and yet at the same time cover the entire spectrum of values, be they legal, political, economic, or personal, the case below is certainly that case. In its simplest form the question before the Court was whether "the obligation of contract contained in a charter to a corporation authorizing the construction of a toll bridge was impaired by a charter, subsequently granted to another corporation, authorizing the construction of a free bridge paralleling the toll bridge." The Charles River Bridge Company had been granted a corporate status by the Massachusetts Legislature in 1785 to build a privately-owned bridge between Charlestown and Boston and to collect tolls for a period of 40 years (later extended to 70 years). In 1828 the Legislature incorporated the Warren Bridge Company and authorized it to build a bridge sufficiently close to the Charles River Bridge to pose a threat to the immediate toll receipts of the latter bridge—a threat that was too realistic to ignore because of the provision that within a short period the Warren Bridge was to become free and a part of the public highway system of the Commonwealth. The Charles River Bridge Company, denied an injunction and other relief by the State Court, sought a review on a writ of error. But behind these facts were forces which then, as now, made this case truly a landmark in our Constitutional development. This was a period of tremendous economic growth and development, when new systems of transportation (railroads and canals) were being built and when businessmen with sufficient capital were anxious to invest in new corporate enterprises, but hesitated only because they feared that concealed in old corporate charters were potential claims of monopoly which might be given legal sanction under the ruling of the Dartmouth College case. It was, moreover, a period which had seen the rise of Jacksonian democracy and whose philosophy had been, in this regard, at least, announced in the Bank Bill Veto Message: "If we cannot at once in justice to interests vested under improvident legislation make government what it ought to be, we can at least take a stand against all new grants of monopolies and exclusive privileges." It raised once again the important conflict of the power of the states to regulate and legis-

*late for their local interest, as they conceived that interest to be—that
is, to provide for their own public welfare, as one era gave way to
another, without being bound by the past or hemmed in by constitutional doctrine or ukase, be it strict construction of public contracts
or the supremacy of so-called national interests over so-called states'
rights. It demonstrated the intimate relationship between the political processes and legal consequences as clearly as any case could, for
the case first came up for adjudication in 1831 when Chief Justice
Marshall still dominated the judiciary, but was finally adjudicated in
1837. By this time a new Chief Justice (Taney), twice rejected by
the Senate for other appointments, plus a new Associate Justice (Bar-
bour, who succeeded Duval), had assumed "control" of the Supreme
Court. Thus this case demonstrated the conflict between the "old"
and "new" in a way which perhaps can serve as an introduction to
a similar episode in what is called "court packing" and the New Deal.
In the final analysis, whereas Marshall was undoubtedly correct in
maintaining that "if business is to prosper, men must have assurance
that contracts will be enforced," Taney was equally correct in adding
the proviso that "no community could survive without some authority
to control agreements that jeopardize the public welfare." Yet the
amazing thing is that almost a half century later, in 1885, Sir Henry
Maine, writing about the Constitution of the United States, was able
to say about the contract clause that "it is this prohibition which has
in reality secured full play to the economical forces by which the
achievement of cultivating the soil of the North American Continent
has been performed; it is the bulwark of American individualism
against democratic impatience and Socialist fantasy. [And] . . . that
until this prohibition, as interpreted by the Courts, is got rid of,
certain communistic schemes . . . have about as much prospect of
obtaining practical realization in the United States as the vision of
a cloud-cuckoo borough to be built by the birds between earth and
sky." (See* Essay on Popular Government, *p.* 196.) *Whatever else
may be said, it is perhaps worthy of note that two eleemosynary institutions lent their names (directly in one instance and indirectly in
another) in the determination of principles so vital to the development of American economic life.*

MR. CHIEF JUSTICE TANEY delivered the opinion of the court.

The questions involved in this case are of the gravest character, and
the court have given to them the most anxious and deliberate consideration. The value of the right claimed by the plaintiffs is large
in amount; and many persons may no doubt be seriously affected in
their pecuniary interests by any decisions which the court may pronounce; and the questions which have been raised as to the power of
the several states, in relation to the corporations they have chartered,
are pregnant with important consequences; not only to the individuals who are concerned in the corporate franchises, but to the com-

munities in which they exist. The court are fully sensible that it is their duty, in exercising the high powers conferred on them by the constitution of the United States, to deal with these great and extensive interests with the utmost caution; guarding, as far as they have the power to do so, the rights of property, and at the same time carefully abstaining from any encroachment on the rights reserved to the states. . . .

The plaintiffs in error insist, . . . : *1st.* That by virtue of the grant of 1650, Harvard College was entitled, in perpetuity, to the right of keeping a ferry between Charlestown and Boston; that this right was exclusive; and that the legislature had not the power to establish another ferry on the same line of travel, because it would infringe the rights of the college; and that these rights, upon the erection of the bridge in the place of the ferry, under the charter of 1785, were transferred to, and became vested in "the proprietors of the Charles River Bridge;" and that under, and by virtue of this transfer of the ferry right, the rights of the bridge company were as exclusive in that line of travel, as the rights of the ferry. *2d.* That independently of the ferry right, the acts of the legislature of Massachusetts, of 1785 and 1792, by their true construction, necessarily implied, that the legislature would not authorize another bridge, and especially a free one, by the side of this, and placed in the same line of travel, whereby the franchise granted to the "Proprietors of the Charles River Bridge" should be rendered of no value; and the plaintiffs in error contend, that the grant of the ferry to the college, and of the charter to the proprietors of the bridge, are both contracts on the part of the state; and that the law authorizing the erection of the Warren bridge in 1828, impairs the obligation of one or both of these contracts. . . .

But upon what ground can the plaintiffs in error contend that the ferry rights of the college have been transferred to the proprietors of the bridge? If they have been thus transferred, it must be by some mode of transfer known to the law; and the evidence relied on to prove it, can be pointed out in the record. How was it transferred? It is not suggested that there ever was, in point of fact, a deed of conveyance executed by the college to the bridge company. Is there any evidence in the record from which such a conveyance may, upon legal principle, be presumed? The testimony before the court, so far from laying the foundation for such a presumption, repels it in the most positive terms. The petition to the legislature, in 1785, on which the charter was granted, does not suggest an assignment, nor any agreement or consent on the part of the college; and the petitioners do not appear to have regarded the wishes of that institution, as by any means necessary to ensure their success. They place their application entirely on considerations of public interest and public convenience, and the superior advantages of a communication across Charles river by a bridge, instead of a ferry. . . .

This brings us to the act of the legislature of Massachusetts, of

1785, by which the plaintiffs were incorporated by the name of "The Proprietors of the Charles River Bridge;" and it is here, and in the law of 1792, prolonging their charter, that we must look for the extent and nature of the franchise conferred upon the plaintiffs.

Much has been said in the argument of the principles of construction by which this law is to be expounded, and what undertakings, on the part of the state, may be implied. The court think there can be no serious difficulty on that head. It is the grant of certain franchises by the public to a private corporation, and in a matter where the public interest is concerned. The rule of construction in such cases is well settled, both in England and by the decisions of our own tribunals. In 2 Barn. & Adol., 793, in the case of the *Proprietors of the Stourbridge Canal* v. *Wheeley* and others, the court say, "The canal having been made under an act of parliament, the rights of the plaintiffs are derived entirely from that act. This, like many other cases, is a bargain between a company of adventurers and the public, the terms of which are expressed in the statute; and the rule of construction, in all such cases, is now fully established to be this; that any ambiguity in the terms of the contract must operate against the adventurers, and in favor of the public, and the plaintiffs can claim nothing that is not clearly given them by the act." And the doctrine thus laid down is abundantly sustained by the authorities referred to in this decision.

. . . The argument in favour of the proprietors of the Charles river bridge, is . . . that the power claimed by the state, if it exists, may be so used as to destroy the value of the franchise they have granted to the corporation. . . . The object and end of all government is to promote the happiness and prosperity of the community by which it is established; and it can never be assumed, that the government intended to diminish its power of accomplishing the end for which it was created. And in a country like ours, free, active, and enterprising, continually advancing in numbers and wealth, new channels of communication are daily found necessary, both for travel and trade; and are essential to the comfort, convenience, and prosperity of the people. A state ought never to be presumed to surrender this power, because, like the taxing power, the whole community have an interest in preserving it undiminished. And when a corporation alleges, that a state has surrendered, for seventy years, its power of improvement and public accommodation, in a great and important line of travel, along which a vast number of its citizens must daily pass, the community have a right to insist, in the language of this court above quoted, "that its abandonment ought not to be presumed in a case in which the deliberate purpose of the state to abandon it does not appear." The continued existence of a government would be of no great value, if by implications and presumptions it was disarmed of the powers necessary to accomplish the ends of its creation; and the functions it was designed to perform, transferred to the hands of privileged corporations. The rule of construction announced by the court was not confined to the taxing power; nor is it so limited in the opinion delivered. On the contrary, it was distinctly placed on the ground that the interests of the community were concerned in preserving, undiminished, the power then in question; and whenever any power of the state is said to be surrendered or diminished, whether it be the taxing power or any other affecting the public interest, the same principle applies, and the rule of construction must be the same. No one will question that the interests of the great body of the people of the state would, in this instance, be affected by the surrender of this great line of travel to a single corporation, with the right to exact toll, and exclude competition for seventy years. While the rights of private property are sacredly guarded, we must not forget that the community also have rights, and that the happiness and well-being of every citizen depends on their faithful preservation.

Adopting the rule of construction above stated as the settled one, we proceed to apply it to the charter of 1785, to the proprietors of the Charles river bridge. This act of incorporation is in the usual form, and the privileges such as are commonly given to corporations of that kind. It confers on them the ordinary faculties of a corporation, for the purpose of building the bridge; and establishes certain rates of toll, which the company are authorized to take: this is the whole grant. There is no exclusive privilege given to them over the waters of Charles river, above or below their bridge; no right to erect another bridge themselves, nor to prevent other persons from erecting one, no engagement from the state, that another shall not be erected; and no undertaking not to sanction competition, nor to make improvements that may diminish the amount of its income. Upon all these subjects, the charter is silent; and nothing is said in it about a line of travel, so much insisted on in the argument, in which they are to have exclusive privileges. No words are used from which an intention to grant any of these rights can be inferred; if the plaintiff is entitled to them, it must be implied, simply, from the nature of the grant; and cannot be inferred, from the words by which the grant is made.

The relative position of the Warren bridge has already been described. It does not interrupt the passage over the Charles river bridge, nor make the way to it, or from it, less convenient. None of the faculties or franchises granted to that corporation, have been revoked by the legislature; and its right to take the tolls granted by the charter remains unaltered. In short, all the franchises and rights of property, enumerated in the charter, and there mentioned to have been granted to it, remain unimpaired. But its income is destroyed by the Warren bridge; which, being free, draws off the passengers and property which would have gone over it, and renders their franchise of no value. This is the gist of the complaint. For it is not pretended, that the erection of the Warren bridge would have done them any injury, or in any degree affected their right of property, if it had not diminished the amount of their tolls. In order, then, to entitle themselves to relief, it is necessary to show, that the legislature contracted not to do the act of which they complain; and that they impaired, or in other words, violated, that contract by the erection of the Warren bridge.

The inquiry, then, is, does the charter contain such a contract on the part of the state? Is there any such stipulation to be found in that instrument? It must be admitted on all hands, that there is none; no words that even relate to another bridge, or to the diminution of their tolls, or to the line of travel. If a contract on that subject can be gathered from the charter, it must be by implication; and cannot be found in the words used. Can such an agreement be implied? The rule of construction before stated is an answer to the question; in charters of this description, no rights are taken from the public, or given to the corporation, beyond those which the words of the charter, by their natural and proper construction, purport to convey. There are no words which import such a contract as the plaintiffs in error contend for, and none can be implied. . . .

Indeed, the practice and usage of almost every state in the Union, old enough to have commenced the work of internal improvement, is opposed to the doctrine contended for on the part of the plaintiffs in error. Turnpike roads have been made in succession, on the same line of travel; the later ones interfering materially with the profits of the first. These corporations have, in some instances, been utterly ruined by the introduction of newer and better modes of transportation and travelling. In some cases, railroads have rendered the turnpike roads on the same line of travel so entirely useless, that the franchise of the turnpike corporation is not worth preserving. Yet in none of these cases have the corporations supposed that their privileges were invaded, or any contract violated on the part of the state. Amid the multitude of cases which have occurred, and have been daily occurring for the last forty or fifty years, this is the first instance in which such an implied contract has been contended for, and this court called upon to infer it, from an ordinary act of incorporation, containing nothing more than the usual stipulations and provisions to be found in every such law. The absence of any such controversy, when there must have been so many occasions to give rise to it, proves that neither states, nor individuals, nor corporations, ever imagined that such a contract could be implied from such charters. It shows, that the men who voted for these laws never imagined that they were forming such a contract; and if we maintain that they have made it, we must create it by a legal fiction, in opposition to the truth of the fact, and the obvious intention of the party. We cannot deal thus with the rights reserved to the states; and by legal intendments and mere technical reasoning, take away from them any portion of that power over their own internal police and improvement, which is so necessary to their well-being and prosperity.

And what would be the fruits of this doctrine of implied contracts, on the part of the states, and of property in a line of travel by a corporation, if it should now be sanctioned by this court? To what results would it lead us? If it is to be found in the charter to this bridge, the same process of reasoning must discover it, in the various acts which have been passed, within the last forty years, for turnpike companies. And what is to be the extent of the privileges of exclusion on the different sides of the road? The counsel who have so ably argued this case, have not attempted to define it by any certain boundaries. How far must the new improvement be distant from the old one? How near may you approach, without invading its rights in the privileged line? If this court should establish the principles now contended for, what is to become of the numerous railroads established on the same line of travel with turnpike companies; and which have rendered the franchises of the turnpike corporations of no value? Let it once be understood, that such charters carry with them these implied contracts, and give this unknown and undefined property in a line of travelling; and you will soon find the old turnpike corporations awakening from their sleep and calling upon this court to put down the improvements which have taken their place. The millions of property which have been invested in railroads and canals, upon lines of travel which had been before occupied by turnpike corporations, will be put in jeopardy. We shall be thrown back to the improvements of the last century, and obliged to stand still, until the claims of the old turnpike corporations shall be satisfied; and they shall consent to permit these states to avail themselves of the lights of modern science, and to partake of the benefit of those improvements which are now adding to the wealth and prosperity, and the convenience and comfort, of every other part of the civilized world. Nor is this all. This court will find itself compelled to fix, by some arbitrary rule, the width of this new kind of property in a line of travel; for if such a right of property exists, we have no lights to guide us in marking out its extent, unless, indeed, we resort to the old feudal grants, and to the exclusive rights of ferries, by prescription, between towns; and are prepared to decide that when a turnpike road from one town to another, had been made, no railroad or canal, between these two points, could afterwards be established. This court are not prepared to sanction principles which must lead to such results. . . .

The judgment of the supreme judicial court of the commonwealth of Massachusetts, dismissing the plaintiffs' bill, must therefore, be affirmed, with costs. . . .

MR. JUSTICE STORY, dissenting. . . .

The present . . . is not the case of a royal grant, but of a legislative grant, by a public statute. The rules of the common law in relation to royal grants have, therefore, in reality, nothing to do with the case. We are to give this act of incorporation a rational and fair construction, according to the general rules which govern in all cases of the exposition of public statutes. We are to ascertain the legislative intent; and that once ascertained, it is our duty to give it a full and liberal operation. . . .

I admit, that where the terms of a grant are to impose burthens upon the public, or to create a restraint injurious to the public interest, there is sound reason for interpreting the terms, if ambiguous, in favour of the public. But at the same time, I insist, that there is not the slightest reason for saying, even in such a case, that the grant is not to be construed favourably to the grantee, so as to secure him in the enjoyment of what is actually granted. . . .

. . . Our legislatures neither have, nor affect to have any royal prerogatives. There is no provision in the constitution authorizing their grants to be construed differently from the grants of private persons, in regard to the like subject matter. The policy of the common law, which gave the crown so many exclusive privileges, and extraordinary claims, different from those of the subject, was founded in a good measure, if not altogether, upon the divine right of kings, or at least upon a sense of their exalted dignity and preeminence over all subjects, and upon the notion, that they are entitled to peculiar favour, for the protection of their kingly privileges. They were always construed according to common sense and common reason, upon their language and their intent. What reason is there, that our legislative act should not receive a similar interpretation? Is it not at least as important in our free governments, that a citizen should have as much security for his rights and estate derived from the grants of the legislature, as he would have in England? What solid ground is there to say, that the words of a grant in the mouth of a citizen, shall mean one thing, and in the mouth of the legislature shall mean another thing? That in regard to the grant of a citizen, every word shall in case of any question of interpretation or implication be construed against him, and in regard to the grant of the government, every word shall be construed in its favour? That language shall be construed, not according to its natural import and implications from its own proper sense, and the objects of the instrument; but shall change its meaning, as it is spoken by the whole people, or by one of them? . . .

But it has been argued, and the argument has been pressed in every form which ingenuity could suggest, that if grants of this nature are to be construed liberally, as conferring any exclusive rights on the grantees, it will interpose an effectual barrier against all general improvements of the country. . . . For my own part, I can conceive of no surer plan to arrest all public improvements, founded on private capital and enterprise, than to make the outlay of that capital uncertain, and questionable both as to security, and as to productiveness. No man will hazard his capital in any enterprise, in which, if there be a loss, it must be borne exclusively by himself; and if there be success, he has not the slightest security of enjoying the rewards of that success for a single moment. . . .

Upon the whole, my judgment is that the act of the legislature of Massachusetts granting the charter of Warren bridge, is an act impairing the obligation of the prior contract and grant to the proprietors of Charles river bridge; and, by the Constitution of the United States, it is, therefore, utterly void. I am for reversing the decree of the state court, (dismissing the bill), and for remanding the cause to the state court for further proceedings. . . .

MR. JUSTICE THOMPSON concurred in this opinion. . . .

BANK OF AUGUSTA v. EARLE

13 Peters 519, 10 L.Ed. 274 (1839)

This case involves the power of a corporation to enter into a contract outside of the state in which it was incorporated. In essence the plaintiff was a banking corporation chartered in Georgia which purchased and/or discounted, through agents in Alabama, bills of exchange in that state. The makers of the bills of exchange (the defendant) refused payment because they maintained that the Bank of Augusta lacked power to do business as a banking corporation in Alabama since it was incorporated in Georgia. Judge McKinley of the United States Circuit Court of Alabama upheld the defendant and at the same time granted "either party to have the right of Appeal or writ of error to the Supreme Court." The importance of the decision can be measured only if one sees its relationship to the commercial and business development of the United States and recalls at the same time that though the charter of the Bank of the United States had expired in 1836, the Bank was still a going concern, having been incorporated by the State of Pennsylvania.

MR. CHIEF JUSTICE TANEY delivered the opinion of the court: . . .

The questions presented to the court arise upon a case stated in the Circuit Court in the following words:

The defendant defends this action upon the following facts, that are admitted by the plaintiffs: that plaintiffs are a corporation, incorporated by an act of the Legislature of the State of Georgia, and have power usually conferred upon banking institutions, such as to purchase bills of exchange, &c. That the bill sued on was made and indorsed, for the purpose of purchasing bills, which funds were derived from bills and notes discounted in Georgia by said plaintiffs, and payable in Mobile; and the said M'Gran, agent as aforesaid, did so discount and purchase the said bill sued on, in the city of Mobile, State aforesaid, for the benefit of said bank, and with their funds, and to remit said funds to the said plaintiffs.

If the court shall say that the facts constitute a defense to this action, judgment will be given for the defendant, otherwise for plaintiffs, for the amount of the bill, damages, interest, and cost; either party to have the right of appeal or writ of error to the Supreme Court upon this statement of facts, and the judgment thereon.

Upon this statement of facts the court gave judgment for the defendant; being of opinion that a bank incorporated by the laws of Georgia, with a power, among other things, to purchase bills of exchange, could not lawfully exercise that power in the State of Alabama; and that the contract for this bill was therefore void, and did not bind the parties to the payment of the money.

It will at once be seen that the questions brought here for decision are of a very grave character, and they have received from the court an attentive examination. A multitude of corporations for various purposes have been chartered by the several States; a large portion of certain branches of business has been transacted by incorporated companies, or through their agency; and contracts to a very great amount have undoubtedly been made by different corporations out of the jurisdiction of the particular State by which they were created. In deciding the case before us, we in effect determine whether these numerous contracts are valid or not. And if, as has been argued at the bar, a corporation, from its nature and character, is incapable of making such contracts; or if they are inconsistent with the rights and sovereignty of the States in which they are made, they cannot be enforced in the courts of justice. . . .

But it has been urged in the argument that, notwithstanding the powers thus conferred by the terms of the charter, a corporation, from the very nature of its being, can have no authority to contract out of the limits of the State; that the laws of a State can have no extraterritorial operation; and that as a corporation is the mere creature of a law of the State, it can have no existence beyond the limits in which that law operates; and that it must necessarily be incapable of making a contract in another place.

It is very true that a corporation can have no legal existence out of the boundaries of the sovereignty by which it is created. It exists only in contemplation of law, and by force of the law; and where that law ceases to operate, and is no longer obligatory, the corporation can have no existence. It must dwell in the place of its creation, and cannot migrate to another sovereignty. But although it must live and have its being in that State only, yet it does not by any means follow that its existence there will not be recognized in other places; and its residence in one State creates no insuperable objection to its power of contracting in another. It is, indeed, a mere artificial being, invisible and intangible; yet it is a person, for certain purposes in contemplation of law, and has been recognized as such by the decisions of this court. . . . Now, natural persons, through the intervention of agents, are continually making contracts in countries in which they do not reside, and where they are not personally present when the contract is made; and nobody has ever doubted the validity of these agreements. And what greater objection can there be to the capacity of an artificial person, by its agents, to make a contract within the scope of its limited powers, in a sovereignty in which it does not reside; provided such contracts are permitted to be made by them by the laws of the place?

The corporation must no doubt show that the law of its creation gave it authority to make such contracts, through such agents. Yet, as in the case of a natural person, it is not necessary that it should actually exist in the sovereignty in which the contract is made. It is sufficient that its existence as an artificial person, in a State of its creation, is acknowledged and recognized by the law of the nation where the dealing takes place; and that it is permitted by the laws of that place to exercise there the powers with which it is endowed.

Every power, however, of the description of which we are speaking, which a corporation exercises in another State, depends for its validity upon the laws of the sovereignty in which it is exercised; and a corporation can make no valid contract without their sanction, express or implied. And this brings us to the question which has been so elaborately discussed; whether, by the comity of nations and between these States, the corporations of one State are permitted to make contracts in another. . . .

But it cannot be necessary to pursue the argument further. We think it is well settled that by the law of comity among nations, a corporation created by one sovereignty is permitted to make contracts in another, and to sue in its courts; and that the same law of comity prevails among the several sovereignties of this Union. The public and well known, and long continued usages of trade; the general acquiescence of the States; the particular legislation of some of them, as well as the legislation of Congress; all concur in proving the truth of this proposition.

But we have already said that this comity is presumed from the silent acquiescence of the State. Whenever a State sufficiently indicates that contracts which derive their validity from its comity are repugnant to its policy, or are considered as injurious to its interest, the presumption in favor of its adoption can no longer be made. . . .

MR. JUSTICE BALDWIN concurred separately; MR. JUSTICE McKINLEY dissented.

COOLEY v. BOARD OF WARDENS OF THE
PORT OF PHILADELPHIA

12 Howard 299, 13 L.Ed. 996 (1851)

Vital and important as GIBBONS v. OGDEN *was at the time of its pronouncement, it actually created more questions than it solved. Though a superficial reading of the case lends itself to concluding that its result was still another stone in the building of Mr. Chief Justice Marshall's nationalistic doctrines, it really was, in the words of Felix Frankfurter (writing as a Professor of Law), "either unconsciously or calculatedly confused." Moreover, a nation's growth, be it economic or geographic, is not entirely an unmixed blessing, for while it is a sign of progress it also adds a degree of complexity which inevitably brings forth increased problems that cry out for regulations of one kind or another. And it is here that Marshall's decision comes to the fore again, for the regulations being local in character and nature came again in conflict with the meaning of the commerce clause. (See, for example,* THE LICENSE CASES *of 1847, in 5 Howard 504, and* THE PASSENGER CASES *of 1849 in 7 Howard 283.) The result was a form of legal jargon that compounded the confusion, albeit in the name and under the banner of* GIBBONS v. OGDEN. *In turn, judges, lawyers, political scientists, and other writers on constitutional law (and especially, of course, with respect to the commerce clause) attempted to translate what the Court was doing when confronted by the extent and validity of these local commerce regulations into concepts and theories. Chief among these were: (1) "The Concurrent Power Theory" which, as the name implies, accepted the fact that both the states and the national government had power to deal with all aspects of commerce, except that in case of conflict federal statute would prevail under the so-called supremacy clause of the Constitution (see Art. VI, Sec. 2); (2) "The Dormant Power Theory" which maintained that the power to control commerce belonged to the federal government and lies dormant even when unexercised, so that any state regulation on the subject must be considered void; (3) "The Mutual Exclusiveness Theory" which again implied that both the states and the federal government had power over commerce, and where one begins and the other ends is clear enough to conclude that the powers being mutually exclusive each must stay out of the orbit of the other. And so the legal battle lines ranged themselves until 1851 when the case below came before the Court setting up a new theory, followed even today. In this case, which came to the Supreme Court on a writ of error, Cooley claimed that the Act of 1803 passed by Pennsylvania—requiring all ships using the Port of Philadelphia to engage a local pilot, and that failure to do so would result in a fine equal to one-half the cost of pilotage, payable to the board of wardens of the port—denied him a right he had under the Constitution of the United States: viz., to be exempt from such payment because the state law contravenes several provisions of the Constitution. Having paid the fine, Cooley attempted to recover the fees. While the result of the decision is the creation of a so-called "Selective Exclusiveness Theory," the real impact is that it would always be the Courts, and especially the Supreme Court, which would determine in the final analysis whether the "selections" made by the political processes (national or state) and which affect commerce, would be valid or void.*

Mr. Justice Curtis delivered the opinion of the court: . . .

[The Court rejected contentions that the law was invalid as a duty on imports, exports, or tonnage, or constituted a preference to a port.]

It remains to consider the objection, that it is repugnant to the third clause of the eighth section of the first article. "The Congress shall have power to regulate commerce with foreign nations and among the several States, and with the Indian tribes."

That the power to regulate commerce includes the regulation of navigation, we consider settled. And when we look to the nature of the service performed by pilots, to the relations which that service and its compensations bear to navigation between the several States, and between the ports of the United States, and foreign countries, we are brought to the conclusion, that the regulation of the qualifications of pilots, of the modes and times of offering and rendering their services, of the responsibilities which shall rest upon them, of the powers they shall possess, of the compensation they may demand, and of the penalties by which their rights and duties may be enforced, do constitute regulations of navigation, and consequently of commerce, within the just meaning of this clause of the Constitution. . . .

The Act of 1789, 1 Stat. at Large, 54, . . . contains a clear legislative exposition of the Constitution by the first Congress, to the effect that the power to regulate pilots was conferred on Congress by the Constitution; as does also the Act of March the 2nd, 1837, ... The weight to be allowed to this contemporaneous construction, and the practice of Congress under it, has, in another connection, been adverted to. And a majority of the court are of opinion that a regulation of pilots is a regulation of commerce, within the grant to Congress of the commercial power, contained in the third clause of the eighth section of the first article of the Constitution.

It becomes necessary, therefore, to consider whether this law of Pennsylvania, being a regulation of commerce, is valid.

The Act of Congress of the 7th of August, 1789, sec. 4, is as follows:

That all pilots in the bays, inlets, rivers, harbors, and ports of the United States, shall continue to be regulated in conformity with the existing laws of the States, respectively, wherein such pilots may be, or with such laws as the States may respectively hereafter enact for the purpose, until further legislative provision shall be made by Congress.

If the law of Pennsylvania, now in question, had been in existence at the date of this Act of Congress, we might hold it to have been adopted by Congress, and thus made a law of the United States, and so valid. Because this Act does, in effect, give the force of an Act of Congress, to the then existing state laws on this subject, so long as they should continue unrepealed by the State which enacted them.

But the law on which these actions are founded was not enacted till 1803. What effect, then, can be attributed to so much of the Act of 1789 as declares that pilots shall continue to be regulated in conformity "with such laws as the States may respectively hereafter enact for the purpose, until further legislative provision shall be made by Congress?"

If the States were divested of the power to legislate on this subject by the grant of the commercial power to Congress, it is plain this Act could not confer upon them power thus to legislate. If the Constitution excluded the States from making any law regulating commerce, certainly Congress cannot regrant, or in any manner reconvey to the States that power. And yet this act of 1789 gives its sanction only to laws enacted by the States. This necessarily implies a constitutional power to legislate; for only a rule created by the sovereign power of a state acting in its legislative capacity, can be deemed a law, enacted by a state; and if the State has so limited its sovereign power that it no longer extends to a particular subject, manifestly it cannot, in any proper sense, be said to enact laws thereon. Entertaining these views we are brought directly and unavoidably to the consideration of the question, whether the grant of the commercial power to Congress, did *per se* deprive the States of all power to regulate pilots. This question has never been decided by this court, nor, in our judgment, has any case depending upon all the considerations which must govern this one, come before this court. The grant of commercial power to Congress does not contain any terms which expressly exclude the States from exercising an authority over its subject matter. If they are excluded it must be because the nature of the power, thus granted to Congress, requires that a similar authority should not exist in the States. If it were conceded on the one side, that the nature of this power, like that to legislate for the District of Columbia, is absolutely and totally repugnant to the existence of similar power in the States, probably no one would deny that the grant of the power to Congress, as effectually and perfectly excludes the States from all future legislation on the subject, as if expressed words had been used to exclude them. And on the other hand, if it were admitted that the existence of this power in Congress, like the power of taxation, is compatible with the existence of a similar power in the States, then it would be in conformity with the contemporary exposition of the Constitution (*Federalist*, No. 32), and with the judicial construction, given from time to time by this court, after the most deliberate consideration, to hold that the mere grant of such a power to Congress, did not imply a prohibition on the States to exercise the same power: that it is not the mere existence of such a power, but its exercise by Congress, which may be incompatible with the exercise of the same power by the States, and that the States may legislate in the absence of congressional regulations. *Sturges* v. *Crowninshield*, 4 Wheat. 193; *Moore* v. *Houston*, 5 Wheat. 1; *Wilson* v. *Black Bird Creek Marsh Co.*, 2 Peters, 251.

The diversities of opinion, therefore, which have existed on this subject, have arisen from the different views taken of the nature of this power. But when the nature of a power like this is spoken of, when it is said that the nature of the power requires that it should be exercised exclusively by Congress, it must be intended to refer to the subjects of that power, and to say they are of such a nature as to require exclusive legislation by Congress. Now, the power to regulate commerce, embraces a vast field, containing not only many, but exceedingly various subjects, quite unlike in their nature; some imperatively demanding a single uniform rule, operating equally on the commerce of the United States in every port; and some, like the subject now in question, as imperatively demanding that diversity, which alone can meet the local necessities of navigation.

Either absolutely to affirm, or deny, that the nature of this power requires exclusive legislation by Congress, is to lose sight of the nature of the subjects of this power, and to assert concerning all of them, what is really applicable but to a part. Whatever subjects of this power are in their nature national, or admit only of one uniform system, or plan of regulation, may justly be said to be of such a nature as to require exclusive legislation by Congress. That this cannot be affirmed of laws for the regulation of pilots and pilotage is plain. The Act of 1789 contains a clear and authoritative declaration by the first Congress, that the nature of this subject is such, that until Congress should find it necessary to exert its power, it should be left to the legislation of the States; that it is local and not national; that it is likely to be the best provided for, not by one system, or plan of regulations, but by as many as the legislative discretion of the several States should deem applicable to the local peculiarities of the ports within their limits.

Viewed in this light, so much of this Act of 1789 as declares that pilots shall continue to be regulated "by such laws as the States may respectively hereafter enact for that purpose," instead of being held to be inoperative, as an attempt to confer on the States a power to legislate, of which the Constitution had deprived them, is allowed an appropriate and important signification. It manifests the understanding of Congress, at the outset of the government, that the nature of this subject is not such as to require its exclusive legislation. The practice of the States, and of the national government, has been in conformity with this declaration, from the origin of the national government to this time; and the nature of the subject, when examined, is such as to leave no doubt of the superior fitness and propriety, not to say the absolute necessity, of different systems of regulation, drawn from local knowledge and experience, and conformed to local wants. How, then, can we say, that by the mere grant of power to regulate commerce, the States are deprived of all the power to legislate on this subject, because from the nature of the power the legislation of Congress must be exclusive. . . .

It is the opinion of a majority of the court that the mere grant to Congress of the power to regulate commerce, did not deprive the States of power to regulate pilots, and that although Congress has legislated on this subject, its legislation manifests an intention, with a single exception, not to regulate this subject, but to leave its regulation to the several States. To these precise questions, which are all we are called on to decide, this opinion must be understood to be confined. It does not extend to the question what other subjects, under the commercial power, are within the exclusive control of Congress, or may be regulated by the States in the absence of all congressional legislation; nor to the general question how far any regulation of a subject by Congress may be deemed to operate as an exclusion of all legislation by the States upon the subject. We decide the precise questions before us, upon what we deem sound principles, applicable to this particular subject in the state in which the legislation of Congress has left it. We go no farther. . . .

[Judgments affirmed.]

MR. JUSTICE MCLEAN [joined by MR. JUSTICE WAYNE] delivered a dissenting opinion. . . .

Congress adopted the pilot-laws of the states, because it was well understood, that they could have had no force, as regulations of foreign commerce or of commerce among the states, if not so adopted. By their adoption they were made acts of Congress, and ever since they have been so considered and enforced. . . . From this race of legislation between Congress and the states, and between the states, if this principle be maintained, will arise a conflict similar to that which existed before the adoption of the Constitution. The states favorably situated, as Louisiana, may levy a contribution upon the commerce of other states which shall be sufficient to meet the expenditures of the states. . . .

Mr. Justice Daniel concurring with the Court in the result. . . .

The power and the practice of enacting pilot-laws, which has been exercised by the states from the very origin of their existence, although it is one in some degree connected with commercial intercourse, does not come essentially and regularly within that power of commercial regulation vested by the Constitution in Congress, and which by the Constitution must, when exercised by Congress, be enforced with perfect equality, and without any kind of discrimination, local or otherwise in its application. . . . [pilotage was inherently a right of the States] not one merely to be tolerated, or held subject to the sanction of the federal government.

Part III: 1868-1931

State Action

SLAUGHTER-HOUSE CASES

16 Wallace 36, 21 L.Ed. 394 (1873)

On March 8, 1869, the "carpet-bag" Legislature of Louisiana, perhaps "under the influence of corruption and bribery," passed "An Act to Protect the Health of the City of New Orleans, to Locate the Stock-landings and Slaughter-houses, and to Incorporate the Crescent City Line Stock Landing and Slaughter-House Company." Toward this end it gave the Company so created exclusive slaughtering privileges in New Orleans for a twenty-five year period, provided that all other butchers could slaughter only at the said Company's abattoir, that a fee, fixed by the law, was to be paid to the said Company for such privilege, and that all other slaughter-houses in the parishes affected by the law must be closed by the first day of June, 1869. The effect of this law was that over one thousand persons were deprived of their right to engage in the slaughter-house business in favor of one corporation. Maintaining that such a "monopoly" constituted "gross injustice to the public and an invasion of private rights," the case comes to the Supreme Court by writs of error to the Supreme Court of the State of Louisiana which had upheld the State law over the protest of the non-favored butchers. The full flavor of this case will come to the fore if it be kept in mind that the Supreme Court is here construing the scope of the 14th Amendment for the first time (though it was passed in 1868) and that it constitutes a vital bench mark within the Court as a reaction against an era of nationalism (only four Acts of Congress had been declared invalid from 1789 to 1869) in favor of State powers. But of even more importance are the very significant differences in approaching the amendment as set forth by Mr. Justice Miller and Mr. Justice Field—differences which vied with each other for acceptance in the Court itself over the next decades, and differences which were felt even in the early part of the New Deal.

Mr. Justice Miller delivered the opinion of the Court: . . .

It is not, and cannot be successfully controverted, that it is both the right and the duty of the legislative body—the supreme power of the State or municipality—to prescribe and determine the localities where the business of slaughtering for a great city may be conducted. To do this effectively it is indispensable that all persons who

71

slaughter animals for food shall do it in those places *and nowhere else*.

The statute under consideration defines these localities and forbids slaughtering in any other. It does not, as has been asserted, prevent the butcher from doing his own slaughtering. On the contrary, the Slaughter-House Company is required, under a heavy penalty, to permit any person who wishes to do so, to slaughter in their houses; and they are bound to make ample provision for the convenience of all slaughtering for the entire city. The butcher then is still permitted to slaughter, to prepare, and to sell his own meats; but he is required to slaughter at a specified place and to pay reasonable compensation for the use of the accommodations furnished him at that place.

The wisdom of the monopoly granted by the legislature may be open to question, but it is difficult to see a justification for the assertion that the butchers are deprived of the right to labor in their occupation, or the people of their daily service in preparing food, or how this statute, with the duties and guards imposed upon the company, can be said to destroy the business of the butcher, or seriously interfere with its pursuit.

The power here exercised by the legislature of Louisiana is, in its essential nature, one which has been, up to the present period in the constitutional history of this country, always conceded to belong to the States, however it may *now* be questioned in some of its details. . . .

Unless, therefore, it can be maintained that the exclusive privilege granted by this charter to the corporation is beyond the power of the legislature of Louisiana, there can be no just exception to the validity of the statute. And in this respect we are not able to see that these privileges are especially odious or objectionable. The duty imposed as a consideration for the privilege is well defined, and its enforcement well guarded. The prices or charges to be made by the company are limited by the statute, and we are not advised that they are on the whole exhorbitant or unjust.

The proposition is, therefore, reduced to these terms: Can any exclusive privileges be granted to any of its citizens, or to a corporation, by the legislature of a State? . . .

The plaintiffs in error accepting this issue, allege that the statute is a violation of the Constitution of the United States in these several particulars:

That it creates an involuntary servitude forbidden by the thirteenth article of amendment;

That it abridges the privileges and immunities of citizens of the United States;

That it denies to the plaintiffs the equal protection of the law; and

That it deprives them of their property without due process of law; contrary to the provisions of the first section of the fourteenth article of amendment.

This court is thus called upon for the first time to give construction to these articles.

We do not conceal from ourselves the great responsibility which this duty devolves upon us. No questions so far-reaching and pervading in their consequences, so profoundly interesting to the people of this country, and so important in their bearing upon the relations of the United States, and of the several States to each other and to the citizens of the States and of the United States, have been before this court during the official life of any of its present members. We have given every opportunity for a full hearing at the bar; we have discussed it freely and compared views among ourselves; we have taken ample time for careful deliberation, and we now propose to announce the judgments which we have formed in the construction of those articles, so far as we have found them necessary to the decision of the cases before us, and beyond that we have neither the inclination nor the right to go. . . .

On the most casual examination of the language of these [Civil War] amendments, no one can fail to be impressed with the one pervading purpose found in them all, lying at the foundation of each, and without which none of them would have been even suggested; we mean the freedom of the slave race, the security and firm establishment of that freedom, and the protection of the newly-made freeman and citizen from the oppressions of those who had formerly exercised unlimited dominion over him. It is true that only the fifteenth amendment, in terms, mentions the Negro by speaking of his color and his slavery. But it is just as true that each of the other articles was addressed to the grievances of that race, and designed to remedy them as the fifteenth.

We do not say that no one else but the Negro can share in this protection. Both the language and spirit of these articles are to have their fair and just weight in any question of construction. Undoubtedly while Negro slavery alone was in the mind of the Congress which proposed the thirteenth article, it forbids any other kind of slavery, now or hereafter. If Mexican peonage or the Chinese cooly labor system shall develop slavery of the Mexican or Chinese race within our territory, this amendment may safely be trusted to make it void. And so if other rights are assailed by the States which properly and necessarily fall within the protection of these articles, that protection will apply, though the party interested may not be of African descent. But what we do say, and what we wish to be understood is, that in any fair and just construction of any section or phrase of these amendments, it is necessary to look to the purpose which we have said was the pervading spirit of them all, the evil which they were designed to remedy, and the process of continued addition to the Constitution, until that purpose was supposed to be accomplished, as far as constitutional law can accomplish it. . . .

The next observation is more important in view of the arguments of counsel in the present case. It is, that the distinction between citizenship of the United States and citizenship of a State is clearly recognized and established. Not only may a man be a citizen of the United States without being a citizen of a State, but an important element is necessary to convert the former into the latter. He must reside within the State to make him a citizen of it, but it is only necessary that he should be born or naturalized in the United States to be a citizen of the Union.

It is quite clear, then, that there is a citizenship of the United States, and a citizenship of a State, which are distinct from each other, and which depend upon different characteristics or circumstances in the individual.

We think this distinction and its explicit recognition in this amendment of great weight in this argument, because the next paragraph of this same section, which is the one mainly relied on by the plaintiffs in error, speaks only of privileges and immunities of citizens of the United States, and does not speak of those of citizens of the several States. The argument, however, in favor of the plaintiffs rests wholly on the assumption that the citizenship is the same, and the privileges and immunities guaranteed by the clause are the same.

The language is, "No State shall make or enforce any law which shall abridge the privileges or immunities of citizens of *the United States*." It is a little remarkable, if this clause was intended as a protection to the citizen of a State against the legislative power of his own State, that the word citizen of the State should be left out when it is so carefully used, and used in contradistinction to citizens of the United States, in the very sentence which precedes it. It is too clear for argument that the change in phraseology was adopted understandingly and with a purpose.

Of the privileges and immunities of the citizen of the United States, and of the privileges and immunities of the citizen of the State, and what they respectively are, we will presently consider; but we wish to state here that it is only the former which are placed by this clause under the protection of the Federal Constitution, and that the latter, whatever they may be, are not intended to have any additional protection by this paragraph of the amendment.

If, then, there is a difference between the privileges and immunities belonging to a citizen of the United States as such, and those belonging to the citizen of the State as such the latter must rest for their security and protection where they have heretofore rested; for they are not embraced by this paragraph of the amendment. . . .

Fortunately we are not without judicial construction of [the state citizenship clause in Art. 4, Sec. 2] of the Constitution. The first and the leading case on the subject is that of *Corfield* v. *Coryell*, 6 Fed. Cas. 3230, decided by Mr. Justice Washington in the Circuit Court for the District of Pennsylvania in 1823.

"The inquiry," he says, "is, what are the privileges and immunities of citizens of the several States? We feel no hesitation in confining these expressions to those privileges and immunities which are fundamental; which belong of right to the citizens of all free governments, and which have at all times been enjoined by citizens of the several States which compose this Union, from the time of their becoming free, independent, and sovereign. What these fundamental principles are, it would be more tedious than difficult to enumerate. They may all, however, be comprehended under the following general heads: protection by the government, with the right to acquire and possess property of every kind, and to pursue and obtain happiness and safety, subject, nevertheless, to such restraints as the government may prescribe for the general good of the whole." . . .

It would be the vainest show of learning to attempt to prove by citations of authority, that up to the adoption of the recent amendments, no claim or pretense was set up that those rights depended on the Federal government for their existence or protection, beyond the very few express limitations which the Federal Constitution imposed upon the States—such, for instance, as the prohibition against ex post facto laws, bills of attainder, and laws impairing the obligation of contracts. But with the exception of these and a few other restrictions, the entire domain of the privileges and immunities of citizens of the States, as above defined, lay within the constitutional and legislative power of the States, and without that of the Federal government. Was it the purpose of the fourteenth amendment, by the simple declaration that no State should make or enforce any law which shall abridge the privileges and immunities *of citizens of the United States*, to transfer the security and protection of all the civil rights which we have mentioned, from the States to the Federal government? And where it is declared that Congress shall have the power to enforce that article, was it intended to bring within the power of Congress the entire domain of civil rights heretofore belonging exclusively to the States?

All this and more must follow, if the proposition of the plaintiffs in error be sound. For not only are these rights subject to the control of Congress whenever in its discretion any of them are supposed to be abridged by State legislation, but that body may also pass laws in advance, limiting and restricting the exercise of legislative power by the States, in their most ordinary and usual functions, as in its judgment it may think proper on all such subjects. And still further, such a construction followed by the reversal of the judgments of the Supreme Court of Louisiana in these cases, would constitute this court a perpetual censor upon all legislation of the States, on the civil rights of their own citizens, with authority to nullify such as it did not approve as consistent with those rights, as they existed at the time of the adoption of this amendment. The argument we admit is not always the most conclusive which is drawn from the consequences urged against the adoption of a particular construction of an instrument. But when, as in the case before us, these consequences are so serious, so far-reaching and pervading, so great a departure from the structure and spirit of our institutions; when the effect is to fetter and degrade the State governments by subjecting them to the control of Congress, in the exercise of powers heretofore universally conceded to them of the most ordinary and fundamental character; when in fact it radically changes the whole theory of the relations of the State and Federal governments to each other and of both these governments to the people; the argument has a force that is irresistible, in the absence of language which expresses such a purpose too clearly to admit of doubt.

We are convinced that no such results were intended by the Congress which proposed these amendments, nor by the legislatures of the States which ratified them.

Having shown that the privileges and immunities relied on in the argument are those which belong to citizens of the States as such, and that they are left to the State governments for security and protection, and not by this article placed under the special care of the Federal government, we may hold ourselves excused from defining the privileges and immunities of citizens of the United States which no State can abridge, until some case involving those privileges may make it necessary to do so.

But lest it be said that no such privileges and immunities are to be found if those we have been considering are excluded, we venture to suggest some which owe their existence to the Federal government, its National character, its Constitution, or its laws.

One of these is well described in the case of *Crandall* v. *Nevada*, 6 Wall. 35. It is said to be the right of the citizens of this great country, protected by implied guaranties of its Constitution, "to come to the seat of government to assert any claim he may have upon that government, to transact any business he may have with it, to seek its protection, to share its offices, to engage in administering its functions. He has the right of free access to its seaports, through which all operations of foreign commerce are conducted, to the subtreasuries, land offices, and courts of justice in the several States." And quoting from the language of Chief Justice Taney in another case, it is said "that for all the great purposes for which the Federal government was established, we are one people, with one common country, we are all citizens of the United States;" and it is, as such citizens, that their rights are supported in this court in *Crandall* v. *Nevada*.

Another privilege of a citizen of the United States is to demand the care and protection of the Federal government over his life, liberty, and property when on the high seas or within the jurisdiction of a foreign government. Of this there can be no doubt, nor that the right depends upon his character as a citizen of the United States. The right to peaceably assemble and petition for redress of grievances, the privilege of the writ of *habeas corpus*, are rights of the citizen guaranteed by the Federal Constitution. The right to use the navigable waters of the United States, however they may penetrate the territory of the several States, all rights secured to our citizens by treaties with foreign nations, are dependant upon citizenship of the United States, and not citizenship of a State. One of these privileges is conferred by the very article under consideration. It is that a citizen of the United States can, of his own volition, become a citizen of any State of the Union by a *bona fide* residence therein, with the same rights as other citizens of that State. To these may be added the rights secured by the thirteenth and fifteenth articles of amendment, and by the other clause of the fourteenth, next to be considered.

But it is useless to pursue this branch of the inquiry, since we are of opinion that the rights claimed by these plaintiffs in error, if they have any existence, are not privileges and immunities of citizens of the United States within the meaning of the clause of the fourteenth amendment under consideration. . . .

The argument has not been much pressed in these cases that the defendant's charter deprives the plaintiffs of their property without due process of law, or that it denies to them the equal protection of the law. The first of these paragraphs has been in the Constitution since the adoption of the fifth amendment, as a restraint upon the federal power. It is also to be found in some form of expression in the constitutions of nearly all the States, as a restraint upon the power of the States. This law, then, has practically been the same as it now is during the existence of the government, except so far as the present amendment may place the restraining power over the States in this matter in the hands of the Federal government.

We are not without judicial interpretation, therefore, both State and National, of the meaning of this clause. And it is sufficient to say that under no construction of that provision that we have ever seen, or any that we deem admissible, can the restraint imposed by the State of Louisiana upon the exercise of their trade by the butchers of New Orleans be held to be a deprivation of property within the meaning of that provision.

"Nor shall any State deny to any person within its jurisdiction the equal protection of the laws."

In the light of the history of these amendments, and the pervading purpose of them, which we have already discussed, it is not difficult to give a meaning to this clause. The existence of laws in the States where the newly emancipated Negroes resided, which discriminated with gross injustice and hardship against them as a class, was the evil to be remedied by this clause, and by it such laws are forbidden.

If, however, the States did not conform their laws to its requirements, then by the fifth section of the article of amendment Congress was authorized to enforce it by suitable legislation. We doubt very much whether any action of a State not directed by way of discrimination against the Negroes as a class, or on account of their race, will ever be held to come within the purview of this provision. It is so clearly a provision for that race and that emergency that a strong case would be necessary for its application to any other. But as it is a State that is to be dealt with, and not alone the validity of its laws, we may safely leave that matter until Congress shall have exercised its power, or some case of State oppression, by denial of equal justice in its courts, shall have claimed a decision at our hands. We find no such case in the one before us, and do not deem it necessary to go over the argument again, as it may have relation to this particular clause of the amendment. . . .

The judgments of the Supreme Court of Louisiana in these cases are affirmed.

MR. JUSTICE FIELD, dissenting: . . .

The question presented is . . . one of the gravest importance, not merely to the parties here, but to the whole country. It is nothing less than the question whether the recent amendments to the Federal Constitution protect the citizens of the United States against the deprivation of their common rights by State legislation. In my judgment the fourteenth amendment does afford such protection, and was so intended by the Congress which framed and the States which adopted it.

The amendment does not attempt to confer any new privileges or immunities upon citizens, or to enumerate or define those already existing. It assumes that there are such privileges and immunities which belong of right to citizens as such, and ordains that they shall not be abridged by State legislation. If this inhibition has no reference to privileges and immunities of this character, but only refers, as held by the majority of the court in their opinion, to such privileges and immunities as were before its adoption specially designated in the constitution or necessarily implied as belonging to the citizens of the United States, it was a vain and idle enactment, which accomplished nothing, and most unnecessarily excited Congress and the people on its passage. With privileges and immunities thus designated or implied no State could ever have interfered by its laws, and no new constitutional provision was required to inhibit such interference. The supremacy of the Constitution and the laws of the United States always controlled any State legislation of that character. But if the amendment refers to the natural and inalienable rights which belong to all citizens, the inhibition has a profound significance and consequence.

What, then, are the privileges and immunities which are secured against abridgment by State legislation? . . .

The terms, privileges and immunities, are not new in the Amendment; they were in the Constitution before the Amendment was adopted. They are found in the Second Section of the Fourth article, which declares that "the citizens of each State shall be entitled to all privileges and immunities of citizens in the several States," and they have been the subject of frequent consideration in judicial decisions. In *Corfield* v. *Coryell*, Mr. Justice Washington said he had "no hesitation in confining these expressions to those privileges and immunities which were, in their nature, fundamental; which belong of right to citizens of all free governments, and which have at all times been enjoyed by the citizens of the several States which compose the Union, from the time of their becoming free, independent, and sovereign;" and, in considering what those fundamental privileges were, he said that perhaps it would be more tedious than difficult to enumerate them, but that they might be "all comprehended under the following general heads; protection by the government; the enjoyment of life and liberty, with the right to acquire and possess property of every kind, and to pursue and obtain happiness and safety, subject, nevertheless, to such restraints as the government may justly prescribe for the general good of the whole." This appears to me to be a sound construction of the clause in question. The privileges and immunities designated are those *which of right belong to the citizens of all free governments*. Clearly among these must be placed the right to pursue a lawful employment in a lawful manner, without other restraint than such as equally affects all persons. In the discussions in Congress upon the passage of the Civil Rights Act repeated reference was made to this language of Mr. Justice Washington. It was cited by Senator Trumbull with the observation that it enumerated the very rights belonging to a citizen of the United States set forth in the first section of the act, and with the statement that all persons born in the United States, being declared by the act citizens of the United States, would thenceforth be entitled to the rights of citizens, and that these were the great fundamental rights set forth in the act; and that they were set forth "as appertaining to every freeman." . . .

This equality of right, with exemption from all disparaging and partial enactments, in the lawful pursuits of life, throughout the whole country, is the distinguishing privilege of citizens of the United States. To them, everywhere, all pursuits, all professions, all avocations are open without other restrictions than such as are imposed equally upon all others of the same age, sex, and condition. The State may prescribe such regulations for every pursuit and calling of life as will promote the public health, secure the good order and advance the general prosperity of society, but when once prescribed, the pursuit or calling must be free to be followed by every citizen who is within the conditions designated, and will conform to the regulations. This is the fundamental idea upon which our institutions rest, and unless adhered to in the legislation of the country our government will be a republic only in name. The fourteenth amendment, in my judgment, makes it essential to the validity of the legislation of every State that this equality of right should be respected. How widely this equality has been departed from, how entirely rejected and trampled upon by the act of Louisiana, I have already shown. And it is to me a matter of profound regret that its validity is recognized by a majority of this court, for by it the right of free labor, one of the most sacred and imprescriptible rights of man, is violated. . . .

I am authorized by the CHIEF JUSTICE [CHASE], MR. JUSTICE SWAYNE, and MR. JUSTICE BRADLEY, to state that they concur with me in this dissenting opinion.

JUSTICES BRADLEY and SWAYNE delivered separate dissenting opinions.

MUNN v. ILLINOIS

94 U.S. 113, 24 L.Ed. 77 (1876)

Everyone is familiar with the Granger movement. Its remnants in the form of farm granges are still to be found in the United States. What has perhaps been forgotten is that the movement dramatized the fact that there were problems in railroads and in other aspects of business enterprise that free competition could not solve. It aroused the American people to attempt to use the power inherent in representative government to make sure that property owners were less "free" and hence more "competitive." While even at this early stage this was labeled "rank Communism," the Illinois Constitution, adopted in 1870, required the Legislature to pass laws "for the protection of producers, shippers, and receivers of grain and produce." In compliance thereof an Illinois statute was passed in 1871 fixing the maximum charges in all grain elevators and public warehouses and requiring a license to operate them. Munn and others, in business as public warehousemen, refused to get such license on the ground that the fixing of rates of storage was unconstitutional. Having been found guilty in the Criminal Court of Cook County, Illinois, they bring this case on a writ of error to the Supreme Court of the State of Illinois.

Mr. Chief Justice Waite delivered the opinion of the court.

The question to be determined in this case is whether the general assembly of Illinois can, under the limitations upon the legislative powers of the States imposed by the Constitution of the United States, fix by law the maximum of charges for the storage of grain in warehouses at Chicago and other places in the State having not less than one hundred thousand inhabitants, "in which grain is stored in bulk, and in which the grain of different owners is mixed together, or in which grain is stored in such a manner that the identity of different lots or parcels cannot be accurately preserved."

It is claimed that such a law is repugnant—

1. To that part of sect. 8, art. I, of the Constitution of the United States which confers upon Congress the power "to regulate commerce with foreign nations and among the several States;"

2. To that part of sect. 9 of the same article, which provides that "no preference shall be given by any regulation of commerce or revenue to the ports of one State over those of another;" and

3. To that part of amendment 14 which ordains that no State shall "deprive any person of life, liberty, or property, without due process of law, nor deny to any person within its jurisdiction the equal protection of the laws."

We will consider the last of these objections first. . . .

The Constitution contains no definition of the word "deprive," as used in the Fourteenth Amendment. To determine its signification, therefore, it is necessary to ascertain the effect which usage has given it, when employed in the same or a like connection.

While this provision of the amendment is new in the Constitution of the United States, as a limitation upon the powers of the States, it is old as a principle of civilized government. It is found in Magna Carta, and, in substance if not in form, in nearly or quite all the constitutions that have been from time to time adopted by the several States of the Union. By the Fifth Amendment, it was introduced into the Constitution of the United States as a limitation upon the powers of the national government, and by the Fourteenth, as a guaranty against any encroachments upon an acknowledged right of citizenship by the legislatures of the States. . . .

When one becomes a member of society, he necessarily parts with some rights or privileges which, as an individual not affected by his relations to others, he might retain. "A body politic," as aptly defined in the preamble of the Constitution of Massachusetts, "is a social compact by which the whole people covenants with each citizen, and each citizen with the whole people, that all shall be governed by certain laws for the common good." This does not confer power upon the whole people to control rights which are purely and exclusively private, but it does authorize the establishment of laws requiring each citizen to so conduct himself, and so use his own property, as not unnecessarily to injure another. This is the very essence of government, and has found expression in the maxim, *sic utere tuo ut alienum non laedas*. From this source come the police powers, which, as was said by Mr. Chief Justice Taney in the *License Cases*, 5 How. 583, "are nothing more or less than the powers of government inherent in every sovereignty, . . . that is to say, . . . the power to govern men and things." Under these powers the government regulates the conduct of its citizens one towards another, and the manner in which each shall use his own property, when such regulation becomes necessary for the public good. In their exercise it has been customary in England from time immemorial, and in this country from its first colonization, to regulate ferries, common carriers, hackmen, bakers, millers, wharfingers, innkeepers, &c., and in so doing to fix a maximum of charge to be made for services rendered, accommodations furnished, and articles sold. To this day, statutes are to be found in many of the States upon some or all these subjects; and we think it has never yet been successfully contended that such legislation came within any of the constitutional prohibitions against interference with private property. With the Fifth Amendment in force, Congress in 1820, conferred power upon the city of Washington "to regulate . . . the rates of wharfage at private wharves, . . . the sweeping of chimneys, and to fix the rates of fees therefore, . . . and the weight and quality of bread"; and, in 1848, "to make all necessary regulations respecting hackney carriages and the rates of fare of the same, and the rates of hauling by cartmen, wagoners, carmen, and draymen, and the rates of commission of auctioneers."

From this it is apparent that, down to the time of the adoption of the Fourteenth Amendment, it was not supposed that statutes regulating the use, or even the price of the use, of private property necessarily deprived an owner of his property without due process of law. Under some circumstances they may, but not under all. The amendment does not change the law in this particular: it simply prevents the States from doing that which will operate as such a deprivation.

This brings us to inquire as to the principles upon which this power of regulation rests, in order that we may determine what is within and what is without its operative effect. Looking, then, to the common law, from whence came the right which the Constitution protects, we find that when private property is "affected with a public interest, it ceases to be *juris privati* only." This was said by Lord Chief Justice Hale more than two hundred years ago, in his treatise *De Portibus Maris*, 1 Harg. Law Tracts, 78, and has been accepted without objection as an essential element in the law of property ever since. Property does become clothed with a public interest when used in a manner to make it of public consequence, and affect the community at large. When, therefore, one devotes his property to a use in which the public has an interest, he, in effect, grants to the public an interest in that use, and must submit to be controlled by the public for the common good, to the extent of the interest he has thus created. He may withdraw his grant by discontinuing the use; but, so long as he maintains the use, he must submit to the control. . . .

From the same source comes the power to regulate the charges of common carriers, which was done in England as long ago as the third year of the reign of William and Mary, and continued until within a comparatively recent period. And in the first statute we find the following suggestive preamble, to wit:—

"And whereas divers wagoners and other carriers, by combination amongst themselves, have raised the prices of carriage of goods in many places to excessive rates, to the great injury of the trade: Be it, therefore, enacted," &c. 3 W. & M. c. 12, Sec. 24; 3 Stat. at Large (Great Britain), 481.

Common carriers exercise a sort of public office, and have duties to perform in which the public is interested. *New Jersey Nav. Co.* v. *Merchants' Bank,* 6 How. 382. Their business is, therefore, "affected with a public interest," within the meaning of the doctrine which Lord Hale has so forcibly stated.

But we need not go further. Enough has already been said to show that, when private property is devoted to a public use, it is subject to public regulation. It remains only to ascertain whether the warehouses of these plaintiffs in error, and the business which is carried on there, come within the operation of this principle.

For this purpose we accept as true the statements of fact contained in the elaborate brief of one of the counsel of the plaintiffs in error. From these it appears that "the great producing region of the West and Northwest sends its grain by water and rail to Chicago, where the greater part of it is shipped by vessel for transportation to the seaboard by the Great Lakes, and some of it is forwarded by railway to the Eastern ports. . . . Vessels, to some extent, are loaded in the Chicago harbor, and sailed through the St. Lawrence directly to Europe. . . . The quantity [of grain] received in Chicago has made it the greatest grain market in the world. This business has created a demand for means by which the immense quantity of grain can be handled or stored, and these have been found in grain warehouses, which are commonly called elevators, because the grain is elevated from the boat or car, by machinery operated by steam, into the bins prepared for its reception, and elevated from the bins, by a like process, into the vessel or car which is to carry it on. . . . In this way the trade in grain is carried on by the inhabitants of seven or eight of the great States of the West with four or five of the States lying on the sea-shore, and forms the largest part of interstate commerce in these States. The grain warehouses or elevators in Chicago are immense structures, holding from 300,000 to 1,000,000 bushels at one time according to size. They are divided into bins of large capacity and great strength. . . . They are located with the river harbor on one side and the railway tracks on the other; and the grain is run through them from car to vessel, or boat to car, as may be demanded in the course of business. It has been found impossible to preserve each owner's grain separate, and this has given rise to a system of inspection and grading, by which the grain of different owners is mixed, and receipts issued for the number of bushels which are negotiable, and redeemable in like kind, upon demand. This mode of conducting the business was inaugurated more than twenty years ago, and has grown to immense proportions. The railways have found it impracticable to own such elevators, and public policy forbids the transaction of such business by the carrier; the ownership has, therefore, been by private individuals who have embarked their capital and devoted their industry to such business as a private pursuit."

In this connection it must also be borne in mind that, although in 1874 there were in Chicago fourteen warehouses adapted to this particular business, and owned by about thirty persons, nine business firms controlled them, and that the prices charged and received for storage were such "as have been from year to year agreed upon and established by the different elevators or warehouses in the city of Chicago, and which rates have been annually published in one or more newspapers printed in said city, in the month of January in each year, as the established rates for the year then next ensuing such publication." Thus it is apparent that all the elevating facilities through which these vast productions "of seven or eight great States of the West" must pass on the way "to four or five of the States on the sea-shore" may be a "virtual" monopoly.

Under such circumstances it is difficult to see why, if the common carrier, or the miller, or the ferryman, or the innkeeper, or the wharfinger, or the baker, or the cartman, or the hackney-coachman, pursues a public employment and exercises "a sort of public office," these plaintiffs in error do not. They stand, to use again the language of their counsel, in the very "gateway of commerce," and take toll from all who pass. Their business most certainly "tends to a common charge, and is become a thing of public interest and use." Every bushel of grain for its passage "pays a toll, which is a common charge," and, therefore, according to Lord Hale, every such warehouseman "ought to be under public regulation, viz., that he . . . take but reasonable toll." Certainly, if any business can be clothed "with a public interest and cease to be *juris privati* only," this has been. It may not be made so by the operation of the Constitution of Illinois or this statute, but it is by the facts. . . .

Neither is it a matter of any moment that no precedent can be found for a statute precisely like this. It is conceded that the business is one of recent origin, that its growth has been rapid, and it is already of great importance. And it must also be conceded that it is a business in which the whole public has a direct and positive interest. It presents, therefore, a case for the application of a long-known and well-established principle in social science, and this statute simply extends the law so as to meet this new development of commercial progress. There is no attempt to compel these owners to grant the public an interest in their property, but to declare their obligations, if they use it in this particular manner.

It matters not in this case that these plaintiffs in error had built their warehouses and established their business before the regulations complained of were adopted. What they did was from the beginning subject to the power of the body politic to require them to conform to such regulations as might be established by the proper authorities for the common good. They entered upon their business and provided themselves with the means to carry it on subject to this condition. If they did not wish to submit themselves to such interference they should not have clothed the public with an interest in their concerns. The same principle applies to them that does to the proprietor of a hackney-carriage, and as to him it has never been supposed that he was exempt from regulating statutes or ordinances because he had purchased his horses and carriage and established his business before the statute or the ordinance was adopted. . . .

Judgment affirmed.

Mr. Justice Field and Mr. Justice Strong dissented. . . .

Mr. Justice Field. I am compelled to dissent from the decision of the court in this case, and from the reasons upon which that decision is founded. The principle upon which the opinion of the majority proceeds is, in my judgment, subversive of the rights of private property, heretofore believed to be protected by constitutional guaranties against legislative interference, and is in conflict with the authorities cited in its support. . . .

If this be sound law, if there be no protection, either in the principles upon which our republican government is founded, or in the prohibitions of the constitution against such invasion of private rights, all property and all business in the State are held at the mercy of a majority of its legislature. The public has no greater interest in the use of buildings for the storage of grain than it has in the use of buildings for the residences of families, nor, indeed, any thing like so great an interest; and, according to the doctrine announced, the legislature may fix the rent of all tenements used for residences, without reference to the cost of their erection. If the owner does not like the rates prescribed, he may cease renting his houses. He has granted to the public, says the court, an interest in the use of the buildings, and "he may withdraw his grant by discontinuing the use; but, so long as he maintains the use, he must submit to the control." The public is interested in the manufacture of cotton, woollen, and silken fabrics, in the construction of machinery, in the printing and publication of books and periodicals, and in the making of utensils of every variety, useful and ornamental; indeed, there is hardly an enterprise or business engaging the attention and labor of any considerable portion of the community, in which the public has not an interest in the sense in which that term is used by the court in its opinion; and the doctrine which allows the legislature to interfere with and regulate the charges which the owners of property thus employed shall make for its use, that is, the rates at which all these different kinds of business shall be carried on, has never before been asserted, so far as I am aware, by any judicial tribunal in the United States. . . .

No State "shall deprive any person of life, liberty, or property without due process of law," says the Fourteenth Amendment to the Constitution. By the term "life," as here used, something more is meant than mere animal existence. The inhibition against its deprivation extends to all those limbs and faculties by which life is enjoyed. The provision equally prohibits the mutilation of the body by the amputation of an arm or leg, or the putting out of an eye, or the destruction of any other organ of the body through which the soul communicates with the outer world. The deprivation not only of life, but of whatever God has given to every one with life, for its growth and enjoyment, is prohibited by the provision in question, if its efficacy be not frittered away by judicial decision.

By the term "liberty," as used in the provision, something more is meant than mere freedom from physical restraint or the bounds of a prison. It means freedom to go where one may choose, and to act in such manner, not inconsistent with the equal rights of others, as his judgment may dictate for the promotion of his happiness; that is, to pursue such callings and avocations as may be most suitable to develop his capacities, and give to them their highest enjoyment.

The same liberal construction which is required for the protection of life and liberty, in all particulars in which life and liberty are of any value, should be applied to the protection of private property. If the legislature of a State, under pretence of providing for the public good, or for any other reason, can determine, against the consent of the owner, the uses to which private property shall be devoted, or the prices which the owner shall receive for its uses, it can deprive him of the property as completely as by a special act for its confiscation or destruction. If, for instance, the owner is prohibited from using his building for the purposes for which it was designed, it is of little consequence that he is permitted to retain the title and possession; or, if he is compelled to take as compensation for its use less than the expenses to which he is subjected by its ownership, he is, for all practical purposes, deprived of the property, as effectually as if the legislature had ordered his forcible dispossession. If it be admitted that the legislature has any control over the compensation, the extent of that compensation becomes a mere matter of legislative discretion. The amount fixed will operate as a partial destruction of the value of the property, if it fall below the amount which the owner would obtain by contract, and, practically, as a complete destruction, if it be less than the cost of retaining its possession. There is, indeed, no protection of any value under the constitutional provision, which does not extend to the use and income of the property, as well as to its title and possession. . . .

HOLDEN v. HARDY

169 U.S. 366, 42 L.Ed. 780 (1898)

The need for reform in this so-called "Age of Reform" was not limited geographically to the Midwest, or professionally to the farmer, or to "rates" to be charged by railroads or grain elevator operators. Its need was also apparent in the large sphere of "employee-employer" relationship, involving such aspects as maximum hours, union membership, and minimum wages. In the case below, while the legislative act involved is clearly set forth in the opinion, it should be pointed out that Holden had been convicted on charges of having employed workmen for more than the eight hours permitted and sentenced to jail. The Supreme Court of Utah denied his application for a writ of habeas corpus and the case comes to the Supreme Court of the United States on a writ of error.

MR. JUSTICE BROWN delivered the opinion of the court:

This case involves the constitutionality of an act of the legislature of Utah of March 30, 1896, chap. 72 entitled "An Act Regulating the Hours of Employment in Underground Mines and in Smelters and Ore Reduction Works." The following are the material provisions:

Sec. 1. The period of employment of workingmen in all underground mines or workings shall be eight hours per day, except in cases of emergency where life or property is in imminent danger.

Sec. 2. The period of employment of workingmen in smelters and all other institutions for the reduction or refining of ores or metals shall be eight hours per day, except in cases of emergency where life or property is in imminent danger.

Sec. 3. Any person, body corporate, agent, manager, or employer, who shall violate any of the provisions of sections one and two of this act, shall be guilty of a misdemeanor. . . .

The validity of the statute in question is . . . challenged upon the ground of an alleged violation of the 14th Amendment to the Constitution of the United States, in that it abridges the privileges or immunities of citizens of the United States; deprives both the employer and the laborer of his property without due process of law, and denies them the equal protection of the laws. As the three questions of abridging their immunities, depriving them of their property, and denying them the protection of the laws, are so connected that the authorities upon each are, to a greater or less extent, pertinent to the others, they may properly be considered together.

Prior to the adoption of the 14th Amendment there was a similar provision against deprivation of life, liberty, or property without due process of law incorporated in the 5th Amendment; but as the first eight amendments to the Constitution were obligatory only upon Congress, the decisions of this court under this amendment have but a partial application to the 14th Amendment, which operates only upon the action of the several states. The 14th Amendment, which was finally adopted July 28, 1868, largely expanded the power of the Federal courts and Congress, and for the first time authorized the former to declare invalid all laws and judicial decisions of the states abridging the rights of citizens or denying them the benefit of due process of law.

This amendment was first called to the attention of this court in 1872, in an attack upon the constitutionality of a law of the state of Louisiana, passed in 1869, vesting in a slaughter-house company therein named the sole and exclusive privilege of conducting and carrying on a live-stock landing and slaughterhouse business, within certain limits specified in the act, and requiring all animals intended for sale and slaughter to be landed at their wharves or landing places. While the court in that case recognized the fact that the primary object of this amendment was to secure to the colored race, then recently emancipated, the full enjoyment of their freedom, the further fact that it was not restricted to that purpose was admitted both in the prevailing and dissenting opinions, and the validity of the act was sustained as a proper police regulation for the health and comfort of the people. A majority of the cases, which have since arisen, have turned, not upon a denial to the colored race of rights therein secured to them, but upon alleged discriminations in matters entirely outside of the political relations of the parties aggrieved.

These cases may be divided, generally, into two classes: First, where a state legislature, or a state court, is alleged to have unjustly discriminated in favor of or against a particular individual or class of individuals, as distinguished from the rest of the community, or denied them the benefit of due process of law; second, where the legislature has changed its general system of jurisprudence by abolishing what had been previously considered necessary to the proper administration of justice, or the protection of the individual. . . .

An examination of both these classes of cases under the 14th Amendment will demonstrate that, in passing upon the validity of state legislation under that Amendment, this court has not failed to recognize the fact that the law is to a certain extent a progressive science; that in some of the states methods of procedure which, at the time the Constitution was adopted, were deemed essential to the protection and safety of the people, or to the liberty of the citizen, have been found to be no longer necessary; that restrictions which had formerly been laid upon the conduct of individuals, or of classes of individuals, had proved detrimental to their interests; while, upon the other hand, certain other classes of persons, particularly those engaged in dangerous or unhealthful employments, have been found to be in need of additional protection. Even before the adoption of the Constitution, much had been done toward mitigating the severity of the common law, particularly in the administration of its criminal branch. The number of capital crimes in this country, at least, had been largely decreased. Trial by ordeal and by battle had never existed here, and had fallen into disuse in England. The earlier practice of the common law, which denied the benefit of witnesses to a person accused of felony, had been abolished by statute, though so far as it deprived him of the assistance of counsel and compulsory process for the attendance of his witnesses, it had not been changed in England. But to the credit of her American colonies let it be said, that so oppressive a doctrine had never obtained a foothold there.

The present century has originated legal reforms of no less importance. The whole fabric of special pleading, once thought to be necessary to the elimination of the real issue between the parties, has crumbled to pieces. The ancient tenures of real estate have been largely swept away, and land is now transferred almost as easily and cheaply as personal property. Married women have been emancipated from the control of their husbands and placed upon a practical equality with them with respect to the acquisition, possession, and transmission of property. Imprisonment for debt has been abolished. Exemptions from execution have been largely added to, and in most of the states homesteads are rendered incapable of seizure and sale upon forced process. Witnesses are no longer incompetent by reason of interest, even though they be parties to the litigation. Indictments have been simplified, and an indictment for the most serious of crimes is now the simplest of all. In several of the states grand juries, formerly the only safeguard against a malicious prosecution, have been largely abolished, and in others the rule of unanimity, so far as applied to civil cases, has given way to verdicts rendered by a three-fourths majority. This case does not call for an expression of opinion as to the wisdom of these changes, or their validity under the 14th Amendment, although the substitution of prosecution by information in lieu of indictment was recognized as valid in *Hurtado* v. *California*, 110 U.S. 516. They are mentioned only for the purpose of calling attention to the probability that other changes of no less importance may be made in the future, and that while the cardinal principles of justice are immutable, the methods by which justice is administered are subject to constant fluctuation, and that the Constitution of the United States, which is necessarily and to a large extent inflexible and exceedingly difficult of amendment, should not be so construed as to deprive the states of the power to so amend their laws as to make them conform to the wishes of the citizens as they may deem best for the public welfare without bringing them into conflict with the supreme law of the land.

Of course, it is impossible to forecast the character or extent of these changes, but in view of the fact that, from the day Magna Charta was signed to the present moment, amendments to the structure of the law have been made with increasing frequency, it is impossible to suppose that they will not continue, and the law be forced to adapt itself to new conditions of society, and, particularly, to the new relations between employers and employees, as they arise. . . .

We do not wish, however, to be understood as holding that this power is unlimited. While the people of the state may doubtless adopt such systems of laws as best conform to their own traditions and customs, the people of the entire country have laid down in the Constitution of the United States certain fundamental principles to which each member of the Union is bound to accede as a condition of its admission as a state. Thus, the government, and the 10th section of the 1st article contains certain other specified limitations upon the power of the several states, the object of which was to secure to Congress paramount authority with respect to matters of universal concern. In addition, the 14th Amendment contains a sweeping provision forbidding the states from abridging the privileges and immunities of citizens of the United States, and denying them the benefit of due process or equal protection of the laws.

This court has never attempted to define with precision the words "due process of law," nor is it necessary to do so in this case. It is sufficient to say that there are certain immutable principles of justice which inhere in the very idea of free government which no member of the Union may disregard, as that no man shall be condemned in his person or property without due notice and an opportunity of being heard in his defense. . . .

It was said by Mr. Justice Miller, in delivering the opinion of this court in *Davidson* v. *New Orleans*, 96 U.S. 97, that the words "law of the land," as used in Magna Charta, implied a conformity with the "ancient and customary laws of the English people," and that it was wiser to ascertain their intent and application by the "gradual process of judicial inclusion and exclusion, as the cases presented for decision shall require, with the reasoning on which such decisions may be founded." Recognizing the difficulty in defining, with exactness, the phrase "due process of law," it is certain that these words imply a conformity with natural and inherent principles of justice, and forbid that one man's property, or right to property, shall be taken for the benefit of another, or for the benefit of the state, without compensation; and that no one shall be condemned in his person or property without an opportunity of being heard in his own defense.

As the possession of property, of which a person cannot be deprived, doubtless implies that such property may be acquired, it is safe to say that a state law, which undertakes to deprive any class of persons of the general power to acquire property, would also be obnoxious to the same provision. Indeed, we may go a step further, and say that as property can only be legally acquired as between living persons by contract, that a general prohibition against entering into contracts with respect to property, or having as their object the acquisition of property, would be equally invalid. . . .

This right of contract, however, is itself subject to certain limitations which the state may lawfully impose in the exercise of its police powers. While this power is inherent in all governments, it has doubtless been greatly expanded in its application during the past century, owing to an enormous increase in the number of occupations which are dangerous, or so far detrimental to the health of employees as to demand special precaution for their well-being and protection, or the safety of adjacent property. While this court has held, notably in the cases of *Davidson* v. *New Orleans*, 96 U.S. 97, and *Yick Wo* v. *Hopkins*, 118 U.S. 356, that the police power cannot be put forward as an excuse for oppressive and unjust legislation, it may be lawfully resorted to for the purpose of preserving the public health, safety, or morals, or the abatement of public nuisances, and a large discretion "is necessarily vested in the legislature to determine, not only what the interests of the public require, but what measures are necessary for the protection of such interests." *Lawton* v. *Steele*, 152 U.S. 133, 136 . . .

While the business of mining coal and manufacturing iron began in Pennsylvania as early as 1716, and in Virginia, North Carolina, and Massachusetts even earlier than this, both mining and manufacturing were carried on in such a limited way and by such primitive methods that no special laws were considered necessary, prior to the adoption of the Constitution, for the protection of the operatives, but, in the vast proportions which these industries have since assumed, it has been found that they can no longer be carried on with due regard to the safety and health of those engaged in them, without special protection against the dangers necessarily incident to these employments. In consequence of this, laws have been enacted in most of the states designed to meet these exigencies and to secure the safety of persons peculiarly exposed to these dangers. Within this general category are ordinances providing for fire escapes for hotels, theaters, factories, and other large buildings, a municipal inspection of boilers, and appliances designed to secure passengers upon railways and steamboats against the dangers necessarily incident to these methods of transportation. In states where manufacturing is carried on to a large extent, provision is made for the protection of dangerous machinery against accidental contact, for the cleanliness and ventilation of working rooms, for the guarding of well holes, stairways, elevator shafts, and for the employment of sanitary appliances. In others, where mining is the principal industry, special provision is made for the shoring up of dangerous walls, for ventilation shafts, bore holes, escapement shafts, means of signaling the surface, for the supply of fresh air and the elimination, as far as possible, of dangerous gases, for safe means of hoisting and lowering cages, for a limitation upon the number of persons permitted to enter a cage, that cages shall be covered, and that there shall be fences and gates around the top of shafts, besides other similar precautions. . . .

But if it be within the power of a legislature to adopt such means for the protection of the lives of its citizens, it is difficult to see why precautions may not also be adopted for the protection of their health and morals. It is as much for the interest of the state that the public health should be preserved as that life should be made secure. With this end in view quarantine laws have been enacted, in most if not all of the states; insane asylums, public hospitals, and institutions for the care and education of the blind established, and special measures taken for the exclusion of infected cattle, rags, and decayed fruit. In other states laws have been enacted limiting the hours during which women and children shall be employed in factories; and while their constitutionality, at least as applied to women, has been doubted in some of the states, they have been generally upheld. Thus, in the case of *Commonwealth* v. *Hamilton Manufacturing Co.*, 120 Mass. 383, it was held that a statute prohibiting the employment of all persons under the age of eighteen, and of all women laboring in any manufacturing establishment more than sixty hours per week, violates no contract of the commonwealth implied in the granting of a charter to a manufacturing company nor any right reserved under the Constitution to any individual citizen, and may be maintained as a health or police regulation.

Upon the principles above stated, we think the act in question may be sustained as a valid exercise of the police power of the state. The enactment does not profess to limit the hours of all workmen, but merely those who are employed in underground mines, or in the smelting, reduction, or refining of ores or metals. These employments when too long pursued the legislature has judged to be detrimental to the health of the employees, and, so long as there are reasonable grounds for believing that this is so, its decision upon this subject cannot be reviewed by the Federal courts.

While the general experience of mankind may justify us in believing that men may engage in ordinary employments more than eight hours per day without injury to their health, it does not follow that labor for the same length of time is innocuous when carried on beneath the surface of the earth, when the operative is deprived of fresh air and sunlight, and is frequently subjected to foul atmosphere and a very high temperature, or to the influence of noxious gases, generated by the processes of refining or smelting. . . .

The legislature has also recognized the fact, which the experience of legislators in many states has corroborated, that the proprietors of these establishments and their operatives do not stand upon an equality, and that their interests are, to a certain extent, conflicting. The former naturally desire to obtain as much labor as possible from their employees, while the latter are often induced by the fear of discharge to conform to regulations which their judgment, fairly exercised, would pronounce to be detrimental to their health or strength. In other words, the proprietors lay down the rules and the laborers are practically constrained to obey them. In such cases self-interest is often an unsafe guide, and the legislature may properly interpose its authority.

It may not be improper to suggest in this connection that although the prosecution in this case was against the employer of labor, who apparently under the statute is the only one liable, his defense is not so much that his right to contract has been infringed upon, but that the act works a peculiar hardship to his employees, whose right to labor as long as they please is alleged to be thereby violated. The argument would certainly come with better grace and greater cogency from the latter class. But the fact that both parties are of full age and competent to contract does not necessarily deprive the state of the power to interfere where the parties do not stand upon an equality, or where the public health demands that one party to the contract shall be protected against himself. "The state still retains an interest in his welfare, however reckless he may be. The whole is no greater than the sum of all the parts, and when the individual health, safety, and welfare are sacrificed or neglected, the state must suffer."

We have no disposition to criticise the many authorities which hold that state statutes restricting the hours of labor are unconstitutional. Indeed, we are not called upon to express an opinion upon this subject. It is sufficient to say of them that they have no application to cases where the legislature had adjudged that a limitation is necessary for the preservation of the health of the employees, and there are reasonable grounds for believing that such determination is supported by the facts. The question in each case is whether the legislature has adopted the statute in exercise of a reasonable discretion, or whether its action be a mere excuse for an unjust discrimination, or the oppression, or spoliation of a particular class. The distinction between these two different classes of enactments cannot be better stated than by a comparison of the views this court found in the opinion in *Barbier* v. *Connolly*, 113 U.S. 27, and *Soon Hing* v. *Crowley*, 113 U.S. 703, with those later expressed in *Yick Wo* v. *Hopkins*, 118 U.S. 356.

We are of opinion that the act in question was a valid exercise of the police power of the state, and the judgments of the Supreme Court of Utah are therefore affirmed.

Mr. Justice Brewer and Mr. Justice Peckham dissented.

LOCHNER v. NEW YORK

198 U.S. 45, 49 L.Ed. 937 (1905)

In the Holden case above the Court seemed to go out of its way in maintaining that "law . . . adapt itself to new conditions of society and, particularly, to the new relations between employers and employees, as they arise. . . ." With this as a "green light" other states began to enact so-called labor legislation. What perhaps was lost sight of was the warning in another part of the Court's opinion which declared: "We do not wish, however, to be understood as holding that this power is unlimited." Though the record of the Court in upholding state legislation passed in pursuance of its so-called "police power" had indeed been remarkable, the "yellow-red" light was there: it would be for the Court to decide these limits.

The New York Legislature in 1897 enacted a labor law which provided, among other things, that no employee "be required or permitted to work in a biscuit, bread or cake bakery or confectionery establishment more than sixty hours in any one week, or more than ten hours in any one day unless for the purpose of making a shorter work day on the last day of the week." Lochner, the defendant in the Courts below, an employer, was convicted for violating the statute, and such convictions were sustained by all the New York Courts through its Court of Appeals. Since the record had been remitted to the County Court of Oneida County where the case began, the writ of error was addressed to that Court.

MR. JUSTICE PECKHAM . . . delivered the opinion of the court. . . .

The statute necessarily interferes with the right of contract between the employer and employees, concerning the number of hours in which the latter may labor in the bakery of the employer. The general right to make a contract in relation to his business is part of the liberty of the individual protected by the Fourteenth Amendment of the Federal Constitution. *Allgeyer* v. *Louisiana,* 165 U.S. 578. . . .

The State . . . has power to prevent the individual from making certain kinds of contracts, and in regard to them the Federal Constitution offers no protection. If the contract be one which the State, in the legitimate exercise of its police power, has the right to prohibit, it is not prevented from prohibiting it by the Fourteenth Amendment. Contracts in violation of a statute, either of the Federal or State government, or a contract to let one's property for immoral purposes, or to do any other unlawful act, could obtain no protection from the Federal Constitution, as coming under the liberty of person or of free contract. Therefore, when the State, by its legislature, in the assumed exercise of its police powers, has passed an act which seriously limits the right to labor or the right of contract in regard to their means of livelihood between persons who are *sui juris* (both employer and employee), it becomes of great importance to determine which shall prevail—the right of the individual to labor for such time as he may choose, or the right of the State to prevent the individual from laboring or from entering into contract to labor, beyond a certain time prescribed by the State.

This court has recognized the existence and upheld the exercise of the police powers of the States in many cases which might fairly be considered as border ones, and it has, in the course of its determination of questions regarding the asserted invalidity of such statutes, on the ground of their violation of the rights secured by the Federal Constitution, been guided by rules of a very liberal nature, the application of which has resulted, in numerous instances, in upholding the validity of state statutes thus assailed. . . .

It must, of course, be conceded that there is a limit to the valid exercise of the police power by the State. . . . In every case that comes before this court, therefore, where legislation of this character is concerned and where the protection of the Federal Constitution is sought, the question necessarily arises: Is this a fair, reasonable and appropriate exercise of the police power of the State, or is it an unreasonable, unnecessary and arbitrary interference with the right of the individual to his personal liberty or to enter into those contracts in relation to labor which may seem to him appropriate or necessary for the support of himself and his family? Of course the liberty of contract relating to labor includes both parties to it. The one has as much right to purchase as the other to sell labor.

This is not a question of substituting the judgment of the court for that of the legislature. If the act be within the power of the State it is valid, although the judgment of the court might be totally opposed to the enactment of such a law. But the question would still remain: Is it within the police power of the State? and that question must be answered by the court.

The question whether this act is valid as a labor law, pure and simple, may be dismissed in a few words. There is no reasonable ground for interfering with the liberty of person or the right of free contract, by determining the hours of labor, in the occupation of a baker. There is no contention that bakers as a class are not equal in intelligence and capacity to men in other trades or manual occupations, or that they are not able to assert their rights and care for themselves without the protecting arm of the State, interfering with their independence of judgment and of action. They are in no sense wards of the State. . . . The law must be upheld, if at all, as a law pertaining to the health of the individual engaged in the occupation of a baker. It does not affect any other portion of the public than those who are engaged in that occupation. Clean and wholesome bread does not depend upon whether the baker works but ten hours a day or only sixty hours a week. The limitation of the hours of labor does not come within the police power on that ground.

It is a question of which of two powers or rights shall prevail—the power of the State to legislate or the right of the individual to liberty of person and freedom of contract. The mere assertion that the subject relates though but in a remote degree to the public health does not necessarily render the enactment valid. The act must have a more direct relation, as a means to an end, and the end itself must be appropriate and legitimate, before an act can be held to be valid which interferes with the general right of an individual to be free in his person and in his power to contract in relation to his own labor.

This case has caused much diversity of opinion in the state courts. In the Supreme Court two of the five judges composing the Appellate Division dissented from the judgment affirming the validity of the act. In the Court of Appeals three of the seven judges also dissented from the judgment upholding the statute. Although found in what is called a labor law of the State, the Court of Appeals has upheld the act as one relating to the public health—in other words, as a health law. One of the judges of the Court of Appeals, in upholding the law, stated that, in his opinion, the regulation in question could not be sustained unless they were able to say, from common knowledge, that working in a bakery and candy factory was an unhealthy employment. The judge held that, while the evidence was not uniform, it still led him to the conclusion that the occupation of a baker or confectioner was unhealthy and tended to result in diseases of the respiratory organs. Three of the judges dissented from that view, and they thought the occupation of a baker was not to such an extent unhealthy as to warrant the interference of the legislature with the liberty of the individual.

We think the limit of the police power has been reached and passed in this case. There is, in our judgment, no reasonable foundation for holding this to be necessary or appropriate as a health law to safeguard the public health or the health of the individuals who are following the trade of a baker. If this statute be valid, and if, therefore, a proper case is made out in which to deny the right of an individual, *sui juris*, as employer or employee, to make contracts for the labor of the latter under the protection of the provisions of the Federal Constitution, there would seem to be no length to which legislation of this nature might not go. . . .

We think that there can be no fair doubt that the trade of a baker, in and of itself, is not an unhealthy one to that degree which would authorize the legislature to interfere with the right to labor, and with the right of free contract on the part of the individual, either as employer or employee. In looking through statistics regarding all trade and occupations, it may be true that the trade of a baker does not appear to be as healthy as some other trades, and is also vastly more healthy than still others. To the common understanding the trade of a baker has never been regarded as an unhealthy one. Very likely physicians would not recommend the exercise of that or of any other trade as a remedy for ill health. Some occupations are more healthy than others, but we think there are none which might not come under the power of the legislature to supervise and control the hours of working therein, if the mere fact that the occupation is not absolutely and perfectly healthy is to confer that right upon the legislative department of the government. It might be safely affirmed that almost all occupations more or less affect the health. . . . But are we all, on that account, at the mercy of legislative majorities? . . .

Statutes of the nature of that under review, limiting the hours in which grown and intelligent men may labor to earn their living, are mere meddlesome interferences with the rights of the individual, and they are not saved from condemnation by the claim that they are passed in the exercise of the police power and upon the subject of the health of the individual whose rights are interfered with, unless there be some fair ground, reasonable in and of itself, to say that there is material danger to the public health or to the health of the employees, if the hours of labor are not curtailed. . . .

It was further urged on the argument that restricting the hours of labor in the case of bakers was valid because it tended to cleanliness on the part of the workers, as a man was more apt to be cleanly when not overworked, and if cleanly then his "output" was also more likely to be so. . . . In our judgment it is not possible in fact to discover the connection between the number of hours a baker may work in the bakery and the healthy quality of the bread made by the workman. The connection, if any exists, is too shadowy and thin to build any argument for the interference of the legislature. If the man works ten hours a day it is all right, but if ten and a half or eleven his health is in danger and his bread may be unhealthful, and, therefore he shall not be permitted to do it. This, we think, is unreasonable and entirely arbitrary. . . .

It is impossible for us to shut our eyes to the fact that many of the laws of this character, while passed under what is claimed to be the police power for the purpose of protecting the public health or welfare, are, in reality, passed from other motives. We are justified in saying so when, from the character of the law and the subject upon which it legislates, it is apparent that the public health or welfare bears but the most remote relation to the law. The purpose of a statute must be determined from the natural and legal effect of the language employed; and whether it is or is not repugnant to the Constitution of the United States must be determined from the natural effect of such statutes when put into operation, and not from their proclaimed purpose. . . . The court looks beyond the mere letter of the law in such cases.

It is manifest to us that the limitation of the hours of labor as provided for in this section of the statute under which the indictment was found, and the plaintiff in error convicted, has no such direct relation to and no such substantial effect upon the health of the employee, as to justify us in regarding the section as really a health law. . . .

The judgment of the Court of Appeals of New York as well as that of the Supreme Court and of the County Court of Oneida County must be reversed and the case remanded to the County Court for further proceedings not inconsistent with this opinion.

Reversed.

MR. JUSTICE HARLAN (with whom MR. JUSTICE WHITE and MR. JUSTICE DAY concurred) dissenting:

While this court has not attempted to mark the precise boundaries of what is called the police power of the state, the existence of the power has been uniformly recognized, equally by the Federal and State courts.

All the cases agree that this power extends at least to the protection of the lives, the health, and the safety of the public against the injurious exercise by any citizen of his own rights. . . .

It is plain that this statute was enacted in order to protect the physical well-being of those who work in bakery and confectionery establishments. It may be that the statute had its origin, in part, in the belief that employers and employees in such establishments were not upon an equal footing, and that the necessities of the latter often compelled them to submit to such exactions as unduly taxed their strength. Be this as it may, the statute must be taken as expressing the belief of the people of New York that, as a general rule, and in the case of the average man, labor in excess of sixty hours during a week in such establishments may endanger the health of those who thus labor. Whether or not this be wise legislation it is not the province of the court to inquire. Under our systems of government the courts are not concerned with the wisdom or policy of legislation. So that, in determining the question of power to interfere with liberty of contract, the court may inquire whether the means devised by the state are germane to an end which may be lawfully accomplished and have a real or substantial relation to the protection of health, as involved in the daily work of the person, male and female, engaged in bakery and confectionery establishments. . . .

Professor Hirt in his treatise on the "Diseases of the Workers" has said: "The labor of the bakers is among the hardest and most laborious imaginable, because it has to be performed under conditions injurious to the health of those engaged in it. It is hard, very hard, work, not only because it requires a great deal of physical exertion in an over-heated workshop and during unreasonably long hours, but more so because of the erratic demands of the public, compelling the baker to perform the greater part of his work at night, thus depriving him of an opportunity to enjoy the necessary rest and sleep,—a fact which is highly injurious to his health." Another writer says: "The constant inhaling of flour dust causes inflammation of the lungs and of the bronchial tubes. The eyes also suffer through this dust, which is responsible for the many cases of running eyes among the bakers. The long hours of toil to which all bakers are subjected produce rheumatism, cramps, and swollen legs. The intense heat in the work-shops induces the workers to resort to cooling drinks, which, together with their habit of exposing the greater part of their bodies to the change in the atmosphere, is another source of a number of diseases of various organs. Nearly all bakers are palefaced and of more delicate health than the workers of other crafts, which is chiefly due to their hard work and their irregular and unnatural mode of living, whereby the power of resistance against disease is greatly diminished. The average age of a baker is below that of other workmen; they seldom live over their fiftieth year, most of them dying between the ages of forty and fifty. During periods of epidemic diseases the bakers are generally the first to succumb to the disease, and the number swept away during such periods far exceeds the number of other crafts in comparison to the men employed in the respective industries. When, in 1720, the plague visited the city of Marseilles, France, every baker in the city succumbed to the epidemic, which caused considerable excitement in the neighboring cities and resulted in measures for the sanitary protection of the bakers." . . .

. . . There are many reasons of a weighty, substantial character, based upon the experience of mankind, in support of the theory that, all things considered, more than ten hours' steady work each day, from week to week, in a bakery or confectionery establishment, may endanger the health and shorten the lives of the workmen, thereby diminishing their physical and mental capacity to serve the state and to provide for those dependent upon them. . . .

I take leave to say that the New York statute, in the particulars here involved, cannot be held to be in conflict with the 14th Amendment, without enlarging the scope of the amendment far beyond its original purpose, and without bringing under the supervision of this court matters which have been supposed to belong exclusively to the legislative departments of the several states when exerting their conceded power to guard the health and safety of their citizens by such regulations as they in their wisdom deem best. Health laws of every description constitute, said Chief Justice Marshall, a part of that mass of legislation which "embraces everything within the territory of a state, not surrendered to the general government; all of which can be most advantageously exercised by the states themselves." *Gibbons* v. *Ogden*, 9 Wheat. 1, 203. A decision that the New York statute is void under the 14th Amendment, will, in my opinion, involve consequences of a far-reaching and mischievous character; for such a decision would seriously cripple the inherent power of the states to care for the lives, health, and well-being of their citizens. Those are matters which can be best controlled by the states. The preservation of the just powers of the states is quite as vital as the preservation of the powers of the general government. . . .

The judgment, in my opinion, should be affirmed.

MR. JUSTICE HOLMES dissenting:

I regret sincerely that I am unable to agree with the judgment in this case, and that I think it my duty to express my dissent.

This case is decided upon an economic theory which a large part of the country does not entertain. If it were a question whether I agreed with that theory, I should desire to study it further and long before making up my mind. But I do not conceive that to be my duty, because I strongly believe that my agreement or disagreement has nothing to do with the right of a majority to embody their opinions in law. It is settled by various decisions of this court that state constitutions and state laws may regulate life in many ways which we as legislators might think as injudicious, or if you like as tyrannical, as this, and which, equally with this, interfere with the liberty to contract. Sunday laws and usury laws are ancient examples. A more modern one is the prohibition of lotteries. The liberty of the citizen to do as he likes so long as he does not interfere with the liberty of others to do the same, which has been a shibboleth for some well-known writers, is interfered with by school laws, by the Postoffice, by every state or municipal institution which takes his money for purposes thought desirable, whether he likes it or not. The 14th Amendment does not enact Mr. Herbert Spencer's Social Statics. The other day we sustained the Massachusetts vaccination law. *Jacobson* v. *Massachusetts*, 197 U.S. 11. United States and state statutes and decisions cutting down the liberty to contract by way of combination are familiar to this court. *Northern Securities Co.* v. *United States*, 193 U.S. 197. Two years ago we upheld the prohibition of sales of stock on margins, or for future delivery, in the Constitution of California. *Otis* v. *Parker*, 187 U.S. 606. The decision sustaining an eight-hour law for miners is still recent. *Holden* v. *Hardy*, 169 U.S. 366. Some of these laws embody convictions or prejudices which judges are likely to share. Some may not. But a Constitution is not intended to embody a particular economic theory, whether of paternalism and the organic relation of the citizen to the state or of laissez faire. It is made for people of fundamentally differing views, and the accident of our finding certain opinions natural and familiar, or novel, and even shocking, ought not to conclude our judgment upon the question whether statutes embodying them conflict with the Constitution of the United States.

General propositions do not decide concrete cases. The decision will depend on a judgment or intuition more subtle than any articulate major premise. But I think that the proposition just stated, if it is accepted, will carry us far toward the end. Every opinion tends to become a law. I think that the word "liberty," in the 14th Amendment, is perverted when it is held to prevent the natural outcome of a dominant opinion, unless it can be said that a rational and fair man necessarily would admit that the statute proposed would infringe fundamental principles as they have been understood by the traditions of our people and our law. It does not need research to show that no such sweeping condemnation can be passed upon the statute before us. A reasonable man might think it a proper measure on the score of health. Men whom I certainly could not pronounce unreasonable would uphold it as a first instalment of a general regulation of the hours of work. Whether in the latter aspect it would be open to the charge of inequality I think it unnecessary to discuss.

[Editor's Note.—The question of the regulation of the hours of labor of women in industry was presented in *Muller* v. *Oregon*, 208 U.S. 412 (1908), which sustained the validity of an Oregon statute which forbade the employment of women for more than ten hours per day in any mechanical establishment, factory, or laundry. The Court, in refusing to follow the precedent of the Lochner case, laid stress upon the distinction between the sexes in respect to the ability to endure long hours of labor and the consequent need of giving special protection to women. Perhaps this was due to the fact that, as in the law of the sea, women and children are given a preferred position. Perhaps it was due to the fact that the case was argued by Louis D. Brandeis, later Mr. Justice Brandeis, and that his "Brandeis brief" (a factual brief) persuaded the Court that there was ample justification for "the widespread belief that woman's physical structure, and the functions she performs in consequence thereof, justify special legislation restricting or qualifying the conditions under which she should be permitted to toil."]

COPPAGE v. KANSAS

236 U.S. 1, 59 L.Ed. 441 (1915)

In the early 1900's it was more or less standard procedure for employers to insert clauses in employment contracts by which employees agreed either to withdraw from or refrain from joining a labor union during the period of employment covered by the contract. These were called by the colorful name of "yellow-dog contracts." Since it would be difficult if not entirely impossible for individual employees to prevent their use, they turned to the state legislatures for help in outlawing such contracts. Thus it was that in 1903 the Legislature of Kansas passed an act making it unlawful for any individual, firm, or corporation, or any agent thereof, "to coerce, require, demand or influence any person or persons to enter into any agreement . . . not to join or become or remain a member of any labor organization or association, as a condition of such person or persons securing employment or continuing in the employment of such individual, firm, or corporation." A man named Hedges was a switchman in the employ of the Frisco Railway. Having refused to sign an agreement to withdraw from the Switchmen's Union while he remained in the service of the Company, he was fired by his superintendent, Coppage. Coppage was then indicted, convicted, and fined. His conviction having been sustained by the Supreme Court of Kansas (two judges dissenting), he brings the case to the Supreme Court of the United States on a writ of error. In commenting on this decision Louis D. Brandeis said in 1916, prior to his joining the Court: *"In the Coppage Case, the Supreme Court showed the potency of mental prepossessions."*

MR. JUSTICE PITNEY delivered the opinion of the court. . . .

In *Adair v. United States,* 208 U.S. 161, this court had to deal with a question not distinguishable in principle from the one now presented. . . . Adair was convicted upon an indictment charging that he, as agent of a common carrier subject to the provisions of the Act, unjustly discriminated against a certain employé by discharging him from the employ of the carrier because of his membership in a labor organization. The court held that portion of the Act upon which the conviction rested to be an invasion of the personal liberty as well as of the right of property guaranteed by the Fifth Amendment, which declares that no person shall be deprived of liberty or property without due process of law. . . . [See p. 134 *infra.*]

Unless it is overruled, this decision is controlling upon the present controversy; for if Congress is prevented from arbitrary interference with the liberty of contract because of the "due process" provision of the Fifth Amendment, it is too clear for argument that the States are prevented from the like interference by virtue of the corresponding clause of the Fourteenth Amendment; and hence if it be unconstitutional for Congress to deprive an employer of liberty or property for threatening an employé with loss of employment or discriminating against him because of his membership in a labor organization, it is unconstitutional for a State to similarly punish an employer for requiring his employé, as a condition to securing or retaining employment, to agree not to become or remain a member of such an organization while so employed. . . .

We are now asked, in effect, to overrule it [the Adair case]; and in view of the importance of the issue we have re-examined the question from the standpoint of both reason and authority. As a result, we are constrained to reaffirm the doctrine there applied. Neither the doctrine nor this application of it is novel; we will endeavor to re-state some of the grounds upon which it rests. The principle is fundamental and vital. Included in the right of personal liberty and the right of private property—partaking of the nature of each—is the right to make contracts for the acquisition of property. Chief among such contracts is that of personal employment, by which labor and other services are exchanged for money or other forms of property. If this right be struck down or arbitrarily interfered with, there is a substantial impairment of liberty in the long-established constitutional sense. The right is as essential to the laborer as to the capitalist, to the poor as to the rich; for the vast majority of persons have no other honest way to begin to acquire property, save by working for money.

An interference with this liberty so serious as that now under consideration, and so disturbing of equality of right, must be deemed to be arbitrary, unless it be supportable as a reasonable exercise of the police power of the State. But, notwithstanding the strong general presumption in favor of the validity of state laws, we do not think the statute in question, as construed and applied in this case, can be sustained as a legitimate exercise of that power. . . . It is equally clear, we think, that to punish an employer or his agent for simply proposing certain terms of employment, under circumstances devoid of coercion, duress, or undue influence, has no reasonable relation to a declared purpose of repressing coercion, duress, and undue influence. Nor can a State, by designating as "coercion" conduct which is not such in truth, render criminal any normal and essentially innocent exercise of personal liberty or of property rights; for to permit this would deprive the Fourteenth Amendment of its effective force in this regard. . . .

As to the interest of the employed, it is said by the Kansas Supreme Court to be a matter of common knowledge that "employés, as a rule, are not financially able to be as independent in making contracts for the sale of their labor as are employers in making contracts of purchase thereof." No doubt, wherever the right of private property exists, there must and will be inequalities of fortune; and thus it naturally happens that parties negotiating about a contract are not equally unhampered by circumstances. This applies to all contracts, and not merely to that between employer and employé. Indeed a little reflection will show that wherever the right of private property and the right of free contract co-exist, each party when contracting is inevitably more or less influenced by the question of whether he has much property, or little, or none; for the contract is made to the very end that each may gain something that he needs or desires more urgently than that which he proposes to give in exchange. And, since it is self-evident that, unless all things are held in common, some persons must have more property than others, it is from the nature of things impossible to uphold freedom of contract and the right of private property without at the same time recognizing as legitimate those inequalities of fortune that are the necessary result of the exercise of those rights. But the Fourteenth Amendment, in declaring that a State shall not "deprive any person of life, liberty or property without due process of law," gives to each of these an equal sanction; it recognizes "liberty" and "property" as co-existent human rights, and debars the States from any unwarranted interference with either. . . .

Of course we do not intend to say, nor to intimate, anything inconsistent with the right of individuals to join labor unions, nor do we question the legitimacy of such organizations so long as they conform to the laws of the land as others are required to do. Conceding the full right of the individual to join the union, he has no inherent right to do this and still remain in the employ of one who is unwilling to employ a union man, any more than the same individual has a right to join the union without the consent of that organization. Can it be doubted that a labor organization—a voluntary association of working men—has the inherent and constitutional right to deny membership to any man who will not agree that during such membership he will not accept or retain employment in company with non-union men? Or that a union man has the constitutional right to decline proffered employment unless the employer will agree not to employ any non-union men? . . . And can there be one rule of liberty for the labor organization and its members, and a different and more restrictive rule for employers? We think not; and since the relation of employer to employé is a voluntary relation, as clearly as is that between the members of a labor organization, the employer has the same inherent right to prescribe the terms upon which he will consent to the relationship, and to have them fairly understood and expressed in advance. . . .

The liberty of making contracts does not include a liberty to procure employment from an unwilling employer, or without a fair understanding. Nor may the employer be foreclosed by legislation from exercising the same freedom of choice that is the right of the employé.

To ask a man to agree, in advance, to refrain from affiliation with the union while retaining a certain position of employment, is not to ask him to give up any part of his constitutional freedom. He is free to decline the employment on those terms, just as the employer may decline to offer employment upon any other; for "It takes two to make a bargain." Having accepted employment on those terms, the man is still free to join the union when the period of employment expires; or, if employed at will, then at any time upon simply quitting the employment. And, if bound by his own agreement to refrain from joining during a stated period of employment, he is in no different situation from that which is necessarily incident to term contracts in general. For constitutional freedom of contract does not mean that a party is to be as free after making a contract as before; he is not free to break it without accountability. Freedom of contract, from the very nature of the thing, can be enjoyed only by being exercised; and each particular exercise of it involves making an engagement which, if fulfilled, prevents for the time any inconsistent course of conduct. . . .

Judgment reversed. . . .

MR. JUSTICE HOLMES, dissenting:

I think the judgment should be affirmed. In present conditions a workman not unnaturally may believe that only by belonging to a union can he secure a contract that shall be fair to him. . . . If that belief, whether right or wrong, may be held by a reasonable man, it seems to me that it may be enforced by law in order to establish the equality of position between the parties in which liberty of contract begins. Whether in the long run it is wise for the workingmen to enact legislation of this sort is not my concern, but I am strongly of the opinion that there is nothing in the Constitution of the United States to prevent it, and that *Adair* v. *United States*, 208 U.S. 161, and *Lochner* v. *New York*, 198 U.S. 45, should be overruled. . . .

MR. JUSTICE DAY, with whom MR. JUSTICE HUGHES concurs, dissenting: . . . That the right of contract is a part of individual freedom within the protection of the amendment, and may not be arbitrarily interfered with, is conceded. While this is true, nothing is better settled . . . than that the right of contract is not absolute and unyielding, but is subject to limitation and restraint in the interests of public health, safety, and welfare . . . declared in legislation of the state. . . . It is constantly emphasized that the case presented is not one of coercion. But in view of the relative positions of employer and employed, who is to deny that the stipulation . . . is essentially coercive. No form of words can strip it of its true character. Whatever our individual opinions may be as to the wisdom of such legislation, we cannot put our judgment in place of that of the legislature. . . . I think that the act now under consideration and kindred ones, are intended to promote the same liberty of action for the employee, as the employer, confessedly enjoys. The law should be as zealous to protect the constitutional liberty of the employee as it is to guard that of the employer. . . . While all stand equal before the law, and are alike entitled to its protection, it ought not to be a reasonable objection that one motive which impelled an enactment was to protect those who might otherwise be unable to protect themselves. . . .

BUNTING v. OREGON

243 U.S. 426, 61 L.Ed. 830 (1917)

The Oregon Legislature enacted a general ten-hour factory law in 1913 with the proviso that three additional hours might be worked

*as overtime at time–and–one-half rate of pay. Bunting employed a
laborer for thirteen hours without payment of overtime as provided by
the law. He was indicted and found guilty and this was sustained by
the Supreme Court of Oregon. It comes to the Supreme Court of the
United States on a writ of error. Standing by itself the case is not too
important, but representing, as it does, a case later in time it raises
the question as to whether the fluctuations between the right of states
to exercise their police power (as in HOLDEN v. HARDY) and the right
of personal liberty [of contract] (as in LOCHNER v. NEW YORK) had
been settled. For since women were dealt with specially in MULLER v.
OREGON, and since it might be argued that a general factory law
includes bakeries and confectionery establishments, the result would
seem to be in favor of state "social justice" legislation. Hence was the
Lochner case, though not mentioned in the opinion below, overruled
sub silentio? But equally as important, does the case put state legislatures on notice that the Court will take a different view in regard to
a wage law where dollars and cents are involved directly?*

MR. JUSTICE McKENNA delivered the opinion of the court. . . .

The consonance of the Oregon law with the Fourteenth Amendment is the question in the case, and this depends upon whether it
is a proper exercise of the police power of the State, as the Supreme
Court of this State decided that it is. . . . The contention presents
two questions: (1) Is the law a wage law, or an hours of service law?
And (2) if the latter, has it equality of operation? . . .

First, as to plaintiff in error's attack upon the law. He says: "The
law is not a ten-hour law; it is a thirteen-hour law designed solely for
the purpose of compelling the employer of labor in mills, factories
and manufacturing establishments to pay more for labor than the
actual market value thereof." And further: "It is a ten-hour law for
the purpose of taking the employer's property from him and giving
it to the employé; it is a thirteen-hour law for the purpose of protecting the health of the employé." To this plaintiff in error adds that he
was convicted, not for working an employee during a busy season for
more than ten hours, but for not paying him more than the market
value of his services. . . .

There is a certain verbal plausibility in the contention that it was
intended to permit 13 hours' work if there be 15½ hours' pay, but
the plausibility disappears upon reflection. The provision for overtime
is permissive, in the same sense that any penalty may be said to be
permissive. Its purpose is to deter by its burden and its adequacy for
this was a matter of legislative judgment under the particular circumstances. . . .

We cannot know all of the conditions that impelled the law or its
particular form. The Supreme Court, nearer to them, describes the
law as follows: "It is clear that the intent of the law is to make 10
hours a regular day's labor in the occupations to which reference is

made. Apparently the provisions for permitting labor for the overtime on express conditions were made in order to facilitate the enforcement of the law, and in the nature of a mild penalty for employing one not more than three hours overtime. It might be regarded as more difficult to detect violations of the law by an employment for a shorter time than for a longer time. This penalty also goes to the employee in case the employer avails himself of the overtime clause."

But we need not cast about for reasons for the legislative judgment. We are not required to be sure of the precise reasons for its exercise or be convinced of the wisdom of its exercise. . . . It is enough for our decision if the legislation under review was passed in the exercise of an admitted power of government; and that it is not as complete as it might be, not as rigid in its prohibitions as might be, gives, perhaps, evasion too much play, is lighter in its penalties than it might be, is no impeachment of its legality. This may be a blemish, giving opportunity for criticism and difference in characterization, but the constitutional validity of legislation cannot be determined by the degree of exactness of its provisions or remedies. New policies are usually tentative in their beginnings, advance in firmness as they advance in acceptance. They do not at a particular moment of time spring full-perfect in extent or means from the legislative brain. Time may be necessary to fashion them to precedent customs and conditions. . . .

There is a contention made that the law, even regarded as regulating hours of service, is not either necessary or useful "for preservation of the health of employés in mills, factories and manufacturing establishments." The record contains no facts to support the contention, and against it is the judgment of the legislature and the Supreme Court, which said: "In view of the well-known fact that the custom in our industries does not sanction a longer service than 10 hours per day, it cannot be held, as a matter of law, that the legislative requirement is unreasonable or arbitrary as to hours of labor. Statistics show that the average daily working time among workingmen in different countries is, in Australia, 8 hours; in Great Britain, 9; in the United States, 9¾; in Denmark, 9¾; in Norway, 10; Sweden, France, and Switzerland, 10½; Germany, 10¼; Belgium, Italy, and Austria, 11; and in Russia, 12 hours."

The next contention of plaintiff in error is that the law discriminates against mills, factories and manufacturing establishments in that it requires that a manufacturer, without reason other than the fiat of the legislature, shall pay for a commodity, meaning labor, one and one-half times the market value thereof while other people purchasing labor in like manner in the open market are not subjected to the same burden. But the basis of the contention is that which we have already disposed of, that is, that the law regulates wages, not hours of service. Regarding it as the latter, there is a basis for the classification.

Further discussion we deem unnecessary.
Judgment affirmed.

The CHIEF JUSTICE [WHITE], MR. JUSTICE VAN DEVANTER and MR. JUSTICE MCREYNOLDS, dissent.

MR. JUSTICE BRANDEIS took no part in the consideration and decision of the case.

ADKINS v. CHILDREN'S HOSPITAL

261 U.S. 525, 67 L.Ed. 785 (1923)

Article I, Section 8, Clause 17, of the Constitution of the United States grants to the Congress of the United States the power "to exercise exclusive Legislation in all Cases whatsover, over such District . . . as may . . . become the Seat of the Government of the United States." The District of Columbia after Home Rule was abolished in the 1870's is completely and directly controlled by the national government with Congress serving as the council (though most of the work is done by the House and Senate Committees on District Affairs), with three commissioners appointed by the President with the consent of the Senate to administer the laws, and with local judges chosen in the same way. It is possible therefore for Congress to enact legislation applicable only to the District of Columbia, and when it does so this legislation, as in the case below, must be looked upon, and equated with, legislation passed by a State Legislature.

On September 19, 1918, Congress passed the Minimum Wage Act (40 Stat. 960) for operation in the District of Columbia. This created a Minimum Wage Board which was to investigate the wages of women and children employed in the different occupations and empowered the Board to set "standards of minimum wages for women . . . to supply the necessary cost of living [and] . . . to maintain them in good health and to protect their morals." Under penalty, employers were forbidden to employ any woman worker for wages lower than those set by the Board. The Children's Hospital which employed women at less than the minimum wage brought suit to restrain the Board (J. C. Adkins and others) from enforcing its order on the ground that such regulation violated the due process clause of the Fifth Amendment.

In what may seem to be a "pincer movement," Willie A. Lyons, a woman of twenty-one, employed as an elevator operator in the Congress Hall Hotel, also brought suit against the Board when she was about to be dismissed from her employment because the hotel could not afford to pay the minimum wage. She claimed that her work was light, healthful; that the hours were short and surroundings clean and moral—in short that she was willing and anxious to work here even at a lesser wage. She was certain that no other employment could be found which would be as good.

Permanent injunctions were granted and the case comes to the Supreme Court of the United States when the Board appealed the mandate from the Court of Appeals of the District of Columbia.

There are obviously many interesting and vital aspects involved in this case, not the least of which is that it sets the "high-water mark" in support of liberty of contract (words, it should be emphasized, which are not included in the Fourteenth Amendment as it appears in the Constitution itself) as against the so-called police power. And in doing so, it clearly sets forth the philosophy and leadership of the antagonists, a philosophy and leadership that were to contest for supremacy well into the New Deal era—a supremacy which was determined only by the interjection of a political weapon.

MR. JUSTICE SUTHERLAND delivered the opinion of the court.

The statute now under consideration is attacked upon the ground that it authorizes an unconstitutional interference with the freedom of contract included within the guaranties of the due process clause of the Fifth Amendment. That the right to contract about one's affairs is a part of the liberty of the individual protected by this clause is settled by the decisions of this Court and is no longer open to question. . . . Within this liberty are contracts of employment of labor. In making such contracts, generally speaking, the parties have an equal right to obtain from each other the best terms they can as the result of private bargaining. . . .

There is, of course, no such thing as absolute freedom of contract. It is subject to a great variety of restraint. But freedom of contract is, nevertheless, the general rule and restraint the exception; and the exercise of legislative authority to abridge it can be justified only by the existence of exceptional circumstances. Whether these circumstances exist in the present case constitutes the question to be answered. It will be helpful to this end to review some of the decisions where the interference has been upheld and consider the grounds upon which they rest.

(1) Those dealing with statutes fixing rates and charges to be exacted by businesses impressed with a public interest. . . . This class of cases may be laid aside as inapplicable.

(2) Statutes relating to contracts for the performance of public work. . . . We may . . . dismiss these decisions from consideration as inapplicable.

(3) Statutes prescribing the character, methods and time for payment of wages. . . . In no sense can they be said to be, or to furnish a precedent for, wage-fixing statutes.

(4) Statutes fixing hours of labor. It is upon this class that the

greatest emphasis is laid in argument and therefore, and because such cases approach most nearly the line of principle applicable to the statute here involved, we shall consider them more at length. . . . [The Court continues citing other cases but relying on *Lochner* v. *New York*, 198 U.S. 45, of which the learned judge said, "Subsequent cases in this Court have been distinguished from that decision, but the principles therein stated have never been disapproved."]

If now, in the light furnished by the foregoing exceptions to the general rule forbidding legislative interference with freedom of contract, we examine and analyze the statute in question, we shall see that it differs from them in every material respect. It is not a law dealing with any business charged with a public interest, or with public work, or to meet and tide over a temporary emergency. It has nothing to do with the character, methods or periods of wage payments. It does not prescribe hours of labor or conditions under which labor is to be done. It is not for the protection of persons under legal disability or for the prevention of fraud. It is simply and exclusively a price-fixing law, confined to adult women (for we are not now considering the provisions relating to minors), who are legally as capable of contracting for themselves as men. It forbids two parties having lawful capacity—under penalties as to the employer—to freely contract with one another in respect of the price for which one shall render service to the other in a purely private employment where both are willing, perhaps anxious, to agree, even though the consequence may be to oblige one to surrender a desirable engagement and the other to dispense with the services of a desirable employee. The price fixed by the board need have no relation to the capacity or earning power of the employee, the number of hours which may happen to constitute the day's work, the character of the place where the work is to be done, or the circumstances or surroundings of the employment; and, while it has no other basis to support its validity than the assumed necessities of the employee, it takes no account of any independent resources she may have. It is based wholly on the opinions of the members of the board and their advisers—perhaps an average of their opinions, if they do not precisely agree—as to what will be necessary to provide a living for a woman, keep her in health and preserve her morals. It applies to any and every occupation in the District without regard to its nature or the character of the work.

The standard furnished by the statute for the guidance of the board is so vague as to be impossible of practical application with any reasonable degree of accuracy. What is sufficient to supply the necessary cost of living for a woman worker and maintain her in good health and protect her morals is obviously not a precise or unvarying sum—not even approximately so. The amount will depend upon a variety of circumstances: the individual temperament, habits of thrift, care, ability to buy necessaries intelligently, and whether the woman live alone or with her family. To those who practice economy, a given sum will afford comfort, while to those of contrary habit the same sum will be wholly inadequate. The cooperative economies of the family group are not taken into account though they constitute an important consideration in estimating the cost of living, for it is obvious that the individual expense will be less in the case of a member of a family than in the case of one living alone. The relation between earnings and morals is not capable of standardization. It cannot be shown that well paid women safeguard their morals more carefully than those who are poorly paid. Morality rests upon other considerations than wages; and there is, certainly, no such prevalent connection between the two as to justify a broad attempt to adjust the latter with reference to the former. As a means of safeguarding morals the attempted classification, in our opinion, is without reasonable basis. No distinction can be made between women who work for others and those who do not; nor is there ground for distinction between women and men, for, certainly, if women require a minimum wage to preserve their morals men require it to preserve their honesty. For these reasons, and others which might be stated, the inquiry in respect of the necessary cost of living and of the income necessary to preserve health and morals, presents an individual and not a composite question, and must be answered for each individual considered by herself and not by a general formula prescribed by a statutory bureau.

This uncertainty of the statutory standard is demonstrated by a consideration of certain orders of the board already made. . . .

The law takes account of the necessities of only one party to the contract. It ignores the necessities of the employer by compelling him to pay not less than a certain sum, not only whether the employee is capable of earning it, but irrespective of the ability of his business to sustain the burden, generously leaving him, of course, the privilege of abandoning his business as an alternative for going on at a loss. Within the limits of the minimum sum, he is precluded, under penalty of fine and imprisonment, from adjusting compensation to the differing merits of his employees. It compels him to pay at least the sum fixed in any event, because the employee needs it, but requires no service of equivalent value from the employee. It therefore undertakes to solve but one-half of the problem. The other half is the establishment of a corresponding standard of efficiency, and this forms no part of the policy of the legislation, although in practice the former half without the latter must lead to ultimate failure, in accordance with the inexorable law that no one can continue indefinitely to take out more than he puts in without ultimately exhausting the supply. The law is not confined to the great and powerful employers but embraces those whose bargaining power may be as weak as that of the employee. It takes no account of periods of stress and business depression, of crippling losses, which may leave the employer himself without adequate means of livelihood. To the extent that the sum fixed exceeds the fair value of the services rendered, it amounts to a compulsory exaction from the employer for the support of a partially indigent person, for whose condition there rests upon him no peculiar responsibility, and therefore, in effect, arbitrarily shifts to his shoulders a burden which, if it belongs to anybody, belongs to society as a whole.

The feature of this statute which, perhaps more than any other, puts upon it the stamp of invalidity is that it exacts from the employer an arbitrary payment for a purpose and upon a basis having no causal connection with his business, or the contract or the work the employee engages to do. The declared basis, as already pointed out, is not the value of the service rendered, but the extraneous circumstance that the employee needs to get a prescribed sum of money to insure her subsistence, health and morals. The ethical right of every worker, man or woman, to a living wage may be conceded. One of the declared and important purposes of trade organizations is to secure it. And with that principle and with every legitimate effort to realize it in fact, no one can quarrel; but the fallacy of the proposed method of attaining it is that it assumes that every employer is bound at all events to furnish it. The moral requirement implicit in every contract of employment, viz., that the amount to be paid and the service to be rendered shall bear to each other some relation of just equivalence, is completely ignored. The necessities of the employee are alone considered and these arise outside of the employment, are the same when there is no employment, and as great in one occupation as in another. Certainly the employer by paying a fair equivalent for the service rendered, though not sufficient to support the employee, has neither caused nor contributed to her poverty. On the contrary, to the extent of what he pays he has relieved it. In principle, there can be no difference between the case of selling labor and the case of selling goods. If one goes to the butcher, the baker or grocer to buy food, he is morally entitled to obtain the worth of his money but he is not entitled to more. If what he gets is worth what he pays he is not justified in demanding more simply because he needs more; and the shopkeeper, having dealt fairly and honestly in that transaction, is not concerned in any peculiar sense with the question of his customer's necessities. Should a statute undertake to vest in a commission power to determine the quantity of food necessary for individual support and require the shopkeeper, if he sell to the individual at all, to furnish that quantity at not more than a fixed maximum, it would undoubtedly fall before the constitutional test. The fallacy of any argument in support of the validity of such a statute would be quickly exposed. The argument in support of that now being considered is equally fallacious, though the weakness of it may not be so plain. A statute requiring an employer to pay in money, to pay at prescribed and regular intervals, to pay the value of the services rendered, even to pay with fair relation to the extent of the benefit obtained from the service, would be understandable. But a statute which prescribes payment without regard to any of these things and solely with relation to circumstances apart from the contract of employment, the business affected by it and the work done under it, is so clearly the product of a naked, arbitrary exercise of power that it cannot be allowed to stand under the Constitution of the United States. . . .

Finally, it may be said that if, in the interest of the public welfare, the police power may be invoked to justify the fixing of a minimum wage, it may, when the public welfare is thought to require it, be invoked to justify a maximum wage. The power to fix high wages connotes, by like course of reasoning, the power to fix low wages. If, in the face of the guaranties of the Fifth Amendment, this form of legislation shall be legally justified, the field for the operation of the police power will have been widened to a great and dangerous degree. If, for example, in the opinion of future lawmakers, wages in the building trades shall become so high as to preclude people of ordinary means from building and owning homes, an authority which sustains the minimum wage will be invoked to support a maximum wage for building laborers and artisans, and the same argument which has been here urged to strip the employer of his constitutional liberty of contract in one direction will be utilized to strip the employee of his constitutional liberty of contract in the opposite direction. A wrong decision does not end with itself: it is a precedent, and, with the swing of sentiment, its bad influence may run from one extremity of the arc to the other.

It has been said that legislation of the kind now under review is required in the interest of social justice, for whose ends freedom of contract may lawfully be subjected to restraint. The liberty of the individual to do as he pleases, even in innocent matters, is not absolute. It must frequently yield to the common good, and the line beyond which the power of interference may not be pressed is neither definite nor unalterable but may be made to move, within limits not well defined, with changing need and circumstance. Any attempt to fix a rigid boundary would be unwise as well as futile. But, nevertheless, there are limits to the power, and when these have been passed, it becomes the plain duty of the courts in the proper exercise of their authority to so declare. To sustain the individual freedom of action contemplated by the Constitution, is not to strike down the common good but to exalt it; for surely the good of society as a whole cannot be better served than by the preservation against arbitrary restraint of the liberties of its constituent members.

It follows from what has been said that the act in question passes the limit prescribed by the Constitution, and, accordingly, the decrees of the court below are affirmed.

MR. JUSTICE BRANDEIS took no part in the consideration or decision of these cases.

MR. CHIEF JUSTICE TAFT, dissenting.

I regret much to differ from the court in these cases.

The boundary of the police power beyond which its exercise becomes an invasion of the guaranty of liberty under the Fifth and Fourteenth Amendments of the Constitution is not easy to mark. Our Court has been laboriously engaged in pricking out a line in successive cases. We must be careful, it seems to me, to follow that line as well as we can and not to depart from it by suggesting a distinction that is formal rather than real.

Legislatures in limiting freedom of contract between employee and employer by a minimum wage proceed on the assumption that employees, in the class receiving least pay, are not upon a full level of equality of choice with their employer and in their necessitous circumstances are prone to accept pretty much anything that is offered. They are peculiarly subject to the overreaching of the harsh and greedy employer. The evils of the sweating system and of the long hours and low wages which are characteristic of it are well known. Now, I agree that it is a disputable question in the field of political economy how far a statutory requirement of maximum hours or minimum wages may be a useful remedy for these evils, and whether it may not make the case of the oppressed employee worse than it was before. But it is not the function of this Court to hold congressional acts invalid simply because they are passed to carry out economic views which the Court believes to be unwise or unsound. . . .

The right of the legislature under the Fifth and Fourteenth Amendments to limit the hours of employment on the score of the health of the employee, it seems to me, has been firmly established. As to that, one would think, the line had been pricked out so that it has become a well formulated rule. In *Holden* v. *Hardy*, 169 U.S. 366, it was applied to miners and rested on the unfavorable environment of employment in mining and smelting. In *Lochner* v. *New York*, 198 U.S. 45, it was held that restricting those employed in bakeries to ten hours a day was an arbitrary and invalid interference with the liberty of contract secured by the Fourteenth Amendment. Then followed a number of cases beginning with *Muller* v. *Oregon*, 208 U.S. 412, sustaining the validity of a limit on maximum hours of labor for women to which I shall hereafter allude, and following these cases came *Bunting* v. *Oregon*, 243 U.S. 426. In that case, this Court sustained a law limiting the hours of labor of any person, whether man or woman, working in any mill, factory or manufacturing establishment to ten hours a day with a proviso as to further hours to which I shall hereafter advert. The law covered the whole field of industrial employment and certainly covered the case of persons employed in bakeries. Yet the opinion in the Bunting Case does not mention the

Lochner Case. No one can suggest any constitutional distinction between employment in a bakery and one in any other kind of a manufacturing establishment which should make a limit of hours in the one invalid, and the same limit in the other permissible. It is impossible for me to reconcile the Bunting Case and the Lochner Case and I have always supposed that the Lochner Case was thus overruled *sub silentio*. Yet the opinion of the Court herein in support of its conclusion quotes from the opinion in the Lochner Case as one which has been sometimes distinguished but never overruled. Certainly there was no attempt to distinguish it in the Bunting Case.

However, the opinion herein does not overrule the Bunting Case in express terms, and therefore I assume that the conclusion in this case rests on the distinction between a minimum of wages and a maximum of hours in the limiting of liberty to contract. I regret to be at variance with the Court as to the substance of this distinction. In absolute freedom of contract the one term is as important as the other, for both enter equally into the consideration given and received, a restriction as to one is not any greater in essence than the other, and is of the same kind. One is the multiplier and the other the multiplicand. . . .

Moreover, there are decisions by this Court which have sustained legislative limitations in respect to the wage term in contracts of employment. In *McLean* v. *Arkansas*, 211 U.S. 539, it was held within legislative power to make it unlawful to estimate the graduated pay of miners by weight after screening the coal. In *Knoxville Iron Co.* v. *Harbison*, 183 U.S. 13, it was held that store orders issued for wages must be redeemable in cash. In *Patterson* v. *Bark Eudora*, 190 U.S. 169, a law forbidding the payment of wages in advance was held valid. . . . While these did not impose a minimum on wages, they did take away from the employee the freedom to agree as to how they should be fixed, in what medium they should be paid, and when they should be paid, all features that might affect the amount or the mode of enjoyment of them. . . .

Without, however, expressing an opinion that a minimum wage limitation can be enacted for adult men, it is enough to say that the case before us involves only the application of the minimum wage to women. If I am right in thinking that the legislature can find as much support in experience for the view that a sweating wage has as great and as direct a tendency to bring about an injury to the health and morals of workers, as for the view that long hours injure their health, then I respectfully submit that *Muller* v. *Oregon*, 208 U.S. 412, controls this case. The law which was there sustained forbade the employment of any female in any mechanical establishment or factory or laundry for more than ten hours. . . . Mr. Justice Brewer, who spoke for the Court in *Muller* v. *Oregon*, based its conclusion on the natural limit to women's physical strength and the likelihood that long hours would therefore injure her health, and we have had since a series of cases which may be said to have established a rule of decision.

But for my inability to agree with some general observations in the forcible opinion of Mr. Justice Holmes who follows me, I should be silent and merely record my concurrence in what he says. It is perhaps wiser for me, however, in a case of this importance, separately to give my reasons for dissenting.

I am authorized to say that MR. JUSTICE SANFORD concurs in this opinion.

MR. JUSTICE HOLMES, dissenting.

The question in this case is a broad one, Whether Congress can establish minimum rates of wages for women in the District of Columbia with due provision for special circumstances, or whether we must say that Congress has no power to meddle in the matter at all. To me, notwithstanding the deference due to the prevailing judgment of the Court, the power of Congress seems absolutely free from doubt. The end, to remove conditions leading to ill health, immorality and the deterioration of the race, no one would deny to be within the scope of constitutional legislation. The means are means that have the approval of Congress, or many States, and of those governments from which we have learned our greatest lessons. When so many intelligent persons who have studied the matter more than any of us can, have thought that the means are effective and are worth the price, it seems to me impossible to deny that the belief reasonably may be held by reasonable men. If the law encountered no other objection than that the means bore no relation to the end or that they cost too much I do not suppose that anyone would venture to say that it was bad. I agree, of course, that a law answering the foregoing requirements might be invalidated by specific provisions of the Constitution. For instance it might take private property without just compensation. But in the present instance the only objection that can be urged is found within the vague contours of the Fifth Amendment, prohibiting the depriving any person of liberty or property without due process of law. To that I turn.

The earlier decisions upon the same words in the Fourteenth Amendment began within our memory and went no farther than an unpretentious assertion of the liberty to follow the ordinary callings. Later that innocuous generality was expanded into the dogma, Liberty of Contract. Contract is not specially mentioned in the text that we have to construe. It is merely an example of doing what you want to do, embodied in the word liberty. But pretty much all law consists in forbidding men to do some things that they want to do, and contract is no more exempt from law than other acts. Without enumerating all the restrictive laws that have been upheld I will mention a few that seem to me to have interfered with liberty of contract quite as seriously and directly as the one before us. Usury laws prohibit contracts by which a man receives more than so much interest for the money that he lends. Statutes of frauds restrict many contracts to certain forms. Some Sunday laws prohibit practically all contracts during one-seventh of our whole life. . . .

I confess that I do not understand the principle on which the power to fix a minimum for the wages of women can be denied by those who admit the power to fix a maximum for their hours of work. I fully assent to the proposition that here as elsewhere the distinctions of the law are distinctions of degree, but I perceive no difference in the kind or degree of interference with liberty, the only matter with which we have any concern, between the one case and the other. The bargain is equally affected whichever half you regulate. *Muller* v. *Oregon*, I take it, is as good law today as it was in 1908. It will need more than the Nineteenth Amendment to convince me that there are no differences between men and women, or that legislation cannot take those differences into account. I should not hesitate to take them into account if I thought it necessary to sustain this act. But after *Bunting* v. *Oregon*, 243 U.S. 426, I had supposed that it was not necessary, and that *Lochner* v. *New York*, 198 U.S. 45, would be allowed a deserved repose.

This statute does not compel anybody to pay anything. It simply forbids employment at rates below those fixed as the minimum requirement of health and right living. It is safe to assume that women will not be employed at even the lowest wages allowed unless they earn them, or unless the employer's business can sustain the burden. In short the law in its character and operation is like hundreds of so-called police laws that have been upheld. I see no greater objection to using a Board to apply the standard fixed by the act than there is to the other commission with which we have become familiar, or than there is to the requirement of a license in other cases. The fact that the statute warrants classification, which like all classifications may bear hard upon some individuals, or in exceptional cases, notwithstanding the power given to the Board to issue a special license, is no greater infirmity than is incident to all law. But the ground on which the law is held to fail is fundamental and therefore it is unnecessary to consider matters of detail.

The criterion of constitutionality is not whether we believe the law to be for the public good. We certainly cannot be prepared to deny that a reasonable man reasonably might have that belief in view of the legislation of Great Britain, Victoria and a number of the States of this Union. The belief is fortified by a very remarkable collection of documents submitted on behalf of the appellants, material here, I conceive, only as showing that the belief reasonably may be held. In Australia the power to fix a minimum for wages in the case of industrial disputes extending beyond the limits of any one State was given to a Court, and its President wrote a most interesting account of its operation. 29 Harv. Law Rev. 13. If a legislature should adopt what he thinks the doctrine of modern economists of all schools, that "freedom of contract is a misnomer as applied to a contract between an employer and an ordinary individual employee," ibid. 25, I could not pronounce an opinion with which I agree impossible to be entertained by reasonable men. If the same legislature should accept his further opinion that industrial peace was best attained by the device of a Court having the above powers, I should not feel myself able to contradict it, or to deny that the end justified restrictive legislation quite as adequately as beliefs concerning Sunday or exploded theories about usury. I should have my doubts, as I have them about this statute—but they would be whether the bill that has to be paid for every gain, although hidden as interstitial detriments, was not greater than the gain was worth: a matter that it is not for me to decide.

I am of opinion that the statute is valid and that the decree should be reversed.

Federal Action

IN RE DEBS

158 U.S. 564, 39 L.Ed. 1092 (1895)

"Government by injunction" was a term echoed by the laboring class with increasing vitality and opprobrium during this period. And the Debs case below was viewed by many as truly representative of the great conflict of the time between "the propertied class" and labor. In its simplest terms an injunction is a judicial process operating against a person or persons, which requires the person or persons to whom it is addressed to do or refrain from doing a particular thing. While some of the cases that precede this one have come about by injunction (as, for example, the Adkins case supra, p. 108), they generally involved some specific legislative enactment which was in essence being challenged through the injunctive process. In the instant case no such legislation existed per se, but rather its use was sought to protect the United States mails and interstate commerce itself.

This case grew out of the Pullman strike of 1894 wherein President Cleveland used the military and civil forces of the United States to end the strike. As part of that force, the Attorney-General of the United States directed the District Attorney for the Northern District of Illinois to file a bill in the Federal Court in Illinois seeking to enjoin Debs and other officers of the American Railway Union from interfering in any manner with the business of twenty-two railroads engaged in interstate commerce and in the transportation of the mails. The request maintained that there was a conspiracy, and that there were, as well, acts of intimidation and violence in support of the employees of the Pullman Company. The injunction was issued in the summer of 1894. In December, Debs and the others were found guilty of violating the injunction and were sentenced to terms of from three to six months for contempt. On being committed to jail they ask the Supreme Court of the United States for a writ of habeas corpus.

MR. JUSTICE BREWER . . . delivered the opinion of the court.

The case presented by the bill is this: The United States, finding that the interstate transportation of persons and property, as well as the carriage of the mails, is forcibly obstructed, and that a combination and conspiracy exists to subject the control of such transportation to the will of the conspirators, applied to one of their courts, sitting as a court of equity, for an injunction to restrain

119

such obstruction and prevent carrying into effect such conspiracy. Two questions of importance are suggested: First. Are the relations of the general government to interstate commerce and the transportation of the mails such as to authorize a direct interference to prevent a forcible obstruction thereof? Second. If authority exists, as authority in government implies both power and duty, has a court of equity jurisdiction to issue an injunction in aid of the performance of such duty?

First. What are the relations of the general government to interstate commerce and the transportation of the mails? They are those of direct supervision, control, and management. While under the dual system which prevails with us the powers of government are distributed between the State and the Nation, and while the latter is properly styled a government of enumerated powers, yet within the limits of such enumeration it has all the attributes of sovereignty, and, in the exercise of those enumerated powers, acts directly upon the citizen, and not through the intermediate agency of the State . . .

Among the powers expressly given to the national government are the control of interstate commerce and the creation and management of a post-office system for the nation. . . . [The Court then recites the statutes passed in the exercise of these powers.]

Obviously these powers given to the national government over interstate commerce and in respect to the transportation of the mails were not dormant and unused. Congress had taken hold of these two matters, and by various and specific acts had assumed and exercised the powers given to it, and was in full discharge of its duty to regulate interstate commerce and carry the mails. The validity of such exercise and the exclusiveness of its control had been again and again presented to this court for consideration. It is curious to note the fact that in a large proportion of the cases in respect to interstate commerce brought to this court the question presented was of the validity of state legislation in its bearings upon interstate commerce, and the uniform course of decision has been to declare that it is not within the competency of a State to legislate in such a manner as to obstruct interstate commerce. If a State with its recognized powers of sovereignty is impotent to obstruct interstate commerce, can it be that any mere voluntary association of individuals within the limits of that State has a power which the State itself does not possess?

As, under the Constitution, power over interstate commerce and the transportation of the mails is vested in the national government, and Congress by virtue of such grant has assumed actual and direct control, it follows that the national government may prevent any unlawful and forcible interference therewith. But how shall this be accomplished? Doubtless, it is within the competency of Congress to prescribe by legislation that any interference with these matters shall be offenses against the United States, and prosecuted and punished by indictment in the proper courts. But is that the only remedy? Have the vast interests of the nation in interstate commerce, and in the transportation of the mails, no other protection than lies in the possible punishment of those who interfere with it? To ask the question is to answer it. By article 3, section 2, clause 3, of the Federal Constitution it is provided: "The trial of all crimes except in cases of impeachment shall be by jury; and such trial shall be held in the State where the said crime shall have been committed." If all the inhabitants of a State, or even a great body of them, should combine to obstruct interstate commerce or the transportation of the mails, prosecutions for such offenses had in such a community would be doomed in advance to failure. And if the certainty of such failure was known, and the national government had no other way to enforce the freedom of interstate commerce and the transportation of the mails than by prosecution and punishment for interference therewith, the whole interests of the nation in these respects would be at the absolute mercy of a portion of the inhabitants of that single State.

But there is no such impotency in the national government. The entire strength of the nation may be used to enforce in any part of the land the full and free exercise of all national powers and the security of all rights entrusted by the Constitution to its care. The strong arm of the national government may be put forth to brush away all obstructions to the freedom of interstate commerce or the transportation of the mails. If the emergency arises, the army of the Nation, and all its militia, are at the service of the Nation to compel obedience to its laws.

But passing to the second question, is there no other alternative than the use of force on the part of the executive authorities whenever obstructions arise to the freedom of interstate commerce or the transportation of the mails? Is the army the only instrument by which rights of the public can be enforced and the peace of the nation preserved? Grant that any public nuisance may be forcibly abated either at the instance of the authorities, or by any individual suffering private damage therefrom, the existence of this right of forcible abatement is not inconsistent with nor does it destroy the right of appeal in an orderly way to the courts for a judicial determination, and an exercise of their powers by writ of injunction and otherwise to accomplish the same result. . . .

So, in the case before us, the right to use force does not exclude the right of appeal to the courts for a judicial determination and for the exercise of all their powers of prevention. Indeed, it is more to the praise than to the blame of the government, that, instead of determining for itself questions of right and wrong on the part of these petitioners and their associates and enforcing that determination by the club of the policeman and the bayonet of the soldier, it submitted all those questions to the peaceful determination of judicial tribunals, and invoked their consideration and judgment as to the measure of its rights and powers and the correlative obligations of those against whom it made complaint. And it is equally to the credit of the latter that the judgment of those tribunals was by the great body of them respected, and the troubles which threatened so much disaster terminated.

Neither can it be doubted that the government has such an interest in the subject-matter as enables it to appear as party plaintiff in this suit. It is said that equity only interferes for the protection of property, and that the government has no property interest. A sufficient reply is that the United States have a property in the mails, the protection of which was one of the purposes of this bill. . . .

We do not care to place our decisions upon this ground alone. . . . The national government, given by the Constitution power to regulate interstate commerce, has by express statute assumed jurisdiction over such commerce when carried upon railroads. It is charged, therefore, with the duty of keeping those highways of interstate commerce free from obstruction, for it has always been recognized as one of the powers and duties of a government to remove obstructions from the highway under its control. . . .

See also *Gilman* v. *Philadelphia*, 3 Wall. 713, 725, in which it was said: "Wherever 'commerce among the States' goes, the power of the nation, as represented in this court, goes with it to protect and enforce its rights."

Up to a recent date commerce, both interstate and international, was mainly by water, and it is not strange that both the legislation of Congress and the cases in the courts have been principally concerned therewith. The fact that in recent years interstate commerce has come mainly to be carried on by railroads and over artificial highways has in no manner narrowed the scope of the constitutional provision, or abridged the power of Congress over such commerce. On the contrary the same fullness of control exists in the one case as in the other, and the same power to remove obstructions from the one as from the other.

Constitutional provisions do not change, but their operation extends to new matters as the modes of business and the habits of life of the people vary with each succeeding generation. The law of the common carrier is the same today as when transportation on land was by coach and wagon, and on water by canal boat and sailing vessel, yet in its actual operation it touches and regulates transportation by modes then unknown, the railroad train and the steamship. Just so is it with the grant to the national government of power over interstate commerce. The Constitution has not changed. The power is the same. But it operates today upon modes of interstate commerce unknown to the fathers, and it will operate with equal force upon any new modes of such commerce which the future may develop. . . .

The petition for a writ of *habeas corpus* is denied.

UNITED STATES v. E. C. KNIGHT

156 U.S. 1, 39 L.Ed. 325 (1895)

Whatever else the Industrial Revolution did, it certainly is directly responsible for the creation of new modes of economic organization. Based on the premise that the individual be free to bargain, and perhaps also to be bargained for, sustained by an economic doctrine of laissez faire, and absorbed into the American way by the law of the land, the organizations grew into monopolies (and later holding companies) with all the concomitants of strength, power, and abuse inherent in the very words. Social Darwinism and the Gospel of Wealth were not quite the opiate they were intended to be, and hence popular efforts toward reform were spelled out in the Sherman Anti-Trust Act passed in 1890.

The instant case is the first presented to the Supreme Court after the Act had become the law of the land. In this case it was brought out that the American Sugar Refining Company produced about 65 per cent of the sugar refined in the United States, and that E. C. Knight and three others produced about 33 per cent. Since the Sherman Act prohibits any person from monopolizing or attempting or conspiring to monopolize any part of the trade or commerce among the several states, or with foreign nations, as well as "every contract, combination, or conspiracy in restraint of such commerce," the question is posed at once: Does the purchase, or agreement to purchase, the stock of the E. C. Knight Company by the American Sugar Company violate the Sherman Act? The United States maintained that it does and hence sought a court order voiding such agreement. The lower court held that a violation of the Act was not established and dismissed the bill. This was affirmed by the Circuit Court and the case comes to the Supreme Court on appeal.

It is well worth comparing the instant case with ADDYSTON PIPE AND STEEL CO. v. UNITED STATES [175 U.S. 211 (1899)] to see the kind of flagrant abuse of economic power that even the Court could not avoid striking down. But lest the obliteration of these practices, which, at this time seemed to be par for the course, upset the economic applecart too quickly or too violently, the Court, by 1911, in UNITED STATES v. STANDARD OIL COMPANY read into the Anti-Trust Act the so-called "rule of reason." (See 222 U.S. 1.)

MR. CHIEF JUSTICE FULLER . . . delivered the opinion of the court.

By the purchase of the stock of the four Philadelphia refineries, with shares of its own stock, the American Sugar Refining Company acquired nearly complete control of the manufacture of refined sugar within the United States. The bill charged that the contracts under which these purchases were made constituted combinations in restraint of trade, and that in entering into them the defendants combined and conspired to restrain the trade and commerce in refined sugar among the several States and with foreign nations, contrary to the act of Congress of July 2, 1890. . . .

The fundamental question is, whether conceding that the existence of a monopoly in manufacture is established by the evidence, that monopoly can be directly suppressed under the act of Congress in the mode attempted by this bill.

It cannot be denied that the power of the State to protect the lives, health and property of its citizens, and to preserve good order and the public morals, "the power to govern men and things within the limits of its dominion," is a power originally and always belonging to the States, not surrendered by them to the general government, nor directly restrained by the Constitution of the United States, and essentially exclusive. The relief of the citizens of each State from the burden of monopoly and the evils resulting from the restraint of trade among such citizens was left with the States to deal with, and this court has recognized their possession of that power even to the extent of holding that an employment or business carried on by private individuals, when it becomes a matter of such public interest and importance as to create a common charge or burden upon the citizen; in other words, when it becomes a practical monopoly, to which the citizen is compelled to resort and by means of which a tribute can be exacted from the community, is subject to regulation by state legislative power. On the other hand, the power of Congress to regulate commerce among the several States is also exclusive. The Constitution does not provide that interstate commerce shall be free, but, by the grant of this exclusive power to regulate it, it was left free except as Congress might impose restraints. Therefore it has been determined that the failure of Congress to exercise this exclusive power in any case is an expression of its will that the subject shall be free from restrictions or impositions upon it by the several States, and if a law passed by a State in the exercise of its acknowledged powers comes into conflict with that will, the Congress and the State cannot occupy the position of equal opposing sovereignties, because the Constitution declares its supremacy and that of the laws passed in pursuance thereof; and that which is not supreme must yield to that which is supreme. "Commerce, undoubtedly, is traffic," said Chief Justice

Marshall, "but it is something more; it is intercourse. It describes the commercial intercourse between nations and parts of nations in all its branches, and is regulated by prescribing rules for carrying on that intercourse." That which belongs to commerce is within the jurisdiction of the United States, but that which does not belong to commerce is within the jurisdiction of the police power of the State. . . .

The argument is that the power to control the manufacture of refined sugar is a monopoly over a necessary of life, to the enjoyment of which by a large part of the population of the United States interstate commerce is indispensable, and that, therefore, the general government in the exercise of the power to regulate commerce may repress such monopoly directly and set aside the instruments which have created it. But this argument cannot be confined to necessaries of life merely, and must include all articles of general consumption. Doubtless the power to control the manufacture of a given thing involves in a certain sense the control of its disposition, but this is a secondary and not the primary sense; and although the exercise of that power may result in bringing the operation of commerce into play, it does not control it, and affects it only incidentally and indirectly. Commerce succeeds to manufacture, and is not a part of it. The power to regulate commerce is the power to prescribe the rule by which commerce shall be governed, and is a power independent of the power to suppress monopoly. But it may operate in repression of monopoly whenever that comes within the rules by which commerce is governed or whenever the transaction is itself a monopoly of commerce. . . .

It is vital that the independence of the commercial power and of the police power, and the delimitation between them, however sometimes perplexing, should always be recognized and observed, for while the one furnishes the strongest bond of union, the other is essential to the preservation of the autonomy of the States as required by our dual form of government; and acknowledged evils, however grave and urgent they may appear to be, had better be borne, than the risk be run, in the effort to suppress them, of more serious consequences by resort to expedients of even doubtful constitutionality. . . .

Contracts, combinations, or conspiracies to control domestic enterprise in manufacture, agriculture, mining, production in all its forms, or to raise or lower prices or wages, might unquestionably tend to restrain external as well as domestic trade, but the restraint would be an indirect result, however inevitable and whatever its extent, and such result would not necessarily determine the object of the contract, combination, or conspiracy.

Again, all the authorities agree that in order to vitiate a contract or combination it is not essential that its result should be a complete monopoly; it is sufficient if it really tends to that end and to deprive the public of the advantages which flow from free competition. Slight reflection will show that if the national power extends to all contracts and combinations in manufacture, agriculture, mining, and other productive industries, whose ultimate result may affect external commerce, comparatively little of business operations and affairs would be left for state control.

It was in the light of well-settled principles that the act of July 2, 1890, was framed. Congress did not attempt thereby to assert the power to deal with monopoly directly as such; or to limit and restrict the rights of corporations created by the States or the citizens of the States in the acquisition, control, or disposition of property; or to regulate or prescribe the price or prices at which such property or the products thereof should be sold; or to make criminal the acts of persons in the acquisition and control of property which the States of their residence or creation sanctioned or permitted. Aside from the provisions applicable where Congress might exercise municipal power, what the law struck at was combinations, contracts, and conspiracies to monopolize trade and commerce among the several States or with foreign nations; but the contracts and acts of the defendants related exclusively to the acquisition of the Philadelphia refineries and the business of sugar refining in Pennsylvania, and bore no direct relation to commerce between the States or with foreign nations. . . . There was nothing in the proofs to indicate any intention to put a restraint upon trade or commerce, and the fact, as we have seen, that trade or commerce might be indirectly affected was not enough to entitle complainants to a decree. . . .

Decree affirmed.

MR. JUSTICE HARLAN, dissenting. . . .

. . . In its consideration of the important constitutional question presented, this court assumes on the record before us that the result of the transactions disclosed by the pleadings and proof was the creation of a monopoly in the manufacture of a necessary of life. If this combination, so far as its operations necessarily or directly affect interstate commerce, cannot be restrained or suppressed under some power granted to Congress, it will be cause for regret that the patriotic statesmen who framed the Constitution did not foresee the necessity of investing the national government with power to deal with gigantic monopolies holding in their grasp, and injuriously controlling in their own interest, the entire trade *among the States* in food products that are essential to the comfort of every household in the land. . . .

What is commerce among the States? The decisions of this court fully answer the question. "Commerce, undoubtedly, is traffic, but it is something more: it is intercourse." It does not embrace the completely interior traffic of the respective States—that which is "carried on between man and man in a State, or between different parts of the same State and which does not extend to or affect other States"—but it does embrace "every species of commercial intercourse" between the United States and foreign nations and among the States, and, therefore, it includes such traffic or trade, buying, selling, and interchange of commodities, as directly affects or necessarily involves the interests of the People of the United States. "Commerce, as the word is used in the Constitution, is a unit," and "cannot stop at the external boundary line of each State, but may be introduced into the interior." "The genius and character of the whole government seem to be, that its action is to be applied to all the external concerns of the nation, *and to those internal concerns which affect the States generally.*"

These principles were announced in *Gibbons* v. *Ogden*, and have often been approved. . . .

In the light of these principles, determining as well the scope of the power to regulate commerce among the States as the nature of such commerce, we are to inquire whether the act of Congress of July 2, 1890 . . . entitled "An act to protect trade and commerce against unlawful restraints and monopolies" . . . is repugnant to the Constitution. . . .

It would seem to be indisputable that no *combination* of corporations or individuals can, *of right*, impose unlawful restraints upon *interstate* trade, whether upon transportation or upon such interstate intercourse and traffic as precede transportation, any more than it can, *of right*, impose unreasonable restraints upon the completely internal traffic of a State. The supposition cannot be indulged that this general proposition will be disputed. If it be true that a *combination* of corporations or individuals may, so far as the power of Congress is concerned, subject interstate trade, in any of its stages, to unlawful restraints, the conclusion is inevitable that the Constitution has failed to accomplish one primary object of the Union, which was to place commerce *among the States* under the control of the common government of all the people, and thereby relieve or protect it against burdens or restrictions imposed, by whatever authority, for the benefit of particular localities or special interests. . . .

The power of Congress covers and protects the absolute freedom of such intercourse and trade among the States as may or must succeed manufacture and precede transportation from the place of purchase. This would seem to be conceded; for, the court in the present case expressly declare that "*contracts to buy*, sell, or exchange goods *to be transported among the several States*, the transportation and its instrumentalities, and articles bought, sold, or exchanged for the purpose of such transit among the States, or put in the way of transit, *may be regulated*, but this is *because they form part of interstate trade or commerce.*" Here is a direct admission— one which the settled doctrines of this court justify—that contracts to buy and the purchasing of goods *to be transported from one State to another*, and transportation, with its instrumentalities, are all *parts* of interstate trade or commerce. Each part of such trade is then under the protection of Congress. And yet, by the opinion and judgment in this case, if I do not misapprehend them, Congress is without power to protect the commercial intercourse that such purchasing necessarily involves against the restraints and burdens arising from the existence of *combinations* that meet purchasers, from whatever State they come, with the threat—for it is nothing more nor less than a threat—that they *shall not* purchase what they desire to purchase, *except at the prices fixed by such combinations*. . . .

In my judgment, the citizens of the several States composing the Union are entitled, of right, to buy goods in the State where they are manufactured, or in any other State, without being confronted by an illegal combination whose business extends throughout the whole country, which by the law everywhere is an enemy to the public interests, and which prevents such buying, except at prices arbitrarily fixed by it. I insist that the free course of trade among the States cannot coexist with such combinations. When I speak of trade I mean the buying and selling of articles of every kind that are recognized articles of interstate commerce. Whatever improperly obstructs the free course of interstate intercourse and trade, as involved in the buying and selling of articles to be carried from one State to another, may be reached by Congress, under its authority to regulate commerce among the States. The exercise of that authority so as to make trade among the States, in all recognized articles of commerce, absolutely free from unreasonable or illegal restrictions imposed by combinations, is justified by an express grant of power to Congress and would redound to the welfare of the whole country. I am unable to perceive that any such result would imperil the autonomy of the States, especially as that result cannot be attained through the action of any one State. . . .

To the general government has been committed the control of commercial intercourse among the States, to the end that it may be free at all times from any restraints except such as Congress may impose or permit for the benefit of the whole country. The common government of all the people is the only one that can adequately deal with a matter which directly and injuriously affects the entire commerce of the country, which concerns equally all the people of the Union, and which, it must be confessed, cannot be adequately controlled by any one State. Its authority should not be so weakened by construction that it cannot reach and eradicate evils that, beyond all question, tend to defeat an object which that government is entitled, by the Constitution, to accomplish. "Powerful and ingenious minds," this court has said, "taking, as postulates, that the powers expressly granted to the government of the Union, are to be contracted by construction into the narrowest possible compass, and that the original powers of the States are retained if any possible construction will retain them, may, by a course of well digested, but refined and metaphysical reasoning, founded on these premises, explain away the Constitution of our country, and leave it, a magnificent structure, indeed, to look at, but totally unfit for use. They may so entangle and perplex the understanding as to obscure principles which were before thought quite plain, and induce doubts where, if the mind were to pursue its own course, none would be perceived." *Gibbons* v. *Ogden.* . . .

POLLOCK v. FARMERS' LOAN AND TRUST CO.

158 U.S. 601, 39 L.Ed. 1108 (1895)

The 1895 term of the Supreme Court was indeed a notable one. Within a period of a few weeks, the Court had sustained the use of national power to end labor strikes (In re Debs); had denied the use of national authority over corporations engaged in manufacturing since it was not interstate commerce (U.S. v. E. C. Knight); and now was confronted by a case involving the constitutionality of the Income Tax imposed by Congress in the Wilson-Gorman Tariff Act of 1894. That these cases set up the "class struggle" of that day cannot be ignored. Indeed, no clearer exposition of it can be found than that stated by Mr. Justice Field at the end of his forty-page concurring opinion in the instant case:

Here I close my opinion. I could not say less in view of the questions of such gravity that go down to the foundations of our government. If the provisions of the Constitution can be set aside by an act of congress, where is this usurpation to end? The present assault upon capital is but the beginning. It will be but the stepping stone to others, larger and more sweeping, till our political contests will become a war of the poor against the rich; a war constantly growing in intensity and bitterness.

In view of the fact that fourteen years before in Springer v. United States, 102 U.S. 586 (1881), the Supreme Court had sustained an income tax law, the issue becomes more clearly defined: Is the political process in a democracy like ours to be permitted to deal with new economic forces as it sees fit, or is the judiciary to be permitted to check such action when it sees fit? And the fact that the issue was, in this case at least, settled by the insertion of an amendment (16th) to the Constitution does not diminish the significance of the issue itself.

The facts of this case are not startling. Charles Pollock, a citizen of Massachusetts, like the rest of us, did not take to paying taxes easily. Congress had passed an Act in 1894 providing for the payment to the United States of two per centum on the net profits of income derived, in part at least, from real estate and bonds. The Farmers' Loan and Trust Company, a New York corporation, was about to pay such tax, when Pollock, a stockholder in the corporation, brought suit on behalf of himself and others to restrain such payment. In his bill he alleged that the Act of 1894 was unconstitutional insofar as its levy on real estate, etc., was a direct tax, and that the tax on bonds of states and municipalities was not subject to the taxing power of the United States.

On April 8, 1895, the Court, one Justice being absent, decided:

A tax on the rents or income of real estate is a direct tax, within the meaning of that term as used in the Constitution of the United States.

A tax upon incomes derived from the interest of bonds issued by a municipal corporation is a tax upon the power of the State and its instrumentalities to borrow money, and is consequently repugnant to the Constitution of the United States.

Upon each of the other questions argued at bar, to wit: 1. Whether the void provision as to rent and income from real estate invalidates the whole act? 2. Whether as to the income from personal property as such, the act is unconstitutional, as laying direct taxes? 3. Whether any part of the tax if considered as a direct tax, is invalid for want of uniformity on either of the grounds suggested?—The Justices who heard the argument are equally divided, and, therefore, no opinion is expressed. (157 U.S. 429)

Inasmuch as the case and that of HYDE v. CONTINENTAL TRUST Co. had not been heard by a full court, and since the question upon which the court was equally divided still lacked authoritative determination, the appellants were granted a rehearing.

MR. CHIEF JUSTICE FULLER delivered the opinion of the court. . . .

Our previous decision was confined to the consideration of the validity of the tax on the income from real estate, and on the income from municipal bonds. The question thus limited was whether such taxation was direct or not, in the meaning of the Constitution; and the court went no farther, as to the tax on the incomes from real estate, than to hold that it fell within the same class as the source whence the income was derived, that is, that a tax upon the realty and a tax upon the receipts therefrom were alike direct; while as to the income from municipal bonds, that could not be taxed because of want of power to tax the source, and no reference was made to the nature of the tax being direct or indirect.

We are now permitted to broaden the field of inquiry, and determine to which of the two great classes a tax upon a person's entire income, whether derived from rents, or products, or otherwise, of real estate, or from bonds, stocks or other forms of personal property, belongs; and we are unable to conclude that the enforced subtraction from the yield of all the owner's real or personal property, in the manner prescribed, is so different from a tax upon the property itself, that it is not a direct, but an indirect tax, in the meaning of the Constitution.

Whatever the speculative views of political economists or revenue reformers may be, can it be properly held that the Constitution, taken in its plain and obvious sense, and with due regard to the circumstances attending the formation of the government, authorizes a general unapportioned tax on the products of the farm and the rents of real estate, although imposed merely because of ownership and with no possible means of escape from payment, as belonging to a totally different class from that which includes the property from whence the income proceeds?

There can be only one answer, unless the constitutional restriction is to be treated as utterly illusory and futile, and the object of its framers defeated. We find it impossible to hold that a fundamental requisition, deemed so important as to be enforced by two provisions, one affirmative and one negative, can be refined away by forced distinctions between that which gives value to property, and the property itself.

Nor can we conceive any ground why the same reasoning does not apply to capital in personalty held for the purpose of income or ordinarily yielding income, and to the income therefrom. All the real estate of the country, and all its invested personal property, are open to the direct operation of the taxing power if an apportionment be made according to the Constitution. The Constitution does not say that no direct tax shall be laid by apportionment on any other property than land; on the contrary, it forbids all unapportioned direct taxes; and we know of no warrant for excepting personal property from the exercise of the power, or any reason why an apportioned direct tax cannot be laid and assessed, as Mr. Gallatin said in his report when Secretary of the Treasury in 1812, "upon the same objects of taxation on which the direct taxes levied under the authority of the State are laid and assessed." . . .

Nor are we impressed with the contention that, because in the four instances in which the power of direct taxation has been exercised, Congress did not see fit, for reasons of expediency, to levy a tax upon personalty, this amounts to such a practical construction of the Constitution that the power did not exist, that we must regard ourselves bound by it. We should regret to be compelled to hold the powers of the general government thus restricted, and certainly cannot accede to the idea that the Constitution has become weakened by a particular course of inaction under it.

The stress of the argument is thrown, however, on the assertion that an income tax is not a property tax at all; that it is not a real estate tax, or a crop tax, or a bond tax; that it is an assessment upon the taxpayer on account of his money-spending power as shown by his revenue for the year preceding the assessment; that rents received, crops harvested, interest collected, have lost all connection with their origin, and although once not taxable have become transmuted in their new form into taxable subject-matter; in other words, that income is taxable irrespective of the source from whence it is derived. . . .

We have unanimously held in this case that, so far as this law operates on the receipts from municipal bonds, it cannot be sustained, because it is a tax on the power of the States, and on their instrumentalities to borrow money, and consequently repugnant to the Constitution. But if, as contended, the interest when received has become merely money in the recipient's pocket, and taxable as such without reference to the source from which it came, the question is immaterial whether it should have been originally taxed at all or not. This was admitted by the Attorney General with characteristic candor; and it follows that, if the revenue derived from municipal bonds cannot be taxed because the source cannot be, the same rule applies to revenue from any other source not subject to the tax; and the lack of power to levy any but an apportioned tax on real estate and personal property equally exists as to the revenue therefrom.

Admitting that this act taxes the income of property irrespective of its source, still we cannot doubt that such a tax is necessarily a direct tax in the meaning of the Constitution. . . .

Being direct, and therefore to be laid by apportionment, is there any real difficulty in doing so? Cannot Congress, if the necessity exist of raising thirty, forty, or any other number of million dollars for the support of the government, in addition to the revenue from duties, imposts, and excises, apportion the quota of each State upon the basis of the census, and thus advise it of the payment which must be made, and proceed to assess that amount on all the real or personal property and the income of all persons in the State, and collect the same if the State does not in the meantime assume and pay its quota and collect the amount according to its own system and in its own way? Cannot Congress do this, as respects either or all these subjects of taxation, and deal with each in such manner as might be deemed expedient, as indeed was done in the act of July 14, 1798, c. 75, 1 Stat. 597? Inconveniences might possibly attend the levy of an income tax, notwithstanding the listing of receipts, when adjusted, furnishes its own valuation; but that it is apportionable is hardly denied, although it is asserted that it would operate so unequally as to be undesirable. . . .

We have considered the act only in respect of the tax on income derived from real estate, and from invested personal property, and have not commented on so much of it as bears on gains or profits from business, privileges, or employments, in view of the instances in which taxation on business, privileges, or employments has assumed the guise of an excise tax and been sustained as such. . . .

Our conclusions may, therefore, be summed up as follows:

First. We adhere to the opinion already announced, that, taxes on real estate being indisputably direct taxes, taxes on the rents or incomes of real estate are equally direct taxes.

Second. We are of opinion that taxes on personal property, or on the income of personal property, are likewise direct taxes.

Third. The tax imposed by sections twenty-seven to thirty-seven, inclusive, of the act of 1894, so far as it falls on the income of real estate and of personal property, being a direct tax within the meaning of the Constitution, and, therefore, unconstitutional and void because not apportioned according to representation, all those sections, constituting one entire scheme of taxation, are necessarily invalid.

The decrees hereinbefore entered in this court will be vacated; the decrees below will be reversed, and the case remanded, with instructions to grant the relief prayed.

[Mr. Justice Harlan, Mr. Justice Brown, Mr. Justice Jackson, and Mr. Justice White delivered dissenting opinions.]

MR. JUSTICE HARLAN, dissenting:

Such a result [the burden put by the decision upon those not deriving rents from real estate or income from personal property] is one to be deeply deplored. It cannot be regarded otherwise than as a disaster to the country. The decree now passed dislocates—principally, for reasons of an economic nature—a sovereign power expressly granted to the general government and long recognized and fully established by judicial decisions and legislative action. It so interprets constitutional provisions, originally designed to protect slave property against oppressive taxation, as to give privileges and immunities never contemplated by the founders of the government. . . .

The practical effect of the decision to-day is to give to certain kinds of property a position of favoritism and advantage inconsistent with the fundamental principles of our social organization, and to invest them with power and influence that may be perilous to that portion of the American people upon whom rests the larger part of the burdens of the government, and who ought not to be subjected to the dominion of aggregated wealth any more than the property of the country should be at the mercy of the lawless.

MR. JUSTICE BROWN, dissenting:

. . . If the question what is and what is not a direct tax were now for the first time presented, I should entertain a grave doubt whether, in view of the definitions of a direct tax given by the courts and writers upon political economy, during the present century, it ought not to be held to apply not only to an income tax, but to every tax, the burden of which is borne, both immediately and ultimately, by the person paying it. It does not, however, follow that this is the definition had in mind by the framers of the Constitution.

. . . whenever this court has been called upon to give a construction to this clause of the Constitution, it has universally held the words "direct taxes" applied only to capitation taxes and taxes upon land.

MR. JUSTICE JACKSON, dissenting: . . .

The decision disregards the well established canons of construction to which I have referred, that an act passed by a coordinate branch of the government has every presumption in its favor, and should never be declared invalid by the courts unless its repugnancy to the Constitution is clear beyond all reasonable doubt.

MR. JUSTICE WHITE, dissenting:

It is, I submit, greatly to be deplored that, after more than one hundred years of our national existence, after the government has withstood the strain of foreign wars and the dread ordeal of civil strife, and its people have become united and powerful, this court should consider itself compelled to go back to a long repudiated and rejected theory of the Constitution by which the government is deprived of an inherent attribute of its being, a necessary power of taxation.

ADAIR v. UNITED STATES

208 U.S. 161, 52 L.Ed. 436 (1908)

The group basis of politics is not a new phenomenon. The Federalist No. 10 speaks of "factions." Charles Beard in his Economic Interpretation of the Constitution *provides further evidence in this direction. The conflict between Jeffersonianism and Hamiltonianism has been throughout our history its living index. What was at stake was the belief that there was somehow a double standard being used: while businesses were being made exempt from the processes of democratic government, workingmen were being subjected to extra-democratic processes—and all under the same protective covering of "laissez faire," "sui juris," "liberty of contract," and the like. And the instant case seemed to provide more grist for the mill. This case comes to the Supreme Court on a writ of error to the District Court of the United States for the Eastern District of Kentucky to review a conviction of an agent of an interstate carrier who discharged an employee from the service of the carrier because of his membership in a labor organization. The Court in this case reversed the con-*

viction and ordered the case dismissed. Since COPPAGE v. KANSAS *(see p. 101, supra) was soon to come, labor found itself in the position perhaps best expressed by a recent writer: " 'Everyone for himself,' said the elephant, as he danced among the chickens."*

MR. JUSTICE HARLAN delivered the opinion of the court: . . .

It thus appears that the criminal offense charged in the count of the indictment upon which the defendant was convicted was, in substance and effect, that, being an agent of a railroad company engaged in interstate commerce, and subject to the provisions of the above act of June 1st, 1898, he discharged one Coppage from its service *because of his membership in a labor organization,*—no other ground for such discharge being alleged.

May Congress make it a criminal offense against the United States—as, by the 10th section of the act of 1898, it does—for an agent or officer of an interstate carrier, having full authority in the premises from the carrier, to discharge an employee from service simply because of his membership in a labor organization? . . .

The first inquiry is whether the part of the 10th section of the act of 1898 upon which the first count of the indictment was based is repugnant to the 5th Amendment of the Constitution, declaring that no person shall be deprived of liberty or property without due process of law. In our opinion that section, in the particular mentioned, is an invasion of the personal liberty, as well as of the right of property, guaranteed by that Amendment. Such liberty and right embrace the right to make contracts for the purchase of the labor of others, and equally the right to make contracts for the sale of one's own labor; each right, however, being subject to the fundamental condition that no contract, whatever its subject-matter, can be sustained which the law, upon reasonable grounds, forbids as inconsistent with the public interests, or as hurtful to the public order, or as detrimental to the common good. This court has said that "in every well-ordered society, charged with the duty of conserving the safety of its members, the rights of the individual in respect of his liberty may, at times, under the pressure of great dangers, be subjected to such restraint, to be enforced by reasonable regulations, as the safety of the general public may demand." *Jacobson* v. *Massachusetts,* 197 U.S. 11, 29, and authorities there cited. Without stopping to consider what would have been the rights of the railroad company under the 5th Amendment, had it been indicted under the act of Congress, it is sufficient in this case to say that, as agent of the railroad company, and, as such, responsible for the conduct of the business of one of its departments, it was the defendant Adair's right—and that right inhered in his personal liberty, and was also a right of property—to serve his employer as best he could, so long as he did nothing that was reasonably forbidden by law as injurious to the public interests. It was the right of the defendant to prescribe the terms upon which the services of Coppage would be accepted, and it was the right of Coppage to become or not, as he chose, an employee of the railroad company upon the terms offered to him. Mr. Cooley, in his treatise on Torts, p. 278, well says: "It is a part of every man's civil rights that he be left at liberty to refuse business relations with any person whomsoever, whether the refusal rests upon reason, or is the result of whim, caprice, prejudice, or malice. With his reasons neither the public nor third persons have any legal concern. It is also his right to have business relations with anyone with whom he can make contracts, and, if he is wrongfully deprived of this right by others, he is entitled to redress." . . .

It was the legal right of the defendant, Adair,—however unwise such a course might have been,—to discharge Coppage because of his being a member of a labor organization, as it was the legal right of Coppage, if he saw fit to do so,—however unwise such a course on his part might have been,—to quit the service in which he was engaged, because the defendant employed some persons who were not members of a labor organization. In all such particulars the employer and the employee have equality or right, and any legislation that disturbs that equality is an arbitrary interference with the liberty of contract which no government can legally justify in a free land. . . .

MR. JUSTICE HOLMES dissenting:

I . . . think that the statute is constitutional, and, but for the decision of my brethren, I should have felt pretty clear about it. . . .

The ground on which this particular law is held bad is not so much that it deals with matters remote from commerce among the States, as that it interferes with the paramount individual rights secured by the 5th Amendment. The section is, in substance, a very limited interference with freedom of contract, no more. It does not require the carriers to employ anyone. It does not forbid them to refuse to employ anyone, for any reason they deem good, even where the notion of a choice of persons is a fiction and wholesale employment is necessary upon general principles that it might be proper to control. The section simply prohibits the more powerful party to exact certain undertakings, or to threaten dismissal or unjustly discriminate on certain grounds against those already employed. I hardly can suppose that the grounds on which a contract lawfully may be made to end are less open to regulation than other terms. So I turn to the general question whether the employment can be regulated at all. I confess that I think that the right to make contracts at will that has been derived from the word "liberty" in the Amendments has been stretched to its extreme by the decisions; but they agree that sometimes the right may be restrained. Where there is, or generally is believed to be, an important ground of public policy for restraint, the Constitution does not forbid it, whether this court agrees or disagrees with the policy pursued. It cannot be doubted that to prevent strikes, and, so far as possible, to foster its scheme of arbitration, might be deemed by Congress an important point of policy, and I think it impossible to say that Congress might not reasonably think that the provision in question would help a good deal to carry its policy along. But suppose the only effect really were to tend to bring about the complete unionizing of such railroad laborers as Congress can deal with, I think that object alone would justify the end. I quite agree that the question what and how much good labor unions do, is one on which intelligent people may differ; I think that laboring men sometimes attribute to them advantages, as many attribute to combinations of capital disadvantages, that really are due to economic conditions of a far wider and deeper kind; but I could not pronounce it unwarranted if Congress should decide that to foster a strong union was for the best interest, not only of the men, but of the railroads and the country at large.

McKenna, J. dissented separately. Moody, J., did not participate.

HAMMER v. DAGENHART

247 U.S. 251, 62 L.Ed. 1101 (1918)

Ask anyone familiar with our governmental system to name some of its basic principles, and "federalism" would most certainly be among the first named. The division of powers between the national government and the state governments as expressed in Article I, Section 8 and in its counterpart, the Tenth Amendment, are in the Constitution for all to see. But since this, like everything else in a society wedded to the doctrine of "the rule of law," is in its application a judicial question, it provides another avenue for the Supreme Court to deal with economic problems. While Congress had used the Commerce Clause to control and regulate common carriers, trusts, and intoxicating liquors, by 1903 the area in which congressional regulations of articles to be transported in interstate commerce began to expand rapidly. This in turn raised the cry of the creation of a Federal police power which, under the guise of regulating interstate commerce, actually regulated the production, manufacture, sale, and transportation of articles and persons which had formerly been under the states and their police power. Taking advantage of the expansion opened to it, Congress was besieged by bills to regulate child labor in the states by debarring the products of such labor from the avenues of interstate commerce. Charging that such action tends to "federalize" and to "centralize" power in the national government, that such power destroys our dual sys-

tem of government, that it makes the police power of the states subservient to that of the national government, the opposing forces met squarely in the case below, the facts of which are clearly presented in the opinion itself.

MR. JUSTICE DAY delivered the opinion of the court:

A bill was filed in the United States district court for the western district of North Carolina by a father in his own behalf and as next friend of his two minor sons, one under the age of fourteen years and the other between the ages of fourteen and sixteen years, employees in a cotton mill at Charlotte, North Carolina, to enjoin the enforcement of the act of Congress intended to prevent interstate commerce in the products of child labor. 39 Stat. at L. 675, chap. 432.

The district court held the act unconstitutional and entered a decree enjoining its enforcement. This appeal brings the case here. . . .

The power essential to the passage of this act, the government contends, is found in the commerce clause of the Constitution, which authorizes Congress to regulate commerce with foreign nations and among the states.

In *Gibbons* v. *Ogden*, 9 Wheat. 1, Chief Justice Marshall, speaking for this court, and defining the extent and nature of the commerce power, said: "It is the power to regulate,—that is, to prescribe the rule by which commerce is to be governed." In other words, the power is one to control the means by which commerce is carried on, which is directly the contrary of the assumed right to forbid commerce from moving and thus destroy it as to particular commodities. But it is insisted that adjudged cases in this court establish the doctrine that the power to regulate given to Congress incidentally includes the authority to prohibit the movement of ordinary commodities, and therefore that the subject is not open for discussion. The cases demonstrate the contrary. They rest upon the character of the particular subjects dealt with and the fact that the scope of governmental authority, state or national, possessed over them, is such that the authority to prohibit is, as to them, but the exertion of the power to regulate.

The first of these cases is *Champion* v. *Ames*, 188 U. S. 321, the so-called Lottery Case, in which it was held that Congress might pass a law having the effect to keep the channels of commerce free from use in the transportation of tickets used in the promotion of lottery schemes. In *Hipolite Egg Co.* v. *United States*, 220 U. S. 45, this court sustained the power of Congress to pass the Pure Food and Drug Act, which prohibited the introduction into the states by means of interstate commerce of impure foods and drugs. In *Hoke* v. *United States*, 227 U. S. 308, this court sustained the constitutionality of the so-called "White Slave Traffic Act," whereby transportation of a woman in interstate commerce for the purpose of prostitution was forbidden. In that case we said, having reference to the authority of Congress, under the regulatory power, to protect the channels of interstate commerce:

> If the facility of interstate transportation can be taken away from the demoralization of lotteries, the debasement of obscene literature, the contagion of diseased cattle or persons, the impurity of food and drugs, the like facility can be taken away from the systematic enticement to and the enslavement in prostitution and debauchery of women, and, more insistently, of girls.

In *Caminetti* v. *United States*, 242 U.S. 470, we held that Congress might prohibit the transportation of women in interstate commerce for the purposes of debauchery and kindred purposes. In *Clark Distilling Co.* v. *Western Maryland R. Co.*, 242 U.S. 311, the power of Congress over the transportation of intoxicating liquors was sustained. . . .

And concluding the discussion which sustained the authority of the government to prohibit the transportation of liquor in interstate commerce, the court said:

> The exceptional nature of the subject here regulated is the basis upon which the exceptional power exerted must rest, and affords no ground for any fear that such power may be constitutionally extended to things which it may not, consistently with the guaranties of the Constitution, embrace.

In each of these instances the use of interstate transportation was necessary to the accomplishment of harmful results. In other words, although the power over interstate transportation was to regulate, that could only be accomplished by prohibiting the use of the facilities of interstate commerce to effect the evil intended.

This element is wanting in the present case. The thing intended to be accomplished by this statute is the denial of the facilities of interstate commerce to those manufacturers in the states who employ children within the prohibited ages. The act in its effect does not regulate transportation among the states, but aims to standardize the ages at which children may be employed in mining and manufacturing within the states. The goods shipped are of themselves harmless. The act permits them to be freely shipped after thirty days from the time of their removal from the factory. When offered for shipment, and before transportation begins, the labor of their production is over, and the mere fact that they were intended for interstate commerce transportation does not make their production subject to Federal control under the commerce power. . . .

Over interstate transportation, or its incidents, the regulatory power of Congress is ample, but the production of articles intended for interstate commerce is a matter of local regulation. . . . If it were otherwise, all manufacture intended for interstate shipment would

be brought under Federal control to the practical exclusion of the
authority of the states,—a result certainly not contemplated by the
framers of the Constitution when they vested in Congress the authority to regulate commerce among the states.

It is further contended that the authority of Congress may be
exerted to control interstate commerce in the shipment of child-
made goods because of the effect of the circulation of such goods
in other states where the evil of this class of labor has been recognized
by local legislation, and the right to thus employ child labor has
been more rigorously restrained than in the state of production.
In other words, that the unfair competition thus engendered may
be controlled by closing the channels of interstate commerce to
manufacturers in those states where the local laws do not meet what
Congress deems to be the more just standard of other states.

There is no power vested in Congress to require the states to exercise their police power so as to prevent possible unfair competition.
Many causes may co-operate to give one state, by reason of local
laws or conditions, an economic advantage over others. The commerce clause was not intended to give to Congress a general authority to equalize such conditions. In some of the states laws have
been passed fixing minimum wages for women; in others the local
law regulates the hours of labor of women in various employments.
Business done in such states may be at an economic disadvantage
when compared with states which have no such regulations; surely,
this fact does not give Congress the power to deny transportation
in interstate commerce to those who carry on business where the
hours of labor and the rate of compensation for women have not
been fixed by a standard in use in other states and approved by
Congress.

The grant of power to Congress over the subject of interstate
commerce was to enable it to regulate such commerce, and not to
give it authority to control the states in their exercise of the police
power over local trade and manufacture. . . .

That there should be limitations upon the right to employ children in mines and factories in the interest of their own and the
public welfare, all will admit. That such employment is generally
deemed to require regulation is shown by the fact that the brief of
counsel states that every state in the Union has a law upon the
subject, limiting the right to thus employ children. In North Carolina,
the state wherein is located the factory in which the employment
was had in the present case, no child under twelve years of age
is permitted to work.

It may be desirable that such laws be uniform, but our Federal
government is one of enumerated powers; "this principle," declared
Chief Justice Marshall in *M'Culloch* v. *Maryland*, 4 Wheat. 316,
"is universally admitted." . . .

In interpreting the Constitution it must never be forgotten that the nation is made up of states, to which are intrusted the powers of local government. And to them and to the people the powers not expressly delegated to the national government are reserved. The power of the states to regulate their purely internal affairs by such laws as seem wise to the local authority is inherent, and has never been surrendered to the general government. . . .

In our view the necessary effect of this act is, by means of a prohibition against the movement in interstate commerce of ordinary commercial commodities, to regulate the hours of labor of children in factories and mines within the states,—a purely state authority. Thus the act in a twofold sense is repugnant to the Constitution. It not only transcends the authority delegated to Congress over commerce, but also exerts a power as to a purely local matter to which the Federal authority does not extend. The far-reaching result of upholding the act cannot be more plainly indicated than by pointing out that if Congress can thus regulate matters intrusted to local authority by prohibition of the movement of commodities in interstate commerce, all freedom of commerce will be at an end, and the power of the states over local matters may be eliminated, and thus our system of government be practically destroyed.

For these reasons we hold that this law exceeds the constitutional authority of Congress. It follows that the decree of the District Court must be affirmed.

MR. JUSTICE HOLMES, dissenting: . . .

The first step in my argument is to make plain what no one is likely to dispute,—that the statute in question is within the power expressly given to Congress if considered only as to its immediate effects, and that if invalid it is so only upon some collateral ground. The statute confines itself to prohibiting the carriage of certain goods in interstate or foreign commerce. Congress is given power to regulate such commerce in unqualified terms. It would not be argued to-day that the power to regulate does not include the power to prohibit. Regulation means the prohibition of something, and when interstate commerce is the matter to be regulated I cannot doubt that the regulations may prohibit any part of such commerce that Congress sees fit to forbid. At all events it is established by the Lottery Case and others that have followed it that a law is not beyond the regulative power of Congress merely because it prohibits certain transportation out and out. *Champion v. Ames,* 188 U.S. 321, 355, 359 et seq. . . .

The question, then, is narrowed to whether the exercise of its otherwise constitutional power by Congress can be pronounced unconstitutional because of its possible reaction upon the conduct of the states in a matter upon which I have admitted that they are free from direct control. I should have thought that that matter had been disposed of so fully as to leave no room for doubt. I should have thought that the most conspicuous decisions of this court had made it clear that the power to regulate commerce and other constitutional powers could not be cut down or qualified by the fact that it might interfere with the carrying out of the domestic policy of any state.

The manufacturing of oleomargarine is as much a matter of state regulation as the manufacture of cotton cloth. Congress levied a tax upon the compound when colored so as to resemble butter that was so great as obviously to prohibit the manufacture and sale. In a very elaborate discussion the present Chief Justice excluded any inquiry into the purpose of an act which, apart from that purpose, was within the power of Congress. *McCray* v. *United States*, 195 U.S. 27. . . . Fifty years ago a tax on state banks, the obvious purpose and actual effect of which was to drive them, or at least their circulation, out of existence, was sustained, although the result was one that Congress had no constitutional power to require. The court made short work of the argument as to the purpose of the act. "The judicial cannot prescribe to the legislative departments of the government limitations upon the exercise of its acknowledged powers." *Veazie Bank* v. *Fenno*, 8 Wall. 533. So it well might have been argued that the corporation tax was intended, under the guise of a revenue measure, to secure a control not otherwise belonging to Congress, but the tax was sustained, and the objection, so far as noticed, was disposed of by citing *McCray* v. *United States; Flint* v. *Stone Tracy Co.* 220 U.S. 107. And to come to cases upon interstate commerce, notwithstanding *United States* v. *E. C. Knight Co.*, 156 U.S. 1, the Sherman Act has been made an instrument for the breaking up of combinations in restraint of trade and monopolies, using the power to regulate commerce as a foothold, but not proceeding because that commerce was the end actually in mind. The objection that the control of the states over production was interfered with was urged again and again, but always in vain.

The Pure Food and Drug Act was sustained in *Hipolite Egg Co.* v. *United States*, 220 U.S. 45, with the intimation that "no trade can be carried on between the states to which it [the power of Congress to regulate commerce] does not extend," applies not merely to articles that the changing opinions of the time condemn as intrinsically harmful, but to others innocent in themselves, simply on the ground that the order for them was induced by a preliminary fraud. *Weeks* v. *United States*, 245 U.S. 618. It does not matter whether the supposed evil precedes or follows the transportation. It is enough that, in the opinion of Congress, the transportation encourages the evil. I may add that in the cases on the so-called White Slave Act it was established that the means adopted by Congress as convenient to the exercise of its power might have the character of police regulations.

The notion that prohibition is any less prohibition when applied to things now thought evil I do not understand. But if there is any matter upon which civilized countries have agreed,—far more unanimously than they have with regard to intoxicants and some other matters over which this country is now emotionally aroused,—it is the evil of premature and excessive child labor. I should have thought that if we were to introduce our own moral conceptions where, in my opinion, they do not belong, this was pre-eminently a case for upholding the exercise of all its powers by the United States.

But I had thought that the propriety of the exercise of a power admitted to exist in some cases was for the consideration of Congress alone, and that this court always had disavowed the right to intrude its judgment upon questions of policy or morals. It is not for this court to pronounce when prohibition is necessary to regulation if it ever may be necessary,—to say that it is permissible as against strong drink, but not as against the product of ruined lives.

The act does not meddle with anything belonging to the states. They may regulate their internal affairs and their domestic commerce as they like. But when they seek to send their products across the state line they are no longer within their rights. If there were no Constitution and no Congress their power to cross the line would depend upon their neighbors. Under the Constitution such commerce belongs not to the states, but to Congress to regulate. It may carry out its views of public policy whatever indirect effect they may have upon the activities of the states. Instead of being encountered by a prohibitive tariff at her boundaries, the state encounters the public policy of the United States which it is for Congress to express. The public policy of the United States is shaped with a view to the benefit of the nation as a whole. If, as has been the case within the memory of men still living, a state should take a different view of the propriety of sustaining a lottery from that which generally prevails, I cannot believe that the fact would require a different decision from that reached in *Champion* v. *Ames.* Yet in that case it would be said with quite as much force as in this that Congress was attempting to intermeddle with the state's domestic affairs. The national welfare as understood by Congress may require a different attitude within its sphere from that of some self-seeking state. It seems to me entirely constitutional for Congress to enforce its understanding by all the means at its command.

Mr. Justice McKenna, Mr. Justice Brandeis, and Mr. Justice Clarke concur in this opinion.

BAILEY v. DREXEL FURNITURE CO.

259 U.S. 20, 66 L.Ed. 817 (1922)

In applying the brakes to the extension of congressional power under the "commerce clause," was the Court in effect saying "that the reserved powers of the states limit the expressly delegated powers of the nation . . . a reversal of the Tenth Amendment"? Perhaps to see whether this was so, perhaps because the pressure on Congress continued unabated, perhaps because the question of social justice was really important, or perhaps because of all of these, Congress turned to the use of its taxing power to deal with the problem of child labor. Accordingly the Revenue Act of 1919, provided in Title XII for a "Tax on Employment of Child Labor" (40 Stat. at Large 1138). This act provided for an "excise tax equivalent to 10 per centum of the entire net profits received or accrued for such year from the sale or disposition of the product" of any mine, quarry, mill, cannery, workshop, factory, or manufacturing establishment in which children under the age of fourteen were employed or permitted to work, or children between fourteen and sixteen were employed or permitted to work for more than eight hours a day or six days a week, during any part of the taxable year. If one did so employ children believing them to be of the prescribed age or having relied on a certificate granted by certain state authorities, or others, the tax would not apply. The Drexel Furniture Company was assessed $6,312.79 for employing a boy under the age of fourteen, paid the tax under protest, and sued to recover from J. W. Bailey, Collector of Internal Revenue. Judgment having been granted to the company, Commissioner Bailey appealed. This case then comes to the Supreme Court on a writ of error to the District Court for the Western District of North Carolina.

MR. CHIEF JUSTICE TAFT delivered the opinion of the court. . . .

The law is attacked on the ground that it is a regulation of the employment of child labor in the States—an exclusively state function under the Federal Constitution and within the reservations of the Tenth Amendment. It is defended on the ground that it is a mere excise tax levied by the Congress of the United States under its broad power of taxation conferred by Sec. 8, Article I, of the Federal Constitution. We must construe the law and interpret the intent and meaning of Congress from the language of the act. The words are to be given their ordinary meaning unless the context shows that they are differently used. Does this law impose a tax with only that incidental restraint and regulation which a tax must inevitably involve? Or does it regulate by the use of the so-called tax as a penalty? If a tax, it is clearly an excise. If it were an excise on a commodity or other thing of value we might not be permitted under previous decisions of this court to infer solely from its heavy burden that the act intends a prohibition instead of a tax. But this act is more. It provides a heavy exaction for a departure from a detailed and specified course of conduct in business. That course of business is that employers shall employ in mines and quarries, children of an age greater than sixteen years; in mills and factories, children of an age greater than fourteen years, and shall prevent children of less than sixteen years in mills and factories from working more than eight hours a day or six days in the week. If an employer departs from this prescribed course of business, he is to pay to the Government one-tenth of his entire net income in the business for a full year. The amount is not to be proportioned in any degree to the extent or frequency of the departures, but is to be paid by the employer in full measure whether he employs five hundred children for a year, or employs only one for a day. Moreover, if he does not know the child is within the named age limit, he is not to pay; that is to say, it is only where he knowingly departs from the prescribed course that payment is to be exacted. Scienter is associated with penalties not with taxes. The employer's factory is to be subject to inspection at any time not only by the taxing officers of the Treasury, the Department normally charged with the collection of taxes, but also by the Secretary of Labor and his subordinates whose normal function is the advancement and protection of the welfare of the workers. In the light of these features of the act, a court must be blind not to see that the so-called tax is imposed to stop the employment of children within the age limits prescribed. Its prohibitory and regulatory effect and purpose are palpable. All others can see and understand this. How can we properly shut our minds to it?

It is the high duty and function of this court in cases regularly brought to its bar to decline to recognize or enforce seeming laws of Congress, dealing with subjects not entrusted to Congress but left or committed by the supreme law of the land to the control of the States. We can not avoid the duty even though it require us to refuse to give effect to legislation designed to promote the highest good. The good sought in unconstitutional legislation is an insidious feature because it leads citizens and legislators of good purpose to promote it without thought of the serious breach it will make in the ark of our covenant, or the harm which will come from breaking down recognized standards. In the maintenance of local self-government, on the one hand, and the national power, on the other, our country has been able to endure and prosper for near a century and a half.

Out of a proper respect for the acts of a coordinate branch of the Government, this court has gone far to sustain taxing acts as such, even though there has been ground for suspecting from the weight of the tax it was intended to destroy its subject. But, in the act before us, the presumption of validity cannot prevail, because the proof of the contrary is found on the very face of its provisions. Grant the validity of this law, and all that Congress would need to do, hereafter, in seeking to take over to its control any one of the great number of subjects of public interest, jurisdiction of which the States have never parted with, and which are reserved to them by the Tenth Amendment, would be to enact a detailed measure of complete regulation of the subject and enforce it by a so-called tax upon departures from it. To give such magic to the word "tax" would be to break down all constitutional limitation of the powers of Congress and completely wipe out the sovereignty of the States.

The difference between a tax and a penalty is sometimes difficult to define and yet the consequences of the distinction in the required method of their collection often are important. Where the sovereign enacting the law has power to impose both tax and penalty the difference between revenue production and mere regulation may be immaterial, but not so when one sovereign can impose a tax only, and the power of regulation rests in another. Taxes are occasionally imposed in the discretion of the legislature on proper subjects with the primary motive of obtaining revenue from them and with the incidental motive of discouraging them by making their continuance onerous. They do not lose their character as taxes because of the incidental motive. But there comes a time in the extension of the penalizing features of the so-called tax when it loses its character as such and becomes a mere penalty with the characteristics of regulation and punishment. Such is the case in the law before us. Although Congress does not invalidate the contract of employment or expressly declare that the employment within the mentioned ages is illegal, it does exhibit its intent practically to achieve the latter result by adopting the criteria of wrongdoing and imposing its principal consequence on those who transgress its standard.

The case before us can not be distinguished from that of *Hammer* v. *Dagenhart*, 247 U.S. 251. Congress there enacted a law to prohibit transportation in interstate commerce of goods made at a factory in which there was employment of children within the same ages and for the same number of hours a day and days in a week as are penalized by the act in this case. This court held the law in that case to be void. It said:

> In our view the necessary effect of this act is, by means of a prohibition against the movement in interstate commerce of ordinary commercial commodities, to regulate the hours of labor of children in factories and mines within the States, a purely state authority.

In this case at the bar, Congress in the name of a tax which on the face of the act is a penalty seeks to do the same thing, and the effort must be equally futile.

The analogy of the Dagenhart Case is clear. The congressional power over interstate commerce is, within its proper scope, just as complete and unlimited as the congressional power to tax, and the legislative motive in its exercise is just as free from judicial suspicion and inquiry. Yet when Congress threatened to stop interstate commerce in ordinary and necessary commodities, unobjectionable as subjects of transportation, and to deny the same to the people of a State in order to coerce them into compliance with Congress's regulation of state concerns, the court said this was not in fact regulation of interstate commerce, but rather that of State concerns and was invalid. So here the so-called tax is a penalty to coerce people of a State to act as Congress wishes them to act in respect of a matter completely the business of the state government under the Federal Constitution. This case requires as did the Dagenhart Case the application of the principle announced by Chief Justice Marshall in *McCulloch* v. *Maryland*, 4 Wheat. 316, 423, in a much quoted passage:

Should Congress, in the execution of its powers, adopt measures which are prohibited by the Constitution; or should Congress, under the pretext of executing its powers, pass laws for the accomplishment of objects not intrusted to the government; it would become the painful duty of this tribunal, should a case requiring such a decision come before it, to say, that such an act was not the law of the land.

But it is pressed upon us that this court has gone so far in sustaining taxing measures the effect or tendency of which was to accomplish purposes not directly within congressional power that we are bound by authority to maintain this law. . . .

It should be noted, too, that the court, speaking of the extent of the taxing power, used these cautionary words [in *Veazie Bank* v. *Fenno*, 8 Wall. 533, 547]:

There are, indeed, certain virtual limitations, arising from the principles of the Constitution itself. It would undoubtedly be an abuse of the power if so exercised as to impair the separate existence and independent self-governments of the States, or if exercised for ends inconsistent with the limited grants of power in the Constitution.

But more than this, what was charged to be the object of the excessive tax was within the congressional authority, as appears from the second answer which the court gave to the objection. . . .

The third case is that of *Flint* v. *Stone Tracy Co.*, 220 U.S. 107. It involved the validity of an excise tax levied on the doing of business by all corporations, joint stock companies, associations organized for profit having a capital stock represented by shares, and insurance companies, and measured the excise by the net income of the corporations. There was not in that case the slightest doubt that the tax was a tax, and a tax for revenue. . . .

The fourth case is *United States* v. *Doremus*, 249 U.S. 86. That involved the validity of the Narcotic Drug Act, 38 Stat. 785, which imposed a special tax on the manufacture, importation and sale or gift of opium or coca leaves or their compounds or derivatives. . . . The validity of a special tax in the nature of an excise tax on manufacture, importation and sale of such drugs was, of course, unquestioned. The provisions for subjecting the sale and distribution of the drugs to official supervision and inspection were held to have a reasonable relation to the enforcement of the tax and were therefore held valid.

The court said that the act could not be declared invalid just because another motive than taxation, not shown on the face of the act, might have contributed to its passage. This case does not militate against the conclusion we have reached in respect of the law now before us. The court, there, made manifest its view that the provisions of the so-called taxing act must be naturally and reasonably adapted to the collection of the tax and not solely to the achievement of some other purpose plainly within state power.

For the reasons given, we must hold the Child Labor Tax Law invalid and the judgment of the District Court is

Affirmed.

MR. JUSTICE CLARKE dissents.

Part: IV: 1932—

NEW STATE ICE CO. v. LIEBMANN

285 U.S. 262, 76 L.Ed. 747 (1932)

In one of his great speeches ("The Law and the Court," Harvard Law School Association of New York, February 15, 1913), Oliver Wendell Holmes proclaimed it a "misfortune if a judge reads his conscious or unconscious sympathy with one side or the other prematurely into the law, and forgets that what seems to him to be first principles are believed by half his fellow men to be wrong. I think that we have suffered from this misfortune . . . and that this is another very important truth to be extracted from the popular discontent. When twenty years ago a vague terror went over the earth and the word socialism began to be heard, I thought and still think that fear was translated into doctrines that had no proper place in the Constitution. Judges are apt to be naive, simple-minded men, and they need something of Mephistopheles. We too need education in the obvious—to learn to transcend our own convictions and to leave room for much that we hold dear to be done away with short of revolution by the orderly change of law." If what had taken place up to 1930 was a "misfortune" it seemed, paradoxically, to be a good one, for through this very process America had transformed itself from a frontier to a highly urbanized industrial society where plenty was at hand to fill the needs of all. Yet there must have been something prophetic about Holmes: within less than two decades the Great Depression was upon us and in the midst of plenty there was starvation; in the great factories there was unemployment as never before; and in the financial centers there was bankruptcy and ruin. And even here Holmes's voice comforts us for he had already sounded the alternatives confronting us as clear as a bell: "revolution" or "orderly change."

The case below early set the stage not alone for the problem itself, but also for the basic philosophies inherent therein as well as the exponents thereof. While the facts are set forth clearly in the decision, the questions posed by Mr. Justice Brandeis' decision are in their own way intimately involved in all the cases presented in this section.

MR. JUSTICE SUTHERLAND delivered the opinion of the Court.

The New State Ice Company, engaged in the business of manufacturing, selling and distributing ice under a license or permit duly issued by the Corporation Commission of Oklahoma, brought this suit against Liebmann in the federal district court for the western district of Oklahoma to enjoin him from manufacturing, selling and distributing ice within Oklahoma City without first having obtained a like license or permit from the commission. The license or permit is required by an act of the Oklahoma legislature, c. 147, Session Laws, 1925. That act declares that the manufacture, sale and distri-

151

bution of ice is a public business; that no one shall be permitted to manufacture, sell or distribute ice within the state without first having secured a license for that purpose from the commission; that whoever shall engage in such business without obtaining the license shall be guilty of a misdemeanor, punishable by fine not to exceed $25, each day's violation constituting a separate offense, and that by general order of the commission, a fine not to exceed $500 may be imposed for each violation. . . .

Plainly, a regulation which has the effect of denying or unreasonably curtailing the common right to engage in a lawful private business, such as that under review, cannot be upheld consistent with the Fourteenth Amendment. Under that amendment, nothing is more clearly settled than that it is beyond the power of a state, "under the guise of protecting the public, arbitrarily [to] interfere with private business or prohibit lawful occupations or impose unreasonable and unnecessary restrictions upon them." *Burns Baking Co.* v. *Bryan,* 264 U.S. 504, 513, and authorities cited.

Stated succinctly, a private corporation here seeks to prevent a competitor from entering the business of making and selling ice. It claims to be endowed with state authority to achieve this exclusion. There is no question now before us of any regulation by the state to protect the consuming public either with respect to conditions of manufacture and distribution or to insure purity of produce or to prevent extortion. The control here asserted does not protect against monopoly, but tends to foster it. The aim is not to encourage competition, but to prevent it; not to regulate the business, but to preclude persons from engaging in it. There is no difference in principle between this case and the attempt of the dairyman under state authority to prevent another from keeping cows and selling milk on the ground that there are enough dairymen in the business; or to prevent a shoemaker from making or selling shoes because shoemakers already in that occupation can make and sell all the shoes that are needed. We are not able to see anything peculiar in the business here in question which distinguishes it from ordinary manufacture and production. It is said to be recent; but it is the character of the business and not the date when it began that is determinative. It is not the case of a natural monopoly, or of an enterprise in its nature dependent upon the grant of public privileges. The particular requirement before us was evidently not imposed to prevent a practical monopoly of the business, since its tendency is quite to the contrary. Nor is it a case of the protection of natural resources. There is nothing in the product that we can perceive on which to rest a distinction, in respect of this attempted control, from other products in common use which enter into free competition, subject, of course, to reasonable regulations prescribed for the protection of the public and applied with appropriate impartiality.

And it is plain that unreasonable or arbitrary interference or restrictions cannot be saved from the condemnation of that Amendment merely by calling them experimental. It is not necessary to challenge the authority of the states to indulge in experimental legislation; but it would be strange and unwarranted doctrine to hold that they may do so by enactments which transcend the limitations imposed upon them by the federal Constitution. The principle is imbedded in our constitutional system that there are certain essentials of liberty with which the state is not entitled to dispense in the interest of experiments. This principle has been applied by this court in many cases. *Dorchy* v. *Kansas,* 264 U.S. 286; *Wolff Packing Co.* v. *Industrial Court,* 262 U.S. 522, 267 U.S. 552; *Pierce* v. *Sisters,* 268 U.S. 510; *Nixon* v. *Herndon,* 273 U.S. 536; *Tumey* v. *Ohio,* 273 U.S. 510; *Manley* v. *Georgia,* 279 U.S. 1; *Washington* v. *Roberge,* 278 U.S. 116; *C., St. P., M. & O.* v. *Holmberg,* 282 U.S. 162; *Stromberg* v. *California,* 283 U.S. 359; *Near* v. *Minnesota,* 283 U.S. 697. In the case last cited the theory of experimentation in censorship was not permitted to interfere with the fundamental doctrine of the freedom of the press. The opportunity to apply one's labor and skill in an ordinary occupation with proper regard for all reasonable regulations is no less entitled to protection.

Dissent by MR. JUSTICE BRANDEIS.

. . . *Eighth.* The people of the United States are now confronted with an emergency more serious than war. Misery is wide-spread, in a time, not of scarcity, but of over-abundance. The long-continued depression has brought unprecedented unemployment, a catastrophic fall in commodity prices and a volume of economic losses which threatens our financial institutions. Some people believe that the existing conditions threaten even the stability of the capitalistic system. Economists are searching for the causes of this disorder and are reexamining the bases of our industrial structure. Business men are seeking possible remedies. Most of them realize that failure to distribute widely the profits of industry has been a prime cause of our present plight. But rightly or wrongly, many persons think that one of the major contributing causes has been unbridled competition. Increasingly, doubt is expressed whether it is economically wise, or morally right, that men should be permitted to add to the producing facilities of an industry which is already suffering from over-capacity. In justification of that doubt, men point to the excess-capacity of our productive facilities resulting from their vast expansion without corresponding increase in the consumptive capacity of the people. They assert that through improved methods of manufacture, made possible by advances in science and invention and vast accumulation of capital, our industries had become capable of producing from thirty to one hundred per cent more than was consumed even in days of vaunted prosperity; and that the present capacity will, for a long time, exceed the needs of business. All agree that irregularity in employment—the greatest of our evils—cannot be overcome unless production and consumption are more nearly balanced. Many insist there must be some form of economic control. There are plans for proration. There are many proposals for stabilization. And some thoughtful men of wide business experience insist that all projects for stabilization and proration must prove futile unless, in some way, the equivalent of the certificate of public convenience and necessity is made a prerequisite to embarking new capital in an industry in which the capacity already exceeds the production schedules.

Whether that view is sound nobody knows. The objections to the proposal are obvious and grave. The remedy might bring evils worse than the present disease. The obstacles to success seem insuperable. The economic and social sciences are largely uncharted seas. We have been none too successful in the modest essays in economic control already entered upon. The new proposal involves a vast extension of the area of control. Merely to acquire the knowledge essential as a basis for the exercise of this multitude of judgments would be a formidable task; and each of the thousands of these judgments would call for some measure of prophecy. Even more serious are the obstacles to success inherent in the demands which execution of the project would make upon human intelligence and upon the character of men. Man is weak and his judgment is at best fallible.

Yet the advances in the exact sciences and the achievements in invention remind us that the seemingly impossible sometimes happens. There are many men now living who were in the habit of using the age-old expression: "It is as impossible as flying." The discoveries in physical science, the triumphs in invention, attest the value of the process of trial and error. In large measure, these advances have been due to experimentation. In those fields experimentation has, for two centuries, been not only free but encouraged. Some people assert that our present plight is due, in part, to the limitations set by courts upon experimentation in the fields of social and economic science; and to the discouragement to which proposals for betterment there have been subjected otherwise. There must be power in the States and the Nation to remould, through experimentation, our economic practices and institutions to meet changing social and economic needs. I cannot believe that the framers of the Fourteenth Amendment, or the States which ratified it, intended to deprive us of the power to correct the evils of technological unemployment and excess productive capacity which have attended progress in the useful arts.

To stay experimentation in things social and economic is a grave responsibility. Denial of the right to experiment may be fraught with serious consequences to the Nation. It is one of the happy incidents of the federal system that a single courageous State may, if its citizens choose, serve as a laboratory; and try novel social and economic experiments without risk to the rest of the country. This Court has the power to prevent an experiment. We may strike down the statute which embodies it on the ground that, in our opinion, the measure is arbitrary, capricious or unreasonable. We have power to do this, because the due process clause has been held by the Court applicable to matters of substantive law as well as to matters of procedure. But in the exercise of this high power, we must be ever on our guard, lest we erect our prejudices into legal principles. If we would guide by the light of reason, we must let our minds be bold.

HOME BUILDING AND LOAN ASSOCIATION
v. BLAISDELL

290 U.S. 398, 78 L.Ed. 413 (1934)

The problem of relief of debtors has confronted governments from time immemorial. Shays' Rebellion, though almost two centuries old, is still a vital part of our own folklore. Though the Constitution in Article I, Section 10, specifically states that "No State shall . . . pass any Bill of Attainder, ex post facto Law, or Law impairing the Obligation of Contracts . . . ," it is also well-established doctrine that such power as a state does possess to modify contractual remedies is derived from its police power exercised for the public good. The case below involves the Minnesota Mortgage Moratorium Law passed in 1933. This law was designed to prevent foreclosure of mortgages during the emergency period produced by the economic depression. To prevent the wholesale loss of mortgaged properties by debtors unable to meet their obligations, the law provided that on application from the mortgagor, state courts could extend the period of redemption from foreclosure for an additional limited time and under conditions set by the courts. Blaisdell had mortgaged a lot to the Home Building and Loan Association which they sought to foreclose. Appealing to the courts, Blaisdell was granted an extended redemption period on condition that certain monthly payments be made. When the Supreme Court of Minnesota affirmed this arrangement, the Loan Company appealed to the Supreme Court. Its great value is the judicial attitude expressed in construing "in harmony with each other" the two great powers involved (contract clause versus state police power) when an economic emergency is upon us. And at the same time it expresses the belief that the wisdom of dealing with such an emergency is a matter of policy which does not concern the courts.

MR. CHIEF JUSTICE HUGHES delivered the opinion of the court. . . .

The state court upheld the statute as an emergency measure. Although conceding that the obligations of the mortgage contract were impaired, the court decided that what it thus described as an impairment was, notwithstanding, the contract clause of the Federal Constitution, within the police power of the state as that power was called into exercise by the public economic emergency which the Legislature had found to exist. Attention is thus directed to the preamble and first section of the statute which described the existing emergency in terms that were deemed to justify the temporary relief which the statute affords. The state court, declaring that it could not say that this legislative finding was without basis, supplemented that finding by its own statement of conditions of which it took judicial notice. The court said:

In addition to the weight to be given the determination of the Legislature that an economic emergency exists which demands relief, the court must take notice of other considerations. The members of the Legislature come from every community of the state and from all the walks of life. They are familiar with conditions generally in every calling, occupation, profession, and business in the state. Not only they, but the courts must be guided by what is common knowledge. It is common knowledge that in the last few years land values have shrunk enormously. Loans made a few years ago upon the basis of the then going values cannot possibly be replaced on the basis of present values. We all know that when this law was enacted the large financial companies which had made it their business to invest in mortgages, had ceased to do so. No bank would directly or indirectly loan on real estate mortgages. Life insurance companies, large investors on such mortgages, had even declared a moratorium as to the loan provisions of their policy contracts. The President had closed banks temporarily. The Congress, in addition to many extraordinary measures looking to the relief of the economic emergency, had passed an act to supply funds whereby mortgagors may be able within a reasonable time to refinance their mortgages or redeem from sales where the redemption has not expired. With this knowledge the court cannot well hold that the Legislature had no basis in fact for the conclusion that an economic emergency existed which called for the exercise of the police power to grant relief. . . .

We approach the questions thus presented upon the assumption made below, as required by the law of the state, that the mortgage contained a valid power of sale to be exercised in case of default; that this power was validly exercised; that under the law then applicable the period of redemption from the sale was one year, and that it has been extended by the judgment of the court over the opposition of the mortgagee-purchaser; and that, during the period thus extended, and unless the order for extension is modified, the mortgagee-purchaser will be unable to obtain possession, or to obtain or convey title in fee, as he would have been able to do had the statute not been enacted. The statute does not impair the integrity of the mortgage indebtedness. The obligation for interest remains. The statute does not affect the validity of the sale or the right of a mortgagee-purchaser to title in fee, or his right to obtain a deficiency judgment, if the mortgagor fails to redeem within the prescribed period. Aside from the extension of time, the other conditions of redemption are unaltered. While the mortgagor remains in possession, he must pay the rental value as that value has been determined, upon notice and hearing, by the court. The rental value so paid is devoted to the carrying of the property by the application of the required payments to taxes, insurance, and interest on the mortgage indebtedness. While the mortgagee-purchaser is debarred from actual possession, he has, so far as rental value is concerned, the equivalent of possession during the extended period.

In determining whether the provision for this temporary and conditional relief exceeds the power of the state by reason of the clause in the Federal Constitution prohibiting impairment of the obligations of contracts, we must consider the relation of emergency to constitutional power, the historical setting of the contract clause, the development of the jurisprudence of this Court in the construction of that clause, and the principles of construction which we may consider to be established.

Emergency does not create power. Emergency does not increase granted power or remove or diminish the restrictions imposed upon power granted or reserved. The Constitution was adopted in a period of grave emergency. Its grants of power to the Federal Government and its limitations of the power of the states were determined in the light of emergency, and they are not altered by emergency. What power was thus granted and what limitations were thus imposed are questions which have always been, and always will be, the subject of close examination under our constitutional system.

While emergency does not create power, emergency may furnish the occasion for the exercise of power. "Although an emergency may not call into life a power which has never lived, nevertheless emergency may afford a reason for the exertion of a living power already enjoyed." *Wilson* v. *New*, 243 U.S. 332, 348. The constitutional question presented in the light of an emergency is whether the power possessed embraces the particular exercise of it in response to particular conditions. Thus, the war power of the federal government is not created by the emergency of war, but it is a power given to meet that emergency. It is a power to wage war successfully, and thus it permits the harnessing of the entire energies of the people in a supreme co-operative effort to preserve the nation. But even the war power does not remove constitutional limitations safeguarding essential liberties. When the provisions of the Constitution, in grant or restriction, are specific, so particularized as not to admit of construction, no question is presented. Thus, emergency would not permit a state to have more than two Senators in the Congress, or permit the election of a President by a general popular vote without regard to the number of electors to which the states are respectively entitled, or permit the states to "coin money" or to "make anything but gold and silver coin a tender in payment of debts." But, where constitutional grants and limitations of power are set forth in general clauses, which afford a broad outline, the process of construction is essential to fill in the details. That is true of the contract clause. . . .

In the construction of the contract clause, the debates in the Constitutional Convention are of little aid. But the reasons which led to the adoption of that clause, and of the other prohibitions of Section 10 of Article 1, are not left in doubt, and have frequently been described with eloquent emphasis. The widespread distress following the revolutionary period, and the plight of debtors had called forth in the states an ignoble array of legislative schemes for the defeat of creditors and the invasion of contractual obligations. Legislative interferences had been so numerous and extreme that the confidence essential to prosperous trade had been undermined and the utter destruction of credit was threatened. "The sober people of America" were convinced that some "thorough reform" was needed which would "inspire a general prudence and industry, and give a regular course to the business of society." *The Federalist*, No. 44. . . . But full recognition of the occasion and general purpose of the clause does not suffice to fix its precise scope. . . . To ascertain the scope of the constitutional prohibition, we examine the course of judicial decisions in its application. These put it beyond question that the prohibition is not an absolute one and is not to be read with literal exactness like a mathematical formula. . . .

The inescapable problems of construction have been: What is a contract? What are the obligations of contracts? What constitutes impairment of these obligations? What residuum of power is there still in the states, in relation to the operation of contracts, to protect the vital interests of the community? Questions of this character, "of no small nicety and intricacy, have vexed the legislative halls, as well as the judicial tribunals, with an uncounted variety and frequency of litigation and speculation." Story on the Constitution, Sec. 1375. . . .

It is manifest . . . that there has been a growing appreciation of public needs and of the necessity of finding ground for a rational compromise between individual rights and public welfare. . . . Pressure of a constantly increasing density of population, the interrelation of the activities of our people and the complexity of our economic interests, have inevitably led to an increased use of the organization of society in order to protect the very bases of individual opportunity. Where, in earlier days, it was thought that only the concerns of individuals or of classes were involved, and that those of the state itself were touched only remotely, it has later been found that the fundamental interests of the state are directly affected; and that the question is no longer merely that of one party to a contract as against another, but of the use of reasonable means to safeguard the economic structure upon which the good of all depends.

It is no answer to say that this public need was not apprehended a century ago, or to insist that what the provision of the Constitution meant to the vision of that day it must mean to the vision of our time. If by the statement that what the Constitution meant at the time of its adoption it means to-day, it is intended to say that the great clauses of the Constitution must be confined to the interpretation which the framers, with the conditions and outlook of their time, would have placed upon them, the statement carries its own refutation. It was to guard against such a narrow conception that Chief Justice Marshall uttered the memorable warning: "We must never forget, that it is a *constitution* we are expounding" (*McCulloch* v. *Maryland* . . .); "a constitution intended to endure for ages to come, and, consequently, to be adapted to the various *crises* of human affairs." . . . When we are dealing with the words of the Constitution, said this Court in *Missouri* v. *Holland* . . . "we must realize that they have called into life a being the development of which could not have been foreseen completely by the most gifted of its begetters. . . . The case before us must be considered in the light of our whole experience and not merely in that of what was said a hundred years ago."

Nor is it helpful to attempt to draw a fine distinction between the intended meaning of the words of the Constitution and their intended application. When we consider the contract clause and the decisions which have expounded it in harmony with the essential reserved power of the states to protect the security of their peoples, we find no warrant for the conclusion that the clause has been warped by these decisions from its proper significance or that the founders of our government would have interpreted the clause differently had they had occasion to assume that responsibility in the conditions of the later day. The vast body of law which has been developed was unknown to the fathers, but it is believed to have preserved the essential content and the spirit of the Constitution. With a growing recognition of public needs and the relation of individual right to public security, the court has sought to prevent the perversion of the clause through its use as an instrument to throttle the capacity of the states to protect their fundamental interests. This development is a growth from the seeds which the fathers planted. It is a development forecast by the prophetic words of Justice Johnson in *Ogden* v. *Saunders*. And the germs of the later decisions are found in the early cases of the Charles River Bridge and the West River Bridge, which upheld the public right against strong insistence upon the contract clause. The principle of this development is, as we have seen, that the reservation of the reasonable exercise of the protective power of the state is read into all contracts, and there is no greater reason for refusing to apply this principle to Minnesota mortgages than to New York leases.

Applying the criteria established by our decisions, we conclude:

1. An emergency existed in Minnesota which furnished a proper occasion for the exercise of the reserved power of the state to protect the vital interests of the community. . . .

2. The legislation was addressed to a legitimate end; that is, the

legislation was not for the mere advantage of particular individuals but for the protection of a basic interest of society.

3. In view of the nature of the contracts in question—mortgages of unquestionable validity—the relief afforded and justified by the emergency, in order not to contravene the constitutional provision, could only be of a character appropriate to that emergency, and could be granted only upon reasonable conditions.

4. The conditions upon which the period of redemption is extended do not appear to be unreasonable. . . .

5. The legislation is temporary in operation. It is limited to the exigency which called it forth. . . .

We are of the opinion that the Minnesota statute as here applied does not violate the contract clause of the Federal Constitution. Whether the legislation is wise or unwise as a matter of policy is a question with which we are not concerned. . . .

The judgment of the Supreme Court of Minnesota is affirmed.

Judgment affirmed.

MR. JUSTICE SUTHERLAND, dissenting.

Few questions of greater moment than that just decided have been submitted for judicial inquiry during this generation. He simply closes his eyes to the necessary implications of the decision who fails to see in it the potentiality of future gradual but ever-advancing encroachments upon the sanctity of private and public contracts. The effect of the Minnesota legislation, though serious enough in itself, is of trivial significance compared with the far more serious and dangerous inroads upon the limitations of the Constitution which are almost certain to ensue as a consequence naturally following any step beyond the boundaries fixed by that instrument. . . .

A provision of the Constitution, it is hardly necessary to say, does not admit of two distinctly opposite interpretations. It does not mean one thing at one time and an entirely different thing at another time. If the contract impairment clause, when framed and adopted, meant that the terms of a contract for the payment of money could not be altered *in invitum* by a state statute enacted for the relief of hardly pressed debtors to the end and with the effect of postponing payment of enforcement during and because of an economic or financial emergency, it is but to state the obvious to say that it means the same now. This view, at once so rational in its application to the written word, and so necessary to the stability of constitutional principles, though from time to time challenged, has never, unless recently, been put within the realm of doubt by the decisions of this court. . . .

The provisions of the Federal Constitution, undoubtedly, are pliable in the sense that in appropriate cases they have the capacity of bringing within their grasp every new condition which falls within their meaning. But, their *meaning* is changeless; it is only their *application*

which is extensible. See *South Carolina* v. *United States,* 199 U.S.
437. Constitutional grants of power and restrictions upon the exercise of power are not flexible as the doctrines of the common law are
flexible. These doctrines, upon the principles of the common law
itself, modify or abrogate themselves whenever they are or whenever
they become plainly unsuited to different or changed conditions. . . .

The whole aim of construction, as applied to a provision of the
Constitution, is to discover the meaning, to ascertain and give effect
to the intent, of its framers and the people who adopted it. . . . And
if the meaning be at all doubtful, the doubt should be resolved,
wherever reasonably possible to do so, in a way to forward the evident
purpose with which the provision was adopted. . . .

An application of these principles to the question under review
removes any doubt, if otherwise there would be any, that the contract
impairment clause denies to the several states the power to mitigate
hard consequences resulting to debtors from financial or economic
exigencies by an impairment of the obligation of contracts of indebtedness. A candid consideration of the history and circumstances which
led to and accompanied the framing and adoption of this clause will
demonstrate conclusively that it was framed and adopted with the
specific and studied purpose of preventing legislation designed to relieve debtors *especially* in time of financial distress. Indeed, it is not
probable that any other purpose was definitely in the minds of those
who composed the framers' convention or the ratifying state conventions which followed, although the restriction has been given a wider
application upon principles clearly stated by Chief Justice Marshall in
the Dartmouth College Case. . . .

The present exigency is nothing new. From the beginning of our
existence as a nation, periods of depression, of industrial failure, of
financial distress, of unpaid and unpayable indebtedness, have alter-
nated with years of plenty. The vital lesson that expenditure beyond
income begets poverty, that public or private extravagance, financed
by promises to pay, either must end in complete or partial repudiation
or the promises be fulfilled by self-denial and painful effort, though
constantly taught by bitter experience, seems never to be learned; and
the attempt by legislative devices to shift the misfortune of the debtor
to the shoulders of the creditor without coming into conflict with
the contract impairment clause has been persistent and oft-
repeated.

It is quite true that an emergency may supply the occasion for the
exercise of power, depending upon the nature of the power and the
intent of the Constitution with respect thereto. The emergency of war
furnishes an occasion for the exercise of certain of the war powers.
This the Constitution contemplates, since they cannot be exercised
upon any other occasion. The existence of another kind of emergency
authorizes the United States to protect each of the states of the
Union against domestic violence. Const. Art. IV, clause 4. But we

are here dealing not with a power granted by the Federal Constitution, but with the state police power, which exists in its own right. Hence the question is not whether an emergency furnishes the occasion for the exercise of that state power, but whether an emergency furnishes an occasion for the relaxation of the restrictions upon the power imposed by the contract impairment clause; and the difficulty is that the contract impairment clause forbids state action under any circumstances, if it have the effect of impairing the obligation of contracts. That clause restricts every state power in the particular specified, no matter what may be the occasion. It does not contemplate that an emergency shall furnish an occasion for softening the restriction or making it any the less a restriction upon state action in that contingency than it is under strictly normal conditions.

The Minnesota statute either impairs the obligation of contracts or it does not. If it does not, the occasion to which it relates becomes immaterial, since then the passage of the statute is the exercise of a normal, unrestricted, state power and requires no special occasion to render it effective. If it does, the emergency no more furnishes a proper occasion for its exercise than if the emergency were nonexistent. And so, while, in form, the suggested distinction seems to put us forward in a straight line, in reality it simply carries us back in a circle, like bewildered travelers lost in a wood, to the point where we parted company with the view of the state court. . . .

I quite agree with the opinion of the court that whether the legislation under review is wise or unwise is a matter with which we have nothing to do. Whether it is likely to work well or work ill presents a question entirely irrelevant to the issue. The only legitimate inquiry we can make is whether it is constitutional. If it is not, its virtues, if it have any, cannot save it; if it is, its faults cannot be invoked to accomplish its destruction. If the provisions of the Constitution be not upheld when they pinch as well as when they comfort, they may as well be abandoned. Being unable to reach any other conclusion than that the Minnesota statute infringes the constitutional restriction under review, I have no choice but to say so.

I am authorized to say that MR. JUSTICE VAN DEVANTER, MR. JUSTICE McREYNOLDS and MR. JUSTICE BUTLER concur in this opinion.

NEBBIA v. NEW YORK

291 U.S. 502, 78 L.Ed. 940 (1934)

If it is true, as someone put it, that the American business economy had "evolved under the stress of an environment which demanded excessive specialization in money-making . . . [and that] to this

*money-making attribute all else had been sacrificed," it can readily be
seen why price-fixing legislation was watched over with such maternal
interest. The attitude of the Court in dealing with maximum hours
as compared with its attitude in dealing with minimum wages can,
to a degree at least, be accounted for on this ground. The attempt of
a state to regulate the resale of theatre tickets in 1927 (Tyson Bros.
v. Banton, 273 U.S. 418); to regulate fees charged by employment
agencies in 1928 (Ribnik v. McBride, 277 U.S. 350); and other such
regulations were all declared null and void as interfering essentially
with businesses that were private. Only public utilities, telephones,
busses, railroads, electricity, etc., which were associated with such historical services as innkeepers and, as we have seen, such businesses
that were deemed to be affected with a public interest (grain
elevators, stockyards, tobacco warehouses) were subjected to price
control with full judicial approbation. As Mr. Justice Roberts says
in the case below: "The thought seems to have persisted that there
is something peculiarly sacrosanct about the price one may charge
for what he makes or sells . . . [and that] the state is incapable
of directly controlling the price itself." And he was right, for such
seemed to be the attitude of the Court despite the view of Mr.
Brandeis that any business may become a matter of public concern
and "whether it is, or is not, depends upon the conditions existing
in the Community affected," and if "it is a matter of public concern, it may be regulated, whatever the business." The instant case,
the facts of which are clearly set forth in the opinion, becomes a
landmark by permitting a state milk control board to have power
to fix minimum and maximum retail prices.*

Mr. Justice Roberts delivered the opinion of the Court.

The Legislature of New York established by Chapter 158 of the
Laws of 1933, a Milk Control Board with power, among other
things, to "fix minimum and maximum . . . retail prices to be
charged by . . . stores to consumers for consumption off the premises
where sold." The Board fixed nine cents as the price to be charged
by a store for a quart of milk. Nebbia, the proprietor of a grocery
store in Rochester, sold two quarts and a five cent loaf of bread for
eighteen cents; and was convicted for violating the Board's order.
At his trial he asserted the statute and order contravene the equal
protection clause and due process clause of the Fourteenth Amendment, and renewed the contention in successive appeals to the
county court and the Court of Appeals. Both overruled his claim
and affirmed the conviction.

The question for decision is whether the Federal Constitution
prohibits a state from so fixing the selling price of milk. We first
inquire as to the occasion for the legislation and its history.

During 1932 the prices received by farmers for milk were much
below the cost of production. The decline in prices during 1931

and 1932 was much greater than that of prices generally. The situation of the families of dairy producers had become desperate and called for state aid similar to that afforded the unemployed, if conditions should not improve.

On March 10, 1932, the senate and assembly resolved "That a joint legislative committee is hereby created . . . to investigate the causes of the decline of the price of milk to producers and the resultant effect of the low prices upon the dairy industry and the future supply of milk to the cities of the State; to investigate the cost of distribution of milk and its relation to prices paid to milk producers, to the end that the consumer may be assured of an adequate supply of milk at a reasonable price, both to producer and consumer." The committee organized May 6, 1932, and its activities lasted nearly a year. . . . As a result . . . a report covering 473 closely printed pages, embracing the conclusions and recommendations of the committee, was presented to the legislature April 10, 1933. . . . The conscientious effort and thoroughness exhibited by the report lend weight to the committee's conclusions.

In part those conclusions are:

Milk is an essential item of diet. It cannot long be stored. It is an excellent medium for growth of bacteria. These facts necessitate safeguards in its production and handling for human consumption which greatly increase the cost of the business. Failure of producers to receive a reasonable return for their labor and investment over an extended period threatens a relaxation of vigilance against contamination.

The production and distribution of milk is a paramount industry of the state, and largely affects the health and prosperity of its people. Dairying yields fully one-half of the total income from all farm products. Dairy farm investment amounts to approximately $1,000,000,000. Curtailment or destruction of the dairy industry would cause a serious economic loss to the people of the state. . . .

The fluid milk industry is affected by factors of instability peculiar to itself which call for special methods of control. Under the best practicable adjustment of supply to demand the industry must carry a surplus of about 20 per cent, because milk, an essential food, must be available as demanded by consumers every day in the year, and demand and supply vary from day to day and according to the season; but milk is perishable and cannot be stored. Close adjustment of supply to demand is hindered by several factors difficult to control. Thus surplus milk presents a serious problem, as the prices which can be realized for it for other uses are much less than those obtainable for milk sold for consumption in fluid form or as cream. A satisfactory stabilization of prices for fluid milk requires that the burden of surplus milk be shared equally by all producers and all distributors in the milk-shed. So long as the surplus burden is unequally distributed the pressure to market surplus milk in fluid form will be a serious disturbing factor. The fact that the larger distributors find it necessary to carry large quantities of surplus milk, while the smaller distributors do not, leads to price-cutting and other forms of destructive competition. Smaller distributors, who take no responsibility for the surplus, by purchasing their milk at the blended prices (i.e., an average between the price paid the producer for milk for sale as fluid milk, and the lower surplus milk price paid by the larger organizations) can undersell the larger distributors. Indulgence in this price-cutting often compels the larger dealer to cut the price to his own and the producer's detriment.

Various remedies were suggested, amongst them united action by producers, the fixing of minimum prices for milk and cream by state authority, and the imposition of certain graded taxes on milk dealers proportioned so as to equalize the cost of milk and cream to all dealers and so remove the cause of price-cutting.

The legislature adopted Chapter 158 as a method of correcting the evils, which the report of the committee showed could not be expected to right themselves through the ordinary play of the forces of supply and demand, owing to the peculiar and uncontrollable factors affecting the industry. . . .

Section 312 (e) on which the prosecution in the present case is founded, provides: "After the board shall have fixed prices to be charged or paid for milk in any form . . . it shall be unlawful for a milk dealer to sell or buy or offer to sell or buy milk at any price less or more than such price . . . , and no method or device shall be lawful whereby milk is bought or sold . . . at a price less or more than such price . . . whether by any discount, or rebate, or free service, or advertising allowance, or a combined price for such milk together with another commodity or commodities, or service or services, which is less or more than the aggregate of the prices for the milk and the price or prices for such other commodity or commodities, or service or services, when sold or offered for sale separately or otherwise. . . ."

First. The appellant urges that the order of the Milk Control Board denies him the equal protection of the laws. [The Court found no merit in appellant's contention.]

Second. The more serious question is whether, in the light of the conditions disclosed, the enforcement of Sect. 312 (e) denied the appellant the due process secured to him by the Fourteenth Amendment.

Save the conduct of railroads, no business has been so thoroughly regimented and regulated by the State of New York as the milk industry. Legislation controlling it in the interest of the public health was adopted in 1862 and subsequent statutes have been carried into the general codification known as the Agriculture and Markets Law. A perusal of these statutes discloses that the milk industry has been progressively subjected to a larger measure of control. The producer or dairy farmer is in certain circumstances liable to have his herd quarantined against bovine tuberculosis; is limited in the importation of dairy cattle to those free from Bang's disease; is subject to rules governing the care and feeding of his cows and the care of the milk produced, the condition and surroundings of his barns and buildings used for production of milk, the utensils used, and the persons employed in milking. . . . In addition there is a large volume of legislation intended to promote cleanliness and fair trade practices, affecting all who are engaged in the industry. The challenged amendment of 1933 carried regulation much farther than the prior enactments. Appellant insists that it went beyond the limits fixed by the Constitution.

Under our form of government the use of property and the making of contracts are normally matters of private and not of public concern. The general rule is that both shall be free of governmental interference. But neither property rights nor contract rights are absolute; for government cannot exist if the citizen may at will use his property to the detriment of his fellows, or exercise his freedom of contract to work them harm. Equally fundamental with the private right is that of the public to regulate it in the common interest. . . . These correlative rights, that of the citizen to exercise exclusive dominion over property and freely to contract about his affairs, and that of the state to regulate the use of property and the conduct of business, are always in collision. No exercise of the private right can be imagined which will not in some respect, however slight, affect the public; no exercise of the legislative prerogative to regulate the conduct of the citizen which will not to some extent abridge his liberty or affect his property. But subject only to constitutional restraint the private right must yield to the public need.

The Fifth Amendment, in the field of federal activity, and the Fourteenth, as respects State action, do not prohibit governmental regulation for the public welfare. They merely condition the exertion of the admitted power, by securing that the end shall be accomplished by methods consistent with due process. And the guaranty of due process, as has often been held, demands only that the law shall not be unreasonable, arbitrary or capricious, and that the means selected shall have a real and substantial relation to the object sought to be attained. It results that a regulation valid for one sort of business, or in given circumstances, may be invalid for another sort, or for the same business under other circumstances, because the reasonableness of each regulation depends upon the relevant facts. . . .

The Constitution does not guarantee the unrestricted privilege to engage in a business or to conduct it as one pleases. Certain kinds of business may be prohibited; and the right to conduct a business, or to pursue a calling, may be conditioned. Regulation of a business to prevent waste of the state's resources may be justified. And statutes prescribing the terms upon which those conducting certain businesses may contract, or imposing terms if they do enter into agreements, are within the state's competency.

Legislation concerning sales of goods, and incidentally affecting prices, has repeatedly been held valid. In this class fall laws forbidding unfair competition by the charging of lower prices in one locality than those exacted in another, by giving trade inducements to purchasers, and by other forms of price discrimination. The public policy with respect to free competition has engendered state and federal statutes prohibiting monopolies, which have been upheld. On the other hand, where the policy of the state dictated that a monopoly should be granted, statutes having that effect have been held inoffensive to the constitutional guaranties. . . .

The milk industry in New York has been the subject of longstanding and drastic regulation in the public interest. The legislative investigation of 1932 was persuasive of the fact that for this and other reasons unrestricted competition aggravated existing evils and the normal law of supply and demand was insufficient to correct maladjustments detrimental to the community. . . . In the order of which complaint is made the Milk Control Board fixed a price of ten cents per quart for sales by a distributor to a consumer, and nine cents by a store to a consumer, thus recognizing the lower costs of the store, and endeavoring to establish a differential which would be just to both. In the light of the facts the order appears not to be unreasonable or arbitrary, or without relation to the purpose to prevent ruthless competition from destroying the wholesale price structure on which the farmer depends for his livelihood, and the community for an assured supply of milk.

But we are told that because the law essays to control prices it denies due process. Notwithstanding the admitted power to correct existing economic ills by appropriate regulation of business, even though an indirect result may be a restriction of the freedom of contract or a modification of charges for services or the price of commodities, the appellant urges that direct fixation of prices is a type of regulation absolutely forbidden. His position is that the Fourteenth Amendment requires us to hold the challenged statute void for this reason alone. The argument runs that the public control of rates or prices is per se unreasonable and unconstitutional, save as applied to businesses affected with a public interest; that a business so affected is one in which property is devoted to an enterprise of a sort which the public itself might appropriately undertake, or one whose owner relies on a public grant or franchise for the right to conduct the business, or in which he is bound to serve all who apply; in short, such as is commonly called a public utility; or a business in its nature a monopoly. The milk industry, it is said, possesses none of these characteristics, and, therefore, not being affected with a public interest, its charges may not be controlled by the state. Upon the soundness of this contention the appellant's case against the statute depends.

We may as well say at once that the dairy industry is not, in the accepted sense of the phrase, a public utility. We think the appellant is also right in asserting that there is in this case no suggestion of any monopoly or monopolistic practice. It goes without saying that those engaged in the business are in no way dependent upon public grants or franchises for the privilege of conducting their activities. But if, as must be conceded, the industry is subject to regulation in the public interest, what constitutional principle bars the state from correcting existing maladjustments by legislation touching prices? We think there is no such principle. The due process clause makes no mention of sales or of prices any more than it speaks of business or contracts or buildings or other incidents of property. The thought seems nevertheless to have persisted that there is something peculiarly sacrosanct about the price one may charge for what he makes or sells, and that, however able to regulate other elements of manufacture or trade, with incidental effect upon price, the state is incapable of directly controlling the price itself. This view was negatived many years ago. *Munn* v. *Illinois*, 94 U.S. 113. The appellant's claim is, however, that this court, in there sustaining a statutory prescription of charges for storage by the proprietors of a grain elevator, limited permissible legislation of that type to businesses affected with a public interest, and he says no business is so affected except it have one or more of the characteristics he enumerates. But this is a misconception. Munn and Scott held no franchise from the state. They owned the property upon which their elevator was situated and conducted their business as private citizens. No doubt they felt at liberty to deal with whom they pleased and on such terms as they might deem just to themselves. Their enterprise could not fairly be called a monopoly, although it was referred to in the decision as a "virtual monopoly." This meant only that their elevator was strategically situated and that a large portion of the public found it highly inconvenient to deal with others. This court concluded the circumstances justified the legislation as an exercise of the governmental right to control the business in the public interest; that is, as an exercise of the police power. It is true that the court cited a statement from Lord Hale's *De Portibus Maris*, to the effect that when private property is "affected with a public interest, it ceases to be juris privati only"; but the court proceeded at once to define what it understood by the expression, saying: "Property does become clothed with a public interest when used in a manner to make it of public consequence, and affect the community at large" (p. 126). Thus understood, "affected with a public interest" is the equivalent of "subject to the exercise of the police power"; and it is plain that nothing more was intended by the expression. The court had been at pains to define that power ending its discussion in these words:

From this it is apparent that, down to the time of the adoption of the Fourteenth Amendment, it was not supposed that statutes regulating the use, or even the price of the use, of private property necessarily deprived an owner of his property without due process of law. Under some circumstances they may, but not under all. The amendment does not change the law in this particular: it simply prevents the States from doing that which will operate as such a deprivation.

In the further discussion of the principle it is said that when one devotes his property to a use, "in which the public has an interest," he in effect "grants to the public an interest in that use" and must submit to be controlled for the common good. The conclusion is that if Munn and Scott wished to avoid having their business regulated they should not have embarked their property in an industry which is subject to regulation in the public interest.

The true interpretation of the court's language is claimed to be that only property voluntarily devoted to a known public use is subject to regulation as to rates. But obviously Munn and Scott had not voluntarily dedicated their business to a public use. They intended only to conduct it as private citizens, and they insisted that they had done nothing which gave the public an interest in their transactions or conferred any right of regulation. The statement that one has dedicated his property to a public use is, therefore, merely another way of saying that if one embarks in a business which public interest demands shall be regulated, he must know regulation will ensue.

In the same volume the court sustained regulation of railroad rates. After referring to the fact that railroads are carriers for hire, are incorporated as such, and given extaordinary powers in order that they may better serve the public, it was said that they are engaged in employment "affecting the public interest," and therefore, under the doctrine of the Munn case, subject to legislative control as to rates. And in another of the group of railroad cases then heard it was said that the property of railroads is "clothed with a public interest" which permits legislative limitation of the charges for its use. Plainly the activities of railroads, their charges and practices, so nearly touch the vital economic interests of society that the police power may be invoked to regulate their charges, and no additional formula of affection or clothing with a public interest is needed to justify the regulation. And this is evidently true of all business units supplying transportation, light, heat, power and water to communities, irrespective of how they obtain their powers. . . .

It is clear that there is no closed class or category of businesses affected with a public interest, and the function of courts in the application of the Fifth and Fourteenth Amendments is to determine in each case whether circumstances vindicate the challenged regulation as a reasonable exertion of governmental authority or condemn it as arbitrary or discriminatory. *Chas. Wolff Packing Co.* v. *Court of Industrial Relations*, 262 U.S. 522, 535. The phrase "affected with a public interest" can, in the nature of things, mean no more than that an industry, for adequate reason, is subject to control for the public good. In several of the decisions of this court wherein the expressions "affected with a public interest," and "clothed with a public use," have been brought forward as the criteria of the validity of price control, it has been admitted that they are not susceptible of definition and form an unsatisfactory test of the constitutionality of legislation directed at business practices or prices. These decisions must rest, finally, upon the basis that the requirements of due process were not met because the laws were found arbitrary in their operation and effect. But there can be no doubt that upon proper occasion and by appropriate measures the state may regulate a business in any of its aspects, including the prices to be charged for the products or commodities it sells.

So far as the requirement of due process is concerned, and in the absence of other constitutional restriction, a state is free to adopt whatever economic policy may reasonably be deemed to promote public welfare, and to enforce that policy by legislation adapted to its purpose. The courts are without authority either to declare such policy, or, when it is declared by the legislative arm, to override it. If the laws passed are seen to have a reasonable relation to a proper legislative purpose, and are neither arbitrary nor discriminatory, the requirements of due process are satisfied, and judicial determination to that effect renders a court *functus officio.* "Whether the free operation of the normal laws of competition is a wise and wholesome rule for trade and commerce is an economic question which this court need not consider or determine." *Northern Securities Co.* v. *United States*, 193 U.S. 197, 337, 338. And it is equally clear that if the legislative policy be to curb unrestrained and harmful competition by measures which are not arbitrary or discriminatory it does not lie with the courts to determine that the rule is unwise. With the wisdom of the policy adopted, with the adequacy or practicability of the law enacted to forward it, the courts are both incompetent and unauthorized to deal. The course of decision in this court exhibits a firm adherence to these principles. . . . If the law-making body within its sphere of government concludes that the conditions or practices in an industry make unrestricted competition an inadequate safeguard of the consumer's interests, produce waste harmful to the public, threaten ultimately to cut off the supply of a commodity needed by the public, or portend the destruction of the industry itself, appropriate statutes passed in an honest effort to correct the threatened consequences may not be set aside because the regulation adopted fixes prices reasonably deemed by the legislature to be fair to those engaged in the industry and to the consuming public. And this is especially so where, as here, the economic maladjustment is one of price, which threatens harm to the producer at one end of the series and the consumer at the other. The Constitution does not secure to any one liberty to conduct his business in such fashion as to inflict injury upon the public at large, or upon any substantial group of the people. Price control, like any other form of regulation, is unconstitutional only if arbitrary, discriminatory, or demonstrably irrelevant to the policy the legislature is free to adopt, and hence an unnecessary and unwarranted interference with individual liberty.

Tested by these considerations we find no basis in the due process clause of the Fourteenth Amendment for condemning the provisions of the Agriculture and Markets Law here drawn into question.

The judgment is affirmed.

Separate opinion of Mr. Justice McReynolds. . . .

Our question is whether the Control Act, as applied to appellant through the order of the Board . . . deprives him of rights guaranteed by the Fourteenth Amendment. He was convicted of a crime for selling his own property—wholesome milk—in the ordinary course of business at a price satisfactory to himself and the customer. We are not immediately concerned with any other provision of the act or later orders. Prices at which the producer may sell were not prescribed—he may accept any price—nor was production in any way limited. "To stimulate the production of a vital food product" was not the purpose of the statute. There was an oversupply of an excellent article. The affirmation is "that milk has been selling too cheaply . . . and has thus created a temporary emergency; this emergency is remedied by making the sale of milk at a low price a crime." . . .

The theory that legislative action which ordinarily would be ineffective because of conflict with the Constitution may become potent if intended to meet peculiar conditions and properly limited, was lucidly discussed and its weakness disclosed by the dissenting opinion in *Home Bldg. and Loan Asso. v. Blaisdell*, 290 U.S. 398. . . .

. . . Those great and good men [who drafted the Constitution] foresaw that troublous times would arise, when rulers and people would become restive under restraint, and seek by sharp and decisive measures to accomplish ends deemed just and proper; and that the principles of constitutional liberty would be in peril, unless established by irrepealable law. . . . The Constitution of the United States is a law for rulers and people, equally in war and in peace, and covers with the shield of its protection all classes of men, at all times, and under all circumstances. No doctrine, involving more pernicious consequences, was ever invented by the wit of man than that any of its provisions can be suspended during any of the great exigencies of government. Such a doctrine leads directly to anarchy or despotism. [Ex parte Milligan, 4 Wall. 2, 120.]

The Fourteenth Amendment wholly disempowered the several States to "deprive any person of life, liberty or property, without due process of law." The assurance of each of these things is the same. If now liberty or property may be struck down because of difficult circumstances, we must expect that hereafter every right must yield to the voice of an impatient majority when stirred by distressful exigency. . . . Constitutional guaranties are not to be "thrust to and fro and carried about with every wind of doctrine." Rights shielded yesterday should remain indefeasible today and tomorrow. Certain fundamentals have been set beyond experimentation; the Constitution has released them from control by the State. Again and again this Court has so declared. . . .

If she relied upon the existence of emergency, the burden was upon the State to establish it by competent evidence. None was presented at the trial. If necessary for appellant to show absence of the asserted conditions, the little grocer was helpless from the beginning—the practical difficulties were too great for the average man.

What circumstances give force to an "emergency" statute? In how much of the State must they obtain? Everywhere, or will a single county suffice? How many farmers must have been impoverished or threatened violence to create a crisis of sufficient gravity? If three days after this act became effective another "very grievous murrain" had descended and half of the cattle had died, would the emergency then have ended, also the prescribed rates? If prices for agricultural products become high can consumers claim a crisis exists and demand that the Legislature fix less ones? Or are producers alone to be considered, consumers neglected? To these questions we have no answers. When emergency gives potency, its subsidence must disempower; but no test for its presence or absence has been offered. How is an accused to know when some new rule of conduct arrived, when it will disappear?

It is argued that the report of the Legislative Committee, dated April 10th, 1933, disclosed the essential facts. May one be convicted of crime upon such findings? Are federal rights subject to extinction by reports of committees? Heretofore, they have not been. . . .

The exigency is of the kind which inevitably arises when one set of men continue to produce more than all others can buy. The distressing result to the producer followed his ill-advised but voluntary efforts. Similar situations occur in almost every business. If here we have an emergency sufficient to empower the Legislature to fix sales prices, then whenever there is too much or too little of an essential thing—whether of milk or grain or pork or coal or shoes or clothes—constitutional provisions may be declared inoperative and "anarchy and despotism" . . . are at the door. . . .

Regulation to prevent recognized evils in business has long been upheld as permissible legislative action. But fixation of the price at which "A," engaged in an ordinary business, may sell, in order to enable "B," a producer, to improve his condition, has not been regarded as within legislative power. This is not regulation, but management, control, dictation—it amounts to the deprivation of the fundamental right which one has to conduct his own affairs honestly and along customary lines. The argument advanced here would support general prescription of prices for farm products, groceries, shoes, clothing, all the necessities of modern civilization, as well as labor, when some legislature finds and declares such action advisable and for the public good. This Court has declared that a State may not by legislative fiat convert a private business into a public utility . . . , *Smith v. Cahoon*, 283 U.S. 553. And if it be now ruled that one dedicates his property to public use whenever he embarks on an enterprise which the Legislature may think it desirable to bring under control, this is but to declare that rights guaranteed by the Constitution exist only so long as supposed public interest does not require their extinction. To adopt such a view, of course, would put an end to liberty under the Constitution. . . .

The judgment of the court below should be reversed.

Mr. Justice Van Devanter, Mr. Justice Sutherland and Mr. Justice Butler authorize me to say that they concur in this opinion.

NORMAN v. BALTIMORE AND OHIO R.R.

294 U.S. 240, 79 L.Ed. 885 (1935)

Though money is by no means a recent invention, the very nature of economic motivations under a capitalistic system gives it unprecedented importance. Money becomes both a commodity and a source of power intimately concerned with, though not the only determinant of, our economic well-being. It requires only a quick survey of the Constitution to realize that our founding fathers knew the importance of money. To them cheap paper money was to be avoided if possible. Thus states are prohibited from coining money, emitting bills of credit, or making anything but gold or silver legal tender in payment of debts (see Art. I, Sec. 10). Though they did not specifically limit the federal government in this regard, it is also worth noting that there is no express authorization for Congress "to emit bills of credit." Rather, Article I, Section 8, sets up broad congressional powers in regard to money: "to borrow Money on the credit of the United States . . . ; to coin Money, regulate the Value thereof, and of foreign Coin. . . ." While not many cases involving this monetary power have been adjudicated, the few that were have been highlights in our constitutional and political development. McCulloch v. Maryland (4 Wheat. 316) in 1819 permitted the establishment of a national bank; Veazie Bank v. Fenno (8 Wall. 533) in 1869 permitted the use of the federal taxing power to tax state bank notes out of existence; and the Legal Tender Cases (12 Wall. 457) in 1871 affirmed the right of Congress to make "greenbacks" legal tender at face value in the payment of debts between private individuals. Since in 1869 the Court had, in Bronson v. Rodes (7 Wall. 229), intimated strongly, if indeed it did not say so expressly, that whatever be the ultimate result of the Legal Tender Acts they could not be made to apply to those obligations of individuals expressly made payable in gold coin, the stage is set for the case below. For not only did many creditors insist on "gold clauses" in their bonds, but almost all public bonds contained such clauses. The result was a dual system of money and monetary claims. Then came the depression and in order to cheapen money, raise prices, and rescue agriculture and manufacturing, gold payments were suspended by law in both private contracts and government bonds as part of an over-all devaluation program. Though the case below— the facts of which are clearly set forth in the opinion—dealt with private contracts, Perry v. United States (294 U.S. 330), also in 1935, sets up a somewhat different standard for those "gold clause" bonds issued by the government itself in holding that such promise could not be abrogated, since the power to borrow money must be given priority over the power to regulate the value thereof.

Mr. Chief Justice Hughes delivered the opinion of the Court.

These cases present the question of the validity of the Joint Resolution of the Congress, of June 5, 1933, with respect to the "gold clauses" of private contracts for the payment of money. 48 Stat. at L. 112.

This Resolution . . . declares that "every provision contained in or made with respect to any obligation which purports to give the obligee a right to require payment in gold or a particular kind of coin or currency, or in an amount in money of the United States measured thereby" is "against public policy." Such provisions in obligations thereafter incurred are prohibited. The Resolution provides that "Every obligation, heretofore or hereafter incurred, whether or not any such provision is contained therein or made with respect thereto, shall be discharged upon payment, dollar for dollar, in any coin or currency which at the time of payment is legal tender for public and private debts."

In No. 270 the suit was brought upon a coupon of a bond made by the Baltimore and Ohio Railroad Company under date of February 1, 1930, for the payment of $1,000 on February 1, 1960, and interest from date at the rate of 4½ per cent. per annum, payable semi-annually. The bond provided that the payment of principal and interest "will be made . . . in gold coin of the United States of America of or equal to the standard of weight and fineness existing on February 1, 1930. . . . The complaint alleged that on February 1, 1930, the standard weight and fineness of a gold dollar of the United States as a unit of value "was fixed to consist of twenty-five and eight-tenths grains of gold, nine-tenths fine," pursuant to the Act of Congress of March 14, 1900; and that by the Act of Congress known as the "Gold Reserve Act of 1934," and by the order of the President under that Act, the standard unit of value of a gold dollar of the United States "was fixed to consist of fifteen and five-twenty-firsts grains of gold, nine-tenths fine," from and after January 31, 1934. On presentation of the coupon, defendant refused to pay the amount in gold, or the equivalent of gold in legal tender of the United States which was alleged to be, on February 1, 1934, according to the standard of weight and fineness existing on February 1, 1930, the sum of $38.10, and plaintiff demanded judgment for that amount.

Defendant answered that by Acts of Congress, and, in particular, by the Joint Resolution of June 5, 1933, defendant had been prevented from making payment in gold coin "or otherwise than dollar for dollar, in coin or currency of the United States (other than gold coin and gold certificates)" which at the time of payment constituted legal tender. Plaintiff, challenging the validity of the Joint Resolution under the Fifth and Tenth Amendments, and Article I. Sec. 1, of the Constitution of the United States, moved to strike the defense. The motion was denied. Judgment was entered for plaintiff for $22.50, the face of the coupon, and was affirmed upon appeal. The Court of Appeals of the State considered the federal question and decided that the Joint Resolution was valid. 265 N.Y. 37. This Court granted a writ of certiorari, October 8, 1934. . . .

The Joint Resolution of June 5, 1933, was one of a series of measures relating to the currency. . . . On March 6, 1933, the President, stating that there had been "heavy and unwarranted withdrawals of gold and currency from our banking institutions for the purpose of hoarding" and "extensive speculative activity abroad in foreign exchange" which had resulted "in severe drains on the Nation's stocks of gold," and reciting the authority conferred by Sec. 5 (b) of the Act of October 6, 1917, declared "a bank holiday" until March 9, 1933. On the same date the Secretary of the Treasury, with the President's approval, issued instructions to the Treasurer of the United States to make payments in gold in any form only under license issued by the Secretary.

On March 9, 1933, the Congress passed the Emergency Banking Act. All orders issued by the President or the Secretary of the Treasury since March 4, 1933, under the authority conferred by Sec. 5 (b) of the Act of October 6, 1917, were confirmed. That section was amended so as to provide that during any period of national emergency declared by the President, he might "investigate, regulate or prohibit," by means of licenses or otherwise, "any transactions in foreign exchange, transfers of credit between or payments by banking institutions as defined by the President, and export, hoarding, melting, or ear-marking of gold or silver coin or bullion or currency, by any person within the United States or any place subject to the jurisdiction thereof." The Act also amended Sec. 11 of the Federal Reserve Act so as to authorize the Secretary of the Treasury to require all persons to deliver to the Treasurer of the United States "any or all gold coin, gold bullion, and gold certificates" owned by them, and that the Secretary should pay therefor "an equivalent amount of any other form of coin or currency coined or issued under the laws of the United States." By Executive Order of March 10, 1933, the President authorized banks to be reopened as stated, but prohibited the removal from the United States, or any place subject to its jurisdiction, of "any gold coin, gold bullion, or gold certificates, except in accordance with regulations prescribed by or under license issued by the Secretary of the Treasury." By further Executive Order of April 5, 1933, forbidding hoarding, all persons were required to deliver, on or before May 1, 1933, to stated banks "all gold coin, gold bullion and gold certificates," with certain exceptions, the holder to receive "an equivalent amount of any other form of coin or currency coined or issued under the laws of the United States." Another Order of April 20, 1933, contained further requirements with respect to the acquisition and export of gold and to transactions in foreign exchange. . . .

Then followed the Joint Resolution of June 5, 1933. There were further Executive Orders . . . and orders of the Secretary of the Treasury, approved by the President, on December 28, 1933, and January 15, 1934, for the delivery of gold coin, gold bullion and gold certificates to the United States Treasury.

On January 30, 1934, the Congress passed the "Gold Reserve Act of 1934" which, by Sec. 13, ratified and confirmed all the actions, regulations and orders taken or made by the President and the Secretary of the Treasury under the Act of March 9, 1933, or under Sec. 43 of the Act of May 12, 1933, and, by Sec. 12, with respect to the authority of the President to fix the weight of the gold dollar, provided that it should not be fixed "in any event at more than 60 per centum of its present weight." On January 31, 1934, the President issued his proclamation declaring that he fixed "the weight of the gold dollar to be 15 5/21 grains nine-tenths fine," from and after that date.

We have not attempted to summarize all the provisions of these measures. We are not concerned with their wisdom. The question before the Court is one of power, not of policy. And that question touches the validity of these measures at but a single point, that is, in relation to the Joint Resolution denying effect to "gold clauses" in existing contracts. The Resolution must, however, be considered in its legislative setting and in the light of other measures in pari materia.

First. The interpretation of the gold clauses in suit. . . .

We are of the opinion that the gold clauses now before us were not contracts for payment in gold coin as a commodity, or in bullion, but were contracts for the payment of money. The bonds were severally for the payment of one thousand dollars. We also think that, fairly construed, these clauses were intended to afford a definite standard or measure of value, and thus to protect against a depreciation of the currency and against the discharge of the obligation by a payment of lesser value than that prescribed. When these contracts were made they were not repugnant to any action of the Congress. In order to determine whether effect may now be given to the intention of the parties in the face of the action taken by the Congress, or the contracts may be satisfied by the payment dollar for dollar, in legal tender, as the Congress has now prescribed, it is necessary to consider (1) the power of the Congress to establish a monetary system and the necessary implications of that power; (2) the power of the Congress to invalidate the provisions of existing contracts which interfere with the exercise of its constitutional authority; and (3) whether the clauses in question do constitute such an interference as to bring them within the range of that power.

Second. The power of the Congress to establish a monetary system. It is unnecessary to review the historic controversy as to the extent of this power, or again to go over the ground traversed by the Court in reaching the conclusion that the Congress may make treasury notes legal tender in payment of debts previously contracted, as well as of those subsequently contracted, whether that authority be exercised in course of war or in time of peace. *Legal Tender Cases (Knox v. Lee)*, 12 Wall. 457; *Legal Tender Case (Juilliard v. Grenman)*, 110 U.S. 421. We need only consider certain postulates upon which that conclusion rested.

The Constitution grants to the Congress power "To coin money, regulate the value thereof, and of foreign coin." Art. I, Sec. 8, Par. 5. But the Court in the legal tender cases did not derive from that express grant alone the full authority of the Congress in relation to the currency. The Court found the source of that authority in all the related powers conferred upon the Congress and appropriate to achieve "the great objects for which the government was framed," —"a national government, with sovereign powers." *M'Culloch v. Maryland*, 4 Wheat. 316, 404–407. The broad and comprehensive national authority over the subjects of revenue, finance and currency is derived from the aggregate of the powers granted to the Congress, embracing the powers to lay and collect taxes, to borrow money, to regulate commerce with foreign nations and among the several States, to coin money, regulate the value thereof, and of foreign coin, and fix the standards of weights and measures, and the added express power "to make all laws which shall be necessary and proper for carrying into execution" the other enumerated powers. . . .

Moreover, by virtue of this national power, there attach to the ownership of gold and silver those limitations which public policy may require by reason of their quality as legal tender and as a medium of exchange. *Ling Su Fan* v. *United States*, 218 U.S. 302, 310. Those limitations arise from the fact that the law "gives to such coinage a value which does not attach as a mere consequence of intrinsic value." Their quality as legal tender is attributed by the law, aside from their bullion value. Hence the power to coin money includes the power to forbid mutilation, melting and exportation of gold and silver coin,—"to prevent its outflow from the country of its origin."

Dealing with the specific question as to the effect of the legal tender acts upon contracts made before their passage, that is, those for the payment of money generally, the Court, in the legal tender cases, recognized the possible consequences of such enactments in frustrating the expected performance of contracts,—in rendering them "fruitless or partially fruitless." The Court pointed out that the exercise of the powers of Congress may affect "apparent obligations" of contracts in many ways. The Congress may pass bankruptcy acts. The Congress may declare war, or, even in peace, pass non-intercourse acts, or direct an embargo, which may operate seriously upon existing contracts. And the Court reasoned that if the legal tender acts "were justly chargeable with impairing contract obligations, they would not, for that reason, be forbidden, unless a different rule is to be applied to them from that which has hitherto prevailed in the construction of other powers granted by the fundamental law." The conclusion was that contracts must be understood as having been made in reference to the possible exercise of the rightful authority of the Government, and that no obligation of a contract "can extend to the defeat" of that authority.

On similar grounds, the Court dismissed the contention under the Fifth Amendment forbidding the taking of private property for public use without just compensation or the deprivation of it without due process of law. That provision, said the Court, referred only to a direct appropriation. A new tariff, an embargo, or a war, might bring upon individuals great losses; might, indeed, render valuable property almost valueless,—might destroy the worth of contracts. "But whoever supposed," asked the Court, "that, because of this, a tariff could not be changed or a non-intercourse act, or embargo be enacted, or a war be declared." The Court referred to the Act of June 28, 1834, by which a new regulation of the weight and value of gold coin was adopted, and about six per cent. was taken from the weight of each dollar. The effect of the measure was that all creditors were subjected to a corresponding loss, as the debts then due "became solvable with six per cent. less gold than was required to pay them before." But it had never been imagined that there was a taking of private property without compensation or without due process of law. The harshness of such legislation, or the hardship it may cause, afforded no reason for considering it to be unconstitutional.

The question of the validity of the Joint Resolution of June 5, 1933, must be determined in the light of these settled principles.

Third. The power of the Congress to invalidate the provisions of existing contracts which interfere with the exercise of its constitutional authority. The instant cases involve contracts between private parties, but the question necessarily relates as well to the contracts or obligations of States and municipalities, or of their political subdivisions, that is, to such engagements as are within the reach of the applicable national power. The Government's own contracts—the obligations of the United States—are in a distinct category and demand separate consideration. See *Perry* v. *United States*, 294 U.S. 330.

The contention is that the power of the Congress, broadly sustained by the decisions we have cited in relation to private contracts for the payment of money generally, does not extend to the striking down of express contracts for gold payments. The acts before the Court in the legal tender cases, as we have seen, were not deemed to go so far. Those acts left in circulation two kinds of money, both lawful and available, and contracts for payments in gold, one of these kinds, were not disturbed. The Court did not decide that the Congress did not have the constitutional power to invalidate existing contracts of that sort, if they stood in the way of the execution of the policy of the Congress in relation to the currency. Mr. Justice Bradley, in his concurring opinion, expressed the view that the Congress had that power and had exercised it. And, upon that ground, he dissented from the opinion of the Court in *Trebilcock* v. *Wilson* (12 Wall. 699), as to the validity of contracts for payment *"in specie."* It is significant that Mr. Justice Bradley, referring to this difference of opinion in the legal tender cases, remarked (in his concurring opinion) that "of course" the difference arose "from the different construction given to the legal tender acts." "I do not understand," he said, "the majority of the court to decide that an act so drawn as to embrace, in terms, contracts payable in specie, would not be constitutional. Such a decision would completely nullify the power claimed for the government. For it would be very easy, by the use of one or two additional words, to make all contracts payable in specie."

Here, the Congress has enacted an express interdiction. The argument against it does not rest upon the mere fact that the legislation may cause hardship or loss. Creditors who have not stipulated for gold payments may suffer equal hardship or loss with creditors who have so stipulated. The former, admittedly, have no constitutional grievance. And, while the latter may not suffer more, the point is pressed that their express stipulations for gold payments constitute property, and that creditors who have not such stipulations are without that property right. And the contestants urge that the Congress is seeking not to regulate the currency, but to regulate contracts, and thus has stepped beyond the power conferred.

This argument is in the teeth of another established principle. Contracts, however express, cannot fetter the constitutional authority of the Congress. Contracts may create rights of property, but when contracts deal with a subject matter which lies within the control of the Congress, they have a congenital infirmity. Parties cannot remove their transactions from the reach of dominant constitutional power by making contracts about them.

This principle has familiar illustration in the exercise of the power to regulate commerce. If shippers and carriers stipulate for specified rates, although the rates may be lawful when the contracts are made, if Congress through the Interstate Commerce Commission exercises its authority and prescribes different rates, the latter control and override inconsistent stipulations in contracts previously made. This is so, even if the contract be a charter granted by a State and limiting rates, or a contract between municipalities and carriers. . . .

The principle is not limited to the incidental effect of the exercise by the Congress of its constitutional authority. There is no constitutional ground for denying to the Congress the power expressly to prohibit and invalidate contracts although previously made, and valid when made, when they interfere with the carrying out of the policy it is free to adopt. The exercise of this power is illustrated by the provision of Sec. 5 of the Employers' Liability Act of 1908 relating to any contract the purpose of which was to enable a common carrier to exempt itself from the liability which the Act created. Such a stipulation the Act explicitly declared to be void. In the *Second Employers' Liability Cases*, 223 U.S. 1, 52, the Court decided that as the Congress possessed the power to impose the liability, it also possessed the power "to insure its efficacy by prohibiting any contract, rule, regulation or device in evasion of it." And this prohibition the Court has held to be applicable to contracts made before the Act was passed. *Philadelphia, B. and W. R. Co.* v. *Schubert*, 224 U.S. 603. . . .

The same reasoning applies to the constitutional authority of the Congress to regulate the currency and to establish the monetary system of the country. If the gold clauses now before us interfere with the policy of the Congress in the exercise of that authority they cannot stand.

Fourth. The effect of the gold clauses in suit in relation to the monetary policy adopted by the Congress. Despite the wide range of the discussion at the bar and the earnestness with which the arguments against the validity of the Joint Resolution have been pressed, these contentions necessarily are brought, under the dominant principles of which we have referred, to a single and narrow point. That point is whether the gold clauses do constitute an actual interference with the monetary policy of the Congress in the light of its broad power to determine that policy. Whether they may be deemed to be such an interference depends upon an appraisement of economic conditions and upon determinations of questions of fact. With respect to those conditions and determinations, the Congress is entitled to its own judgment. We may inquire whether its action is arbitrary or capricious, that is, whether it has reasonable relation to a legitimate end. If it is an appropriate means to such an end, the decision of the Congress as to the degree of the necessity for the adoption of that means, is final. . . .

Can we say that this determination [by the Committee on Banking and Currency of the House of Representatives and by the Joint Resolution itself] is so destitute of basis that the interdiction of the gold clauses must be deemed to be without any reasonable relation to the monetary policy adopted by the Congress?

. . . The estimates submitted at the bar indicate that when the Joint Resolution was adopted there were outstanding seventy-five billion dollars or more of such obligations, the annual interest charges on which probably amounted to between three and four billion dollars. It is apparent that if these promises were to be taken literally, as calling for actual payment in gold coin, they would be directly opposed to the policy of Congress, as they would be calculated to increase the demand for gold, to encourage hoarding, and to stimulate attempts at exportation of gold coin. . . .

But, if the clauses are treated as "gold value" clauses, that is, as intended to set up a measure or standard of value if gold coin is not available, we think they are still hostile to the policy of the Congress and hence subject to prohibition. . . .

The devaluation of the dollar placed the domestic economy upon a new basis. In the currency as thus provided, States and municipalities must receive their taxes; railroads, their rates and fares; public utilities, their charges for services. The income out of which they must meet their obligations is determined by the new standard. Yet, according to the contentions before us, while that income is thus controlled by law, their indebtedness on their "gold bonds" must be met by an amount of currency determined by the former gold standard. Their receipts, in this view, would be fixed on one basis; their interest charges, and the principal of their obligations, on another. It is common knowledge that the bonds issued by these obligors have generally contained gold clauses, and presumably they account for a large part of the outstanding obligations of that sort. It is also common knowledge that a similar situation exists with respect to numerous industrial corporations that have issued their "gold bonds" and must now receive payments for their products in the existing currency. It requires no acute analysis or profound economic inquiry to disclose the dislocation of the domestic economy which would be caused by such a disparity of conditions in which, it is insisted, those debtors under gold clauses should be required to pay one dollar and sixty-nine cents in currency while respectively receiving their taxes, rates, charges and prices on the basis of one dollar of that currency.

We are not concerned with consequences, in the sense that consequences, however serious, may excuse an invasion of constitutional right. We are concerned with the constitutional power of the Congress over the monetary system of the country and its attempted frustration. Exercising that power, the Congress has undertaken to establish a uniform currency, and parity between kinds of currency, and to make that currency, dollar for dollar, legal tender for the payment of debts. In the light of abundant experience, the Congress was entitled to choose such a uniform monetary system, and to reject a dual system, with respect to all obligations within the range of the exercise of its constitutional authority. The contention that these gold clauses are valid contracts and cannot be struck down proceeds upon the assumption that private parties, and States and municipalities, may make and enforce contracts which may limit that authority. Dismissing that untenable assumption, the facts must be faced. We think that it is clearly shown that these clauses interfere with the exertion of the power granted to the Congress and certainly it is not established that the Congress arbitrarily or capriciously decided that such an interference existed.

The judgment and decree, severally under review, are affirmed.

Mr. Justice McReynolds, Mr. Justice Van Devanter, Mr. Justice Sutherland, and Mr. Justice Butler dissent.

MR. JUSTICE McREYNOLDS, dissenting:

MR. JUSTICE VAN DEVANTER, MR. JUSTICE SUTHERLAND, MR. JUSTICE BUTLER and I conclude that, if given effect, the enactments here challenged will bring about confiscation of property rights and repudiation of national obligations. Acquiescence in the decisions just announced is impossible; the circumstances demand statement of our views. "To let oneself slide down the easy slope offered by the course of events and to dull one's mind against the extent of the danger, . . . that is precisely to fail in one's obligation of responsibility."

Just men regard repudiation and spoliation of citizens by their sovereign with abhorrence; but we are asked to affirm that the Constitution has granted power to accomplish both. No definite delegation of such a power exists; and we cannot believe the farseeing framers, who labored with hope of establishing justice and securing the blessings of liberty, intended that the expected government should have authority to annihilate its own obligations and destroy the very rights which they were endeavoring to protect. Not only is there no permission for such actions; they are inhibited. And no plenitude of words can conform them to our charter. . . .

The fundamental problem now presented is whether recent statutes passed by Congress in respect of money and credits, were designed to attain a legitimate end. Or whether, under the guise of pursuing a monetary policy, Congress really has inaugurated a plan primarily designed to destroy private obligations, repudiate national debts and drive into the Treasury all gold within the country in exchange for inconvertible promises to pay, of much less value.

Considering all the circumstances, we must conclude they show that the plan disclosed is of the latter description and its enforcement would deprive the parties before us of their rights under the Constitution. Consequently the Court should do what it can to afford adequate relief. . . .

This Resolution was not appropriate for carrying into effect any power entrusted to Congress. The gold clauses in no substantial way interfered with the power of coining money or regulating its value or providing an uniform currency. Their existence, as with many other circumstances, might have circumscribed the effect of the intended depreciation and disclosed the unwisdom of it. But they did not prevent the exercise of any granted power. They were not inconsistent with any policy theretofore declared. To assert the contrary is not enough. The Court must be able to see the appropriateness of the thing done before it can be permitted to destroy lawful agreements. . . .

Congress has power to coin money but this cannot be exercised without the possession of metal. Can Congress authorize appropriation, without compensation, of the necessary gold? Congress has power to regulate commerce, to establish post roads, etc. Some approved plan may involve the use or destruction of A's land or a private way. May Congress authorize the appropriation or destruction of these things without adequate payment? Of course not. The limitations prescribed by the Constitution restrict the exercise of all power. . . .

These [Government] bonds are held by men and women in many parts of the world; they have relied upon our honor. Thousands of our own citizens of every degree not doubting the good faith of their sovereign have purchased them. It will not be easy for this multitude to appraise the form of words which establishes that they have suffered no appreciable damage; but perhaps no more difficult for them than for us. And their difficulty will not be assuaged when they reflect that ready calculation of the exact loss suffered by the Philippine government moved Congress to satisfy it by appropriating, in June, 1934, $23,862,750.78 to be paid out of the Treasury of the United States. . . .

Under the challenged statutes it is said the United States have realized profits amounting to $2,800,000,000. But this assumes that gain may be generated by legislative fiat. To such counterfeit profits there would be no limit; with each new debasement of the dollar they would expand. Two billions might be ballooned indefinitely— to twenty, thirty, or what you will.

Loss of reputation for honorable dealing will bring us unending humiliation; the impending legal and moral chaos is appalling.

[Editor's Note.—This dissenting opinion is appended to *Perry* v. *United States*, 294 U.S. 330 (1935) to which it was also directed.]

UNITED STATES v. BUTLER

297 U.S. 1, 80 L.Ed. 477 (1936)

Any collection of cases, especially one dealing with such an extensive and vital subject as "American Economic Life," must inevitably be selective. If the preceding cases seem to indicate a willingness on the part of the Court to submerge its views to the new legislative programs for economic recovery created by the political processes of democratic government, it should be pointed out that the same Court had also held the following legislation invalid: The National Industrial Recovery Act (see PANAMA REFINING COMPANY v. RYAN, *293 U.S. 389, and* SCHECHTER POULTRY CORP. v. U.S., *295 U.S. 495); The Railway Pension Act (see* RAILROAD RETIREMENT BOARD v. ALTON R.R., *295 U.S. 330); The Farm Mortgage Act (see* LOUISVILLE JOINT STOCK LAND BANK v. RADFORD, *295 U.S. 555).*

As part of its comprehensive plan for dealing with the depression, the New Deal had a so-called farm program. Since, as has already been pointed out, this economic crisis was one of dealing with abundance (one can even pun and say abundance in unemployment and the like), the program envisaged crop reduction to be paid for by a tax levied on the first processor of the farm commodity involved, in the hope that such would stabilize prices by cutting production. On its face such a law (the A.A.A. of 1933) should have had ready acceptance since it included within its own provisions both a spend-ing program and a tax for financing the program. But such was not to be the case, for it opened up a whole series of vital constitutional questions including the meaning of the "general welfare" clause in Article I, Section 8 (cf. The Federalist, No. 41); the use of a specific tax to aid a specific group (in this case farmers); and the ever-present invasion of the power of the states by the federal government.

In the instant case, Butler resisted the collection of taxes on cotton processed at the Hoosac Mills of which he was the receiver. As a simple problem of taxation there is every reason to believe that such a tax on processors is a valid one. But once in court, Butler concen-trated on the spending power to which the tax was inextricably con-nected. Ordered to pay by the District Court, told not to pay by the Circuit Court of Appeals, the government appealed to the Supreme Court of the United States. Since the Supreme Court affirmed the decision of the Circuit Court and thus invalidated the whole A.A.A. farm program, it is interesting to note that the same legislation was later re-enacted by Congress using the commerce power and was up-held by a more understanding and co-operative Court (see MULFORD v. SMITH, 307 U.S. 38, and WICKARD v. FILBURN, 317 U.S. 111). In the long range of history, it is possible that the actual facts, de-cision, and even opinion of this case will go down as a mere footnote. But that it will remain in the minds of students of the law, and of the Court, and of those interested in the interrelationship of the law to the political processes cannot be questioned. For the grumblings about the Court, brought on by their reaction to much of the New Deal legislation, were beginning to be heard by the sensitive ears of the Justices themselves, who were, as these cases have illustrated, divided among themselves. As though to forestall possible political recrimina-tion (though, as we shall see, to no avail), Mr. Justice Roberts for "his side" and Mr. Justice Stone for "his side" set forth their concepts of the judicial function and especially how that function should be exercised by the Supreme Court—an argument very much with us even today especially in the field of Civil Rights.

MR. JUSTICE ROBERTS delivered the opinion of the Court. . . .

It is inaccurate and misleading to speak of the exaction from proc-essors prescribed by the challenged act as a tax, or to say that as a tax it is subject to no infirmity. A tax, in the general understanding of the term, and as used in the Constitution, signifies an exaction for the support of the government. The word has never been thought to connote the expropriation of money from one group for the benefit of another. We may concede that the latter sort of imposition is con-stitutional when imposed to effectuate regulation of a matter in which both groups are interested and in respect of which there is a power of legislative regulation. But manifestly no justification for it can be found unless as an integral part of such regulation. The exaction cannot be wrested out of its setting, denominated an excise for raising revenue and legalized by ignoring its purpose as a mere instrumentality for bringing about a desired end. To do this would be to shut our eyes to what all others than we can see and understand. *Child Labor Tax Case [Bailey v. Drexel Furniture Co.]*. . . .

We conclude that the act is one regulating agricultural production; that the tax is a mere incident of such regulation; and that the respondents have standing to challenge the legality of the exaction.

It does not follow that as the act is not an exertion of the taxing power and the exaction not a true tax, the statute is void or the exaction uncollectible. For, to paraphrase what was said in the *Head Money Cases*, 112 U.S. 580, if this is an expedient regulation by Congress, of a subject within one of its granted powers, "and the end to be attained is one falling within that power, the act is not void, because, within a loose and more extended sense than was used in the Constitution," the exaction is called a tax.

The Government asserts that even if the respondents may question the propriety of the appropriation embodied in the statute, their attack must fail because Article 1, Sec. 8 of the Constitution, authorizes the contemplated expenditure of the funds raised by the tax. This contention presents the great and the controlling question in the case. We approach its decision with a sense of our grave responsibility to render judgment in accordance with the principles established for the governance of all three branches of the Government.

There should be no misunderstanding as to the function of this court in such a case. It is sometimes said that the court assumes a power to overrule or control the action of the people's representatives. This is a misconception. The Constitution is the supreme law of the land ordained and established by the people. All legislation must conform to the principles it lays down. When an act of Congress is appropriately challenged in the courts as not conforming to the constitutional mandate the judicial branch of the Government has only one duty,—to lay the article of the Constitution which is invoked beside the statute which is challenged and to decide whether the latter squares with the former. All the court does, or can do, is to announce its considered judgment upon the question. The only power it has, if such it may be called, is the power of judgment. This court neither approves nor condemns any legislative policy. Its delicate and difficult office is to ascertain and declare whether the legislation is in accordance with, or in contravention of, the provisions of the Constitution; and having done that, its duty ends. . . .

Article I, Sec. 8, of the Constitution vests sundry powers in the Congress. But two of its clauses have any bearing upon the validity of the statute under review.

The third clause endows the Congress with power "to regulate commerce . . . among the several States." Despite reference in its first section to a burden upon, and an obstruction of the normal currents of commerce, the act under review does not purport to regulate transactions in interstate or foreign commerce. Its stated purpose is the control of agricultural production, a purely local activity, in an effort to raise the prices paid the farmer. Indeed, the Government does not attempt to uphold the validity of the act on the basis of the commerce clause, which, for the purpose of the present case, may be put aside as irrelevant.

The clause thought to authorize the legislation,—the first,—confers upon the Congress power "to lay and collect Taxes, Duties, Imposts and Excises, to pay the Debts and provide for the common Defence and general Welfare of the United States. . . ." It is not contended that this provision grants power to regulate agricultural production upon the theory that such legislation would promote the general welfare. The government concedes that the phrase "to provide for the general welfare" qualifies the power "to lay and collect taxes." The view that the clause grants power to provide for the general welfare, independently of the taxing power, has never been authoritatively accepted. Mr. Justice Story points out that, if it were adopted, "it is obvious that under color of the generality of the words, to 'provide for the common defence and general welfare,' the government of the United States is, in reality, a government of general and unlimited powers, notwithstanding the subsequent enumeration of specific powers." The true construction undoubtedly is that the only thing granted is the power to tax for the purpose of providing funds for payment of the nation's debts and making provision for the general welfare.

Nevertheless, the Government asserts that warrant is found in this clause for the adoption of the Agricultural Adjustment Act. The argument is that Congress may appropriate and authorize the spending of moneys for the "general welfare"; that the phrase should be liberally construed to cover anything conducive to national welfare; that decision as to what will promote such welfare rests with Congress alone, and the courts may not review its determination; and, finally, that the appropriation under attack was in fact for the general welfare of the United States.

The Congress is expressly empowered to lay taxes to provide for the general welfare. Funds in the Treasury as a result of taxation may be expended only through appropriation. (Article I, Sec. 9, cl. 7.) They can never accomplish the objects for which they were collected, unless the power to appropriate is as broad as the power to tax. The necessary implication from the terms of the grant is that the public funds may be appropriated "to provide for the general welfare of the United States." These words cannot be meaningless, else they would not have been used. The conclusion must be that they were intended to limit and define the granted power to raise and to expend money. How shall they be construed to effectuate the intent of the instrument?

Since the foundation of the nation, sharp differences of opinion have persisted as to the true interpretation of the phrase. Madison asserted it amounted to no more than a reference to the other powers enumerated in the subsequent clauses of the same section; that, as the United States is a government of limited and enumerated powers, the grant of power to tax and spend for the general national welfare must be confined to the enumerated legislative fields committed to the Congress. In this view the phrase is mere tautology, for taxation and appropriation are or may be necessary incidents of the exercise of any of the enumerated legislative powers. Hamilton, on the other hand, maintained the clause confers a power separate and distinct from those later enumerated, is not restricted in meaning by the grant of them, and Congress consequently has a substantive power to tax and to appropriate, limited only by the requirement that it shall be exercised to provide for the general welfare of the United States. Each contention has had the support of those whose views are entitled to weight. This court has noticed the question, but has never found it necessary to decide which is the true construction. Mr. Justice Story, in his Commentaries, espouses the Hamiltonian position. We shall not review the writings of public men and commentators or discuss the legislative practice. Study of all these leads us to conclude that the reading advocated by Mr. Justice Story is the correct one. While, therefore, the power to tax is not unlimited, its confines are set in the clause which confers it, and not in those of section 8 which bestow and define the legislative powers of the Congress. It results that the power of Congress to authorize expenditure of public moneys for public purposes is not limited by the direct grants of legislative power found in the Constitution.

But the adoption of the broader construction leaves the power to spend subject to limitations. . . .

Story says that if the tax be not proposed for the common defence or general welfare, but for other objects wholly extraneous, it would be wholly indefensible upon constitutional principles. And he makes it clear that the powers of taxation and appropriation extend only to matters of national, as distinguished from local welfare. . . .

We are not now required to ascertain the scope of the phrase "general welfare of the United States" or to determine whether an appropriation in aid of agriculture falls within it. Wholly apart from that question, another principle embedded in our Constitution prohibits the enforcement of the Agricultural Adjustment Act. The act invades the reserved rights of the states. It is a statutory plan to regulate and control agricultural production, a matter beyond the powers delegated to the federal government. The tax, the appropriation of the funds raised, and the direction for their disbursement, are but parts of the plan. They are but means to an unconstitutional end.

From the accepted doctrine that the United States is a government of delegated powers, it follows that those not expressly granted, or reasonably to be implied from such as are conferred, are reserved to the states or to the people. To forestall any suggestion to the contrary, the Tenth Amendment was adopted. The same proposition, otherwise stated, is that powers not granted are prohibited. None to regulate agricultural production is given, and therefore legislation by Congress for that purpose is forbidden. . . .

If the taxing power may not be used as the instrument to enforce a regulation of matters of state concern with respect to which the Congress has no authority to interfere, may it, as in the present case, be employed to raise the money necessary to purchase a compliance which the Congress is powerless to command? The Government asserts that whatever might be said against the validity of the plan, if compulsory, it is constitutionally sound because the end is accomplished by voluntary cooperation. There are two different answers to the contention. The regulation is not in fact voluntary. The farmer, of course, may refuse to comply, but the price of such refusal is the loss of benefits. The amount offered is intended to be sufficient to exert pressure on him to agree to the proposed regulation. The power to confer or withhold unlimited benefits is the power to coerce or destroy. If the cotton grower elects not to accept the benefits, he will receive less for his crops; those who receive payments will be able to undersell him. The result may well be financial ruin. The coercive purpose and intent of the statute is not obscured by the fact that it has not been perfectly successful. It is pointed out that, because there still remained a minority whom the rental and benefit payments were insufficient to induce to surrender their independence of action, the Congress has gone further and, in the Bankhead Cotton Act, used the taxing power in a more directly minatory fashion to compel submission. This progression only serves more fully to expose the coercive purpose of the so-called tax imposed by the present act. It is clear that the Department of Agriculture has properly described the plan as one to keep a non-cooperating minority in line. This is coercion by economic pressure. The asserted power of choice is illusory. . . .

Congress has no power to enforce its commands on the farmer to the ends sought by the Agricultural Adjustment Act. It must follow that it may not indirectly accomplish those ends by taxing and spending to purchase compliance. The Constitution and the entire plan of our government negative any such use of the power to tax and to spend as the act undertakes to authorize. It does not help to declare that local conditions throughout the nation have created a situation of national concern; for this is but to say that whenever there is a widespread similarity of local conditions, Congress may ignore constitutional limitations upon its own powers and usurp those reserved to the states. If, in lieu of compulsory regulation of subjects within the states' reserved jurisdiction, which is prohibited, the Congress could invoke the taxing and spending power as a means to accomplish the same end, clause 1 of Sec. 8 of Article 1 would become the instrument for total subversion of the governmental powers reserved to the individual states.

If the act before us is a proper exercise of the federal taxing power, evidently the regulation of all industry throughout the United States may be accomplished by similar exercises of the same power. . . .

Until recently no suggestion of the existence of any such power in the federal government has been advanced. The expressions of the framers of the Constitution, the decisions of this court interpreting that instrument and the writings of great commentators will be searched in vain for any suggestion that there exists in the clause under discussion or elsewhere in the Constitution, the authority whereby every provision and every fair implication from that instrument may be subverted, the independence of the individual states obliterated, and the United States converted into a central government exercising uncontrolled police power in every state of the Union, superseding all local control or regulation of the affairs or concerns of the states. . . .

Affirmed.

MR. JUSTICE STONE, dissenting. . . .

1. The power of courts to declare a statute unconstitutional is subject to two guiding principles of decision which ought never to be absent from judicial consciousness. One is that courts are concerned only with the power to enact statutes, not with their wisdom. The other is that while unconstitutional exercise of power by the executive and legislative branches of the government is subject to judicial restraint, the only check upon our own exercise of power is our own sense of self-restraint. For the removal of unwise laws from the statute books appeal lies not to the courts but to the ballot and to the processes of democratic government.

2. The constitutional power of Congress to levy an excise tax upon the processing of agricultural products is not questioned. The present levy is held invalid, not for any want of power in Congress to lay such a tax to defray public expenditures, including those for the general welfare, but because the use to which its proceeds are put is disapproved.

3. As the present depressed state of agriculture is nation wide in its extent and effects, there is no basis for saying that the expenditure of public money in aid of farmers is not within the specifically granted power of Congress to levy taxes to "provide for the . . . general welfare." The opinion of the Court does not declare otherwise.

4. No question of a variable tax fixed from time to time by fiat of the Secretary of Agriculture, or of unauthorized delegation of legislative power, is now presented. The schedule of rates imposed by the Secretary in accordance with the original command of Congress has since been specifically adopted and confirmed by Act of Congress, which has declared that it shall be the lawful tax. . . .

It is with these preliminary and hardly controverted matters in mind that we should direct our attention to the pivot on which the decision of the Court is made to turn. It is that a levy unquestionably within the taxing power of Congress may be treated as invalid because it is a step in a plan to regulate agricultural production and is thus a forbidden infringement of state power. The levy is not any the less an exercise of taxing power because it is intended to defray an expenditure for the general welfare rather than for some other support of government. Nor is the levy and collection of the tax pointed to as affecting the regulation. While all federal taxes inevitably have some influence on the internal economy of the states, it is not contended that the levy of a processing tax upon manufacturers using agricultural products as raw material has any perceptible regulatory effect upon either their production or manufacture. . . .

Of the assertion that the payments to farmers are coercive, it is enough to say that no such contention is pressed by the taxpayer, and no such consequences were to be anticipated or appear to have resulted from the administration of the Act. The suggestion of coercion finds no support in the record or in any data showing the actual operation of the Act. Threat of loss, not hope of gain, is the essence of economic coercion. . . .

It is upon the contention that state power is infringed by purchased regulation of agricultural production that chief reliance is placed. It is insisted that, while the Constitution gives to Congress, in specific and unambiguous terms, the power to tax and spend, the power is subject to limitations which do not find their origin in any express provision of the Constitution and to which other expressly delegated powers are not subject. . . .

The spending power of Congress is in addition to the legislative power and not subordinate to it. This independent grant of the power of the purse, and its very nature, involving in its exercise the duty to insure expenditure within the granted power, presuppose freedom of selection among divers ends and aims, and the capacity to impose such conditions as will render the choice effective. It is a contradiction in terms to say that there is power to spend for the national welfare, while rejecting any power to impose conditions reasonably adapted to the attainment of the end which alone would justify the expenditure.

The limitation now sanctioned must lead to absurd consequences. The government may give seeds to farmers, but may not condition the gift upon their being planted in places where they are most needed or even planted at all. The government may give money to the unemployed, but may not ask that those who get it shall give labor in return, or even use it to support their families. It may give money to sufferers from earthquake, fire, tornado, pestilence or flood, but may not impose conditions—health precautions designed to prevent the spread of disease, or induce the movement of population to safer or more sanitary areas. All that, because it is purchased regulation infringing state powers, must be left for the states, who are unable or unwilling to supply the necessary relief. . . .

That the governmental power of the purse is a great one is not now for the first time announced. Every student of the history of government and economics is aware of its magnitude and of its existence in every civilized government. Both were well understood by the framers of the Constitution when they sanctioned the grant of the spending power to the federal government, and both were recognized by Hamilton and Story, whose views of the spending power as standing on a parity with the other powers specifically granted, have hitherto been generally accepted.

The suggestion that it must now be curtailed by judicial fiat because it may be abused by unwise use hardly rises to the dignity of argument. So may judicial power be abused. "The power to tax is the power to destroy," but we do not, for that reason, doubt its existence, or hold that its efficacy is to be restricted by its incidental or collateral effects upon the states. . . . The power to tax and spend is not without constitutional restraints. One restriction is that the purpose must be truly national. Another is that it may not be used to coerce action left to state control. Another is the conscience and patriotism of Congress and the Executive. "It must be remembered that legislators are the ultimate guardians of the liberties and welfare of the people in quite as great a degree as the courts." Justice Holmes, in *Missouri, Kansas and Texas Ry. Co.* v. *May*, 194 U.S. 267, 270.

A tortured construction of the Constitution is not to be justified by recourse to extreme examples of reckless congressional spending which might occur if courts could not prevent expenditures which, even if they could be thought to effect any national purpose, would be possible only by action of a legislature lost to all sense of public responsibility. Such suppositions are addressed to the mind accustomed to believe that it is the business of courts to sit in judgment on the wisdom of legislative action. Courts are not the only agency of government that must be assumed to have capacity to govern. Congress and the courts both unhappily may falter or be mistaken in the performance of their constitutional duty. But interpretation of our great charter of government which proceeds on any assumption that the responsibility for the preservation of our institutions is the exclusive concern of any one of the three branches of government, or that it alone can save them from destruction is far more likely, in the long run, "to obliterate the constituent members" of "an indestructible union of indestructible states" than the frank recognition that language, even of a constitution, may mean what it says: that the power to tax and spend includes the power to relieve a nationwide economic maladjustment by conditional gifts of money.

MR. JUSTICE BRANDEIS and MR. JUSTICE CARDOZO join in this opinion.

CARTER v. CARTER COAL CO.

298 U.S. 238, 80 L.Ed. 1160 (1936)

In the so-called "sick chicken case" (SCHECHTER POULTRY CORP.
v. UNITED STATES, *295 U.S. 495*), *reliance was placed on the commerce clause of the Constitution as a means of combating the depression through codes of fair competition. The Court, speaking through
Mr. Chief Justice Hughes, so interpreted interstate commerce as to
limit, if not to kill, the whole NIRA which sought to utilize centralized power to meet the economic emergency. Said the Chief Justice: "It is not the province of the Court to consider economic advantage or disadvantage of such centralized system. It is sufficient to
say that the Federal Constitution does not provide for it."*

*The NIRA was enacted in 1933 and was due to expire by its own
terms in 1935 unless renewed, and there was no intention of doing
so. The decision of the Court in the Schechter case in 1935 simply
stated as a legal fact that which had already been discovered as a
political reality—that the marriage of capital and labor in this way
was not a happy one.*

*But 1935 also showed that economic conditions were getting worse
and that the coal industry was immediately in need of aid lest it crash
completely. Accordingly, the Bituminous Coal Conservation Act was
passed, again under the commerce clause power, in order to create a
code of operation for all coal companies which would, among other
things: stabilize the industry and promote interstate commerce; provide for co-operative marketing of coal; levy a tax on such coal; declare that coal production and distribution is affected with a national
public interest; and conserve coal as a national resource. In the instant
case Carter, a stockholder, brought suit to enjoin the Carter Coal
Company, of which he was also president, from accepting the code
formulated and expressed in the Act of 1935—thus challenging the
constitutional validity of the Act. The District Court for the District
of Columbia dismissed the bill. Pending an appeal to the Court of
Appeals, the Supreme Court of the United States granted certiorari,
the petition for certiorari having been joined by the government.*

*It should, of course, be kept in mind that perhaps the E. C. Knight
case might have been a tip-off. But while production may be local, a
production crisis in every part of the United States, going on at the
same time, might indeed add up to such a national problem that
Congress ought to be able to regulate under the commerce power.
Indeed such seemed to be the view in* ANTHRACITE COAL CO. v.
ADKINS, *310 U.S. 381 (1940).*

MR. JUSTICE SUTHERLAND delivered the opinion of the Court.

The purposes of the "Bituminous Coal Conservation Act of [Au-
gust 30] 1935," involved in these suits, as declared by the title, are to

stabilize the bituminous coal-mining industry and promote its interstate commerce; to provide for cooperative marketing of bituminous
coal; to levy a tax on such coal and provide for a drawback under
certain conditions; to declare the production, distribution, and use of
such coal to be affected with a national public interest; to conserve
the national resources of such coal; to provide for the general welfare,
and for other purposes. . . . The constitutional validity of the act is
challenged in each of the suits. . . .

Third. The so-called excise tax of 15 *per centum* on the sale price
of coal at the mine, or, in the case of captive coal the fair market
value, with its drawback allowance of 13½%, is clearly not a tax but
a penalty. The exaction applies to all bituminous coal produced,
whether it be sold, transported or consumed in interstate commerce,
or transactions in respect of it be confined wholly to the limits of the
state. It also applies to "captive coal"—that is to say, coal produced
for the sole use of the producer.

It is very clear that the "excise tax" is not imposed for revenue but
exacted as a penalty to compel compliance with the regulatory provisions of the act. The whole purpose of the exaction is to coerce
what is called an agreement—which of course, it is not, for it lacks
the essential element of consent. One who does a thing in order to
avoid monetary penalty does not agree; he yields to compulsion precisely the same as though he did so to avoid a term in jail. . . .

Fifth. Since the validity of the act depends upon whether it is a
regulation of interstate commerce, the nature and extent of the power
conferred upon Congress by the commerce clause becomes the determinative question in this branch of the case. The commerce clause
vests in Congress the power—"To regulate Commerce with foreign
Nations, and among the several States, and with the Indian Tribes."
The function to be exercised is that of regulation. The thing to be
regulated is the commerce described. In exercising the authority conferred by this clause of the Constitution, Congress is powerless to do
anything about commerce which is not regulation. We first inquire,
then—What is commerce? The term, as this court many times has
said, is one of extensive import. No all-embracing definition has ever
been formulated. The question is to be approached both affirmatively
and negatively—that is to say, from the points of view as to what it
includes and what it excludes.

In *Gibbons* v. *Ogden,* 9 Wheat. 1, 189–190, Chief Justice Marshall said:

Commerce, undoubtedly, is traffic, but it is something more; it is intercourse. It describes the commercial intercourse between nations, and parts of
nations, in all its branches, and is regulated by prescribing rules for carrying
on that intercourse. . . .

As used in the Constitution, the word "commerce" is the equivalent of the phrase "intercourse for the purposes of trade," and in-

cludes transportation, purchase, sale, and exchange of commodities between the citizens of the different states. And the power to regulate commerce embraces the instruments by which commerce is carried on. In *Adair* v. *United States*, 208 U.S. 161, 177, the phrase "Commerce among the several States" was defined as comprehending "traffic, intercourse, trade, navigation, communication, the transit of persons and the transmission of messages by telegraph—indeed, every species of commercial intercourse among the several States." In *Veazie* v. *Moor*, 14 How. 568, 573–574, this court, after saying that the phrase could never be applied to transactions wholly internal, significantly added: "Nor can it be properly concluded, that, because the products of domestic enterprise in agriculture or manufactures, or in the arts, may ultimately become the subjects of foreign commerce, that the control of the means or the encouragements by which enterprise is fostered and protected, is legitimately within the import of the phrase *foreign commerce*, or fairly implied in any investiture of the power to regulate such commerce. A pretension as far reaching as this, would extend to contracts between citizen and citizen of the same State, would control the pursuits of the planter, the grazier, the manufacturer, the mechanic, the immense operations of the collieries and mines and furnaces of the country; for there is not one of these avocations, the results of which may not become the subjects of foreign commerce, and be borne either by turnpikes, canals, or railroads, from point to point within the several States, towards an ultimate destination, like the one above mentioned. . . ."

And [in *Kidd* v. *Pearson*, 128 U.S. 1] as though foreseeing the present controversy, the opinion proceeds:

Any movement toward the establishment of rules of production in this vast country, with its many different climates and opportunities, could only be at the sacrifice of the peculiar advantages of a large part of the localities in it, if not of every one of them. On the other hand, any movement toward the local, detailed and incongruous legislation required by such interpretation would be about the widest possible departure from the declared object of the clause in question. Nor this alone. Even in the exercise of the power contended for, Congress would be confined to the regulation, not of certain branches of industry, however numerous, but to those instances in each and every branch where the producer contemplated an interstate market. . . . A situation more paralyzing to the state governments, and more provocative of conflicts between the general government and the States, and less likely to have been what the framers of the Constitution intended, it would be difficult to imagine. . . .

That commodities produced or manufactured within a state are intended to be sold or transported outside the state does not render their production or manufacture subject to federal regulation under the commerce clause. As this court said in *Coe* v. *Errol*, 116 U.S. 517, 526, "Though intended for exportation, they may never be exported; the owner has a perfect right to change his mind; and until actually put in motion, for some place out of the State, or committed to the custody of a carrier for transportation to such place, why may they not be regarded as still remaining a part of the general mass of property in the State?" It is true that this was said in respect of a challenged power of the state to impose a tax, but the query is equally pertinent where the question, as here, is with regard to the power of regulation. The case was relied upon in *Kidd* v. *Pearson*. "The application of the principles above announced," it was there said, "to the case under consideration leads to a conclusion against the contention of the plaintiff in error. The police power of a State is as broad and plenary as its taxing power; and property within the State is subject to the operations of the former so long as it is within the regulating restrictions of the latter."

In *Heisler* v. *Thomas Colliery Co.*, 260 U.S. 245, 259–260, we held that the possibility, or even certainty of exportation of a product or article from a state did not determine it to be in interstate commerce before the commencement of its movement from the state. To hold otherwise "would nationalize all industries, it would nationalize and withdraw from state jurisdiction and deliver to federal commercial control the fruits of California and the South, the wheat of the West and its meats, the cotton of the South, the shoes of Massachusetts and the woolen industries of other States, at the very inception of their production or growth, that is, the fruits unpicked, the cotton and wheat ungathered, hides and flesh of cattle yet 'on the hoof,' wool yet unshorn, and coal yet un-mined, because they are in varying percentages destined for and surely to be exported to States other than those of their production."

In *Oliver Iron Min. Co.* v. *Lord*, 262 U.S. 172, 178, we said on the authority of numerous cited cases: "Mining is not interstate commerce, but, like manufacturing, is a local business subject to local regulation and taxation. . . . Its character in this regard is intrinsic, is not affected by the intended use or disposal of the product, is not controlled by contractual engagements, and persists even though the business be conducted in close connection with interstate commerce." . . .

We have seen that the word "commerce" is the equivalent of the phrase "intercourse for the purposes of trade." Plainly the incidents leading up to and culminating in the mining of coal do not constitute such intercourse. The employment of men, the fixing of their wages, hours of labor and working conditions, the bargaining in respect of these things—whether carried on separately or collectively —each and all constitute intercourse for the purposes of production, not of trade. The latter is a thing apart from the relation of employer and employee, which in all producing occupations is purely local in character. Extraction of coal from the mine is the aim and completed result of local activities. Commerce in the coal mined is not brought into being by force of these activities, but by negotiations, agreements, and circumstances entirely apart from production. Mining brings the subject matter of commerce into existence. Commerce disposes of it.

A consideration of the foregoing, and of many cases which might be added to those already cited, renders inescapable the conclusion that the effect of the labor provisions of the act, including those in respect of minimum wages, wage agreements, collective bargaining, and the Labor Board and its powers, primarily falls upon production and not upon commerce; and confirms the further resulting conclusion that production is a purely local activity. It follows that none of these essential antecedents of production constitutes a transaction in or forms any part of interstate commerce. . . .

That the production of every commodity intended for interstate sale and transportation has some effect upon interstate commerce may be, if it has not already been, freely granted; and we are brought to the final and decisive inquiry, whether here that effect is direct, as the "preamble" recites, or indirect. The distinction is not formal, but substantial in the highest degree, as we pointed out in the Schechter Case. . . . "If the commerce clause were construed," we there said, "to reach all enterprises and transactions which could be said to have an indirect effect upon interstate commerce, the federal authority would embrace practically all the activities of the people and the authority of the State over its domestic concerns would exist only by sufferance of the federal government. Indeed, on such a theory, even the development of the State's commercial facilities would be subject to federal control." It was also pointed out that "the distinction between direct and indirect effects of intrastate transactions upon interstate commerce must be recognized as a fundamental one, essential to the maintenance of our constitutional system."

Whether the effect of a given activity or condition is direct or indirect is not always easy to determine. The word "direct" implies that the activity or condition invoked or blamed shall operate proximately —not immediately, remotely, or collaterally—to produce the effect. It connotes the absence of an efficient intervening agency or condition. And the extent of the effect bears no logical relation to its character. The distinction between a direct and an indirect effect turns, not upon the magnitude of either the cause or the effect, but entirely upon the manner in which the effect has been brought about. If the production by one man of a single ton of coal intended for interstate sale and shipment, and actually so sold and shipped, affects interstate commerce indirectly, the effect does not become direct by multiplying the tonnage, or increasing number of men employed, or adding to the expense or complexities of the business, or by all combined. It is quite true that rules of law are sometimes qualified by considerations of degree, as the government argues. But the matter of degree has no bearing upon the question here, since that question is not—What is the *extent* of the local activity or condition, or the *extent* of the effect produced upon interstate commerce? but—What is the *relation* between the activity or condition and the effect?

Much stress is put upon the evils which come from the struggle between employers and employees over the matter of wages, working conditions, the right of collective bargaining, etc., and the resulting strikes, curtailment and irregularity of production and effect on prices; and it is insisted that interstate commerce is *greatly* affected thereby. But, in addition to what has just been said, the conclusive answer is that the evils are all local evils over which the federal government has no legislative control. The relation of employer and employee is a local relation. At common law, it is one of the domestic relations. The wages are paid for the doing of local work. Working conditions are obviously local conditions. The employees are not engaged in or about commerce, but exclusively in producing a commodity. And the controversies and evils, which it is the object of the act to regulate and minimize, are local controversies and evils affecting local work undertaken to accomplish that local result. Such effect as they may have upon commerce, however extensive it may be, is secondary and indirect. An increase in the greatness of the effect adds to its importance. It does not alter its character.

The government's contentions in defense of the labor provisions are really disposed of adversely by our decision in the Schechter Case. The only perceptible difference between that case and this is that in the Schechter Case the federal power was asserted with respect to commodities which had come to rest after their interstate transportation; while here, the case deals with commodities at rest before interstate commerce has begun. That difference is without significance. The federal regulatory power ceases when interstate commercial intercourse ends; and correlatively, the power does not attach until interstate commercial intercourse begins. There is no basis in law or reason for applying different rules to the two situations. No such distinction can be found in anything said in the Schechter Case. On the contrary, the situations were recognized as akin. In the opinion, after calling attention to the fact that if the commerce clause could be construed to reach transactions having an indirect effect upon interstate commerce the federal authority would embrace practically all the activities of the people, and the authority of the state over its domestic concerns would exist only by sufferance of the federal government, we said: "Indeed, on such a theory, even the development of the State's commercial facilities would be subject to federal control." And again, after pointing out that hours and wages have no direct relations to interstate commerce and that if the federal government had power to determine the wages and hours of employees in the internal commerce of a state because of their relation to cost and prices and their indirect effect upon interstate commerce, we said, "All the process of production and distribution that enter into cost could likewise be controlled. If the cost of doing an interstate business is in itself the permitted object of federal control, the extent of the regulation of cost would be a question of discretion and not of power." A reading of the entire opinion makes clear, what we now declare, that the want of power on the part of the federal government is the same whether the wages, hours of service, and working conditions, and the bargaining about them, are related to production before interstate commerce has begun, or to sale and distribution after it has ended. . . .

CHIEF JUSTICE HUGHES concurred specially. CARDOZO, BRANDEIS, and STONE, J. J., dissented.

MR. JUSTICE CARDOZO. . . .

My conclusions compendiously stated are these:

(*a*) Part II of the statute sets up a valid system of price-fixing as applied to transactions in interstate commerce and to those in intrastate commerce where interstate commerce is directly or intimately affected. The prevailing opinion holds nothing to the contrary.

(*b*) Part II, with its system of price-fixing, is separable from Part III, which contains the provisions as to labor considered and condemned in the opinion of the court.

(*c*) Part II being valid, the complainants are under a duty to come in under the code, and are subject to a penalty if they persist in a refusal.

. . .

First: I am satisfied that the Act is within the power of the central government in so far as it provides for minimum and maximum prices upon sales of bituminous coal in the transactions of interstate commerce and in those of intrastate commerce where interstate commerce is directly or intimately affected. Whether it is valid also in other provisions that have been considered and condemned in the opinion of the court, I do not find it necessary to determine at this time. Silence must not be taken as importing acquiescence. Much would have to be written if the subject, even as thus restricted, were to be explored through all its implications, historical and economic as well as strictly legal. The fact that the prevailing opinion leaves the price provisions open for consideration in the future makes it appropriate to forego a fullness of elaboration that might otherwise be necessary. As a system of price fixing the Act is challenged upon three grounds: (1) because the governance of prices is not within the commerce clause; (2) because it is a denial of due process forbidden by the Fifth Amendment; and (3) because the standards for administrative action are indefinite, with the result that there has been an unlawful delegation of legislative power.

(1) With reference to the first objection, the obvious and sufficient answer is, so far as the Act is directed to interstate transactions, that sales made in such conditions constitute interstate commerce, and do not merely "affect" it. . . . To regulate the price for such

transactions is to regulate commerce itself, and not alone its antecedent conditions or its ultimate consequences. The very act of sale is limited and governed. Prices in interstate transactions may not be regulated by the states. *Baldwin* v. *Seelig*, 294 U.S. 511. They must therefore be subject to the power of the nation unless they are to be withdrawn altogether from governmental supervision. . . . If such a vacuum were permitted, many a public evil incidental to interstate transactions would be left without a remedy. This does not mean, of course, that prices may be fixed for arbitrary reasons or in an arbitrary way. The commerce power of the nation is subject to the requirement of due process like the police power of the states. . . . Heed must be given to similar considerations of social benefit or detriment in marking the division between reason and oppression. The evidence is overwhelmingly that Congress did not ignore those considerations in the adoption of this Act. What is to be said in that regard may conveniently be postponed to the part of the opinion dealing with the Fifth Amendment.

Regulation of prices being an exercise of the commerce power in respect of interstate transactions, the question remains whether it comes within that power as applied to intrastate sales where interstate prices are directly or intimately affected. Mining and agriculture and manufacture are not interstate commerce considered by themselves, yet their relation to that commerce may be such that for the protection of the one there is need to regulate the other. *Schechter Poultry Corporation* v. *United States*, 295 U.S. 495, 544, 545, 546. Sometimes it is said that the relation must be "direct" to bring that power into play. In many circumstances such a description will be sufficiently precise to meet the needs of the occasion. But a great principle of constitutional law is not susceptible of comprehensive statement in an adjective. The underlying thought is merely this, that "the law is not indifferent to considerations of degree." . . . It cannot be indifferent to them without an expansion of the commerce clause that would absorb or imperil the reserved powers of the states. At times, . . . the waves of causation will have radiated so far that their undulatory motion, if discernible at all, will be too faint or obscure, too broken by cross-currents, to be heeded by the law. In such circumstances the holding is not directed at prices or wages considered in the abstract, but at prices or wages in particular conditions. The relation may be tenuous or the opposite according to the facts. Always the setting of the facts is to be viewed if one would know the closeness of the tie. Perhaps, if one group of adjectives is to be chosen in preference to another, "intimate" and "remote" will be found to be as good as any. At all events, "direct" and "indirect," even if accepted as sufficient, must not be read too narrowly. Cf. Stone, J., in *DiSanto* v. *Pennsylvania*, 273 U.S. 34, 44. A survey of the cases shows that the words have been interpreted with suppleness of adaptation and flexibility of meaning. The power is as broad as the need that evokes it.

One of the most common and typical instances of a relation characterized as direct has been that between interstate and intrastate rates for carriers by rail where the local rates are so low as to divert business unreasonably from interstate competitors. In such circumstances Congress has the power to protect the business of its carriers against disintegrating encroachments. . . . What the cases really mean is that the causal relation in such circumstances is so close and intimate and obvious as to permit it to be called direct without subjecting the word to an unfair or excessive strain. There is a like immediacy here. Within rulings the most orthodox, the prices for intrastate sales of coal have so inescapable a relation to those for interstate sales that a system of regulation for transactions of the one class is necessary to give adequate protection to the system of regulation adopted for the other. . . .

(2) The commerce clause being accepted as a sufficient source of power, the next inquiry must be whether the power has been exercised consistently with the Fifth Amendment. In the pursuit of that inquiry, *Nebbia* v. *New York*, 291 U.S. 502, lays down the applicable principle. There a statute of New York prescribing a minimum price for milk was upheld against the objection that price fixing was forbidden by the Fourteenth Amendment. We found it a sufficient reason to uphold the challenged system that "the conditions or practices in an industry make unrestricted competition an inadequate safeguard of the consumer's interests, produce waste harmful to the public, threaten ultimately to cut off the supply of a commodity needed by the public, or portend the destruction of the industry itself."

All this may be said, and with equal, if not greater force, of the conditions and practices in the bituminous coal industry, not only at the enactment of this statute in August, 1935, but for many years before. Overproduction was at a point where free competition had been degraded into anarchy. Prices had been cut so low that profit had become impossible for all except a lucky handful. Wages came down along with prices and with profits. There were strikes, at times nationwide in extent, at other times spreading over broad areas and many mines, with the accompaniment of violence and bloodshed and misery and bitter feeling. The sordid tale is unfolded in many a document and treatise. During the twenty-three years between 1913 and 1935, there were nineteen investigations or hearings by Congress or by specially created commissions with reference to conditions in the coal mines. The hope of betterment was faint unless the industry could be subjected to the compulsion of a code. In the weeks immediately preceding the passage of this Act the country was threatened once more with a strike of ominous proportions. The plight of the industry was not merely a menace to owners and to mine workers:

it was and had long been a menace to the public, deeply concerned in a steady and uniform supply of a fuel so vital to the national economy.

Congress was not condemned to inaction in the face of price wars and wage wars so pregnant with disaster. Commerce had been choked and burdened; its normal flow had been diverted from one state to another; there had been bankruptcy and waste and ruin alike for capital and for labor. The liberty protected by the Fifth Amendment does not include the right to persist in this anarchic riot. "When industry is grievously hurt, when producing concerns fail, when unemployment mounts and communities dependent upon profitable production are prostrated, the wells of commerce go dry." *Appalachian Coals, Inc.* v. *United States*, 288 U.S. 344, 372. The free competition so often figured as a social good imports order and moderation and a decent regard for the welfare of the group. . . . After making every allowance for difference of opinion as to the most efficient cure, the student of the subject is confronted with the indisputable truth that there were ills to be corrected, and ills that had a direct relation to the maintenance of commerce among the states without friction or diversion. An evil existing, and also the power to correct it, the lawmakers were at liberty to use their own discretion in the selection of the means.

(3) Finally, and in answer to the third objection to the statute in its price-fixing provisions, there has been no excessive delegation of legislative power. The prices to be fixed by the District Boards and the Commission must conform to the following standards: . . . The standards established by this Act are quite as definite as others that have had the approval of this court. . . . Certainly a bench of judges, not experts in the coal business, cannot say with assurance that members of a commission will be unable, when advised and informed by others experienced in the industry, to make the standards workable, or to overcome through the development of an administrative technique many obstacles and difficulties that might be baffling or confusing to inexperience or ignorance. . . .

Second: The next inquiry must be whether Part I of the statute which creates the administrative agencies, and Part II, which has to do in the main with the price-fixing machinery, as well as preliminary sections levying a tax or penalty are separable from Part III, which deals with labor relations in the industry, with the result that what is earlier would stand if what is later were to fall. . . .

Undoubtedly the rules as to labor relations are important provisions of the statute. Undoubtedly the law-makers were anxious that provisions so important should have the force of law. But they announced with all the directness possible for words that they would keep what they could have if they could not have the whole. Stabilizing prices would go a long way toward stabilizing labor relations by giving the producers capacity to pay a living wage. To hold otherwise is to ignore the whole history of mining. All in vain have official committees inquired and reported in thousands of printed pages if this lesson has been lost. In the face of that history the court is now holding that Congress would have been unwilling to give the force of law to the provisions of Part II, which were to take effect at once, if it could not have Part III, which in the absence of agreement between the employers and the miners would never take effect at all. . . .

A last assault upon the statute is still to be repulsed. The complainants take the ground that the Act may not coerce them through the imposition of a penalty into a seeming recognition or acceptance of the code, if any of the code provisions are invalid, however separable from others. I cannot yield assent to a position so extreme. . . . The penalty in those circumstances is adopted as a lawful sanction to compel submission to a statute having the quality of law. . . . What the code will provide as to wages and hours of labor, or whether it will provide anything, is still in the domain of prophecy. The opinion of the court begins at the wrong end. To adopt a homely form of words, the complainants have been crying before they are really hurt.

My vote is for affirmance.

I am authorized to state that MR. JUSTICE BRANDEIS and MR. JUSTICE STONE join in this opinion.

MOREHEAD v. NEW YORK EX REL. TIPALDO

298 U.S. 587, 80 L.Ed. 1347 (1936)

1936 was certainly not 1923. Great changes had taken place in a very few years. The period in which the Adkins decision was handed down was, if not one of milk and honey, certainly generally prosperous. And if the cases that have preceded this one have demonstrated anything at all, they certainly must have shown that the depression was real, not imaginary; that there was enough factual data to support its existence so that it could not be viewed as merely supposititious to develop legal theory that could be or might be utilized if an economic emergency did develop. In the Adkins case the majority of the Court had viewed the police power of a state solely within the traditional bounds of morals and health and thus seeing the statute "simply and exclusively a price-fixing law, confined to adult women . . . who are legally as capable of contracting for themselves as men" could conclude, as it did, that "a statute which prescribes payment solely with relation to circumstances apart from contract of employment, the business affected by it and the work done under it, is so clearly the product of a naked, arbitrary exercise of power that it cannot be allowed to stand under the Constitution." The case below, the facts of which are sufficiently set forth in the opinion of the Court, deals with a minimum wage law that is typical of the many passed by various states during the intervening years. Yet as far as the majority were concerned nothing had changed "in the years that had intervened" and, hence, they could assert dogmatically that "the State is without power by any form of legislation to prohibit, change or nullify contracts between employers and adult women workers as to the amount of wages paid." That this was challenged by "as distinguished a foursome as ever sat on the high court" (see especially the dissents below), as well as by legislators, economists, social workers and the like, was nothing compared to upholding the banner of freedom of contract in its "purest" form with no ands, buts, and ifs attached for special groups or special circumstances.

MR. JUSTICE BUTLER delivered the opinion of the Court:

This is a habeas corpus case originating in the supreme court of New York. Relator was indicted in the county court of Kings county and sent to jail to await trial upon the charge that as manager of a laundry he failed to obey the mandatory order of the state industrial commissioner prescribing minimum wages for women employees.

The relator's petition for the writ avers that the statute, c.584 of the Laws of 1933 (Cons. Law, c.31, art. 19) under which the commissioner made the order, insofar as it purports to authorize him to fix women's wages, is repugnant to the due process clause, art. 1, sec. 6, of the constitution of the State and the due process clause of the Fourteenth Amendment to the Constitution of the United States. The application for the writ is grounded upon the claim that the state statute is substantially identical with the minimum wage law enacted by Congress for the District of Columbia, which in 1923 was condemned by this court as repugnant to the due process clause of the Fifth Amendment. *Adkins* v. *Children's Hospital*, 261 U.S. 525. (See p. 108, *supra.*)

The warden's return, without disclosing the commissioner's order, the prescribed wages, the findings essential to his jurisdiction to establish them, things done in pursuance of the Act, or the allegations of the indictment, merely shows that under an order of the county court he was detaining relator for trial. The case was submitted on petition and return. The court dismissed the writ. Relator took the case to the Court of Appeals. It held the Act repugnant to the due process clauses of the state and federal constitutions. The remittitur directed that the order appealed from be reversed, the writ sustained and the prisoner discharged; it certified that the federal constitutional question was presented and necessarily passed on. The supreme court entered a judgment as directed. We granted a writ of certiorari.

The Act extends to women and minors in any "occupation" which "shall mean an industry, trade or business or branch thereof or class of work therein in which women or minors are gainfully employed, but shall not include domestic service in the home of the employer or labor on a farm." It is not an emergency law. It does not regulate hours or any conditions affecting safety or protection of employees. It relates only to wages of adult women and minors. As the record is barren of details in respect of investigation, findings, amounts being paid women workers in laundries or elsewhere prior to the order, or of things done to ascertain the minimum prescribed, we must take it as granted that, if the state is permitted as against employers and their women employees to establish and enforce minimum wages, that power has been validly exerted. It is to be assumed that the rates have been fairly made in accordance with the procedure prescribed by the Act and in full compliance with the defined standards. If, consistently with the due process clause, the State may not enter upon regulation of the sort undertaken by the challenged enactment, then plainly it cannot by diligence to insure the establishment of just minima create power to enter that field.

The Adkins Case, unless distinguishable, requires affirmance of the judgment below. The petition for the writ sought review upon the ground that this case is distinguishable from that one. No application has been made for reconsideration of the constitutional question there decided. The validity of the principles upon which that decision rests are not challenged. This court confines itself to the ground upon which the writ was asked or granted. . . .

Thus it appears: The minimum wage provided for in the District Act was one not less than adequate "to supply the necessary cost of living to any such women workers to maintain them in good health and to protect their morals." The New York act defines an oppressive and unreasonable wage as containing two elements. The one first mentioned is: "Less than the fair and reasonable value of the services rendered." The other is: "Less than sufficient to meet the minimum cost of living necessary for health." The basis last mentioned is not to be distinguished from the living wage defined in the District act. The exertion of the granted power to prescribe minimum wages is by the State act conditioned upon a finding by the commissioner or other administrative agency that a substantial number of women in any occupation are receiving wages that are oppressive and unreasonable, i.e., less than value of the service and less than a living wage. That finding is essential to jurisdiction of the commissioner. In the state court there was controversy between the parties as to whether the "minimum fair wage rates" are required to be established solely upon value of service or upon that value and the living wage. Against the contention of the attorney general, the Court of Appeals held that the minimum wage must be based on both elements.

Speaking through its chief judge, that court said: "We find no material difference between the act of Congress and this act of the New York State Legislature. The act of Congress, it is said, was to protect women from conditions resulting from wages which were inadequate to maintain decent standards of living." The opinion then quotes from the brief of the attorney general: "The purpose of the statute in the Adkins Case was to guarantee a wage based solely upon the necessities of the workers. The statute did not provide for the wages to have any relationship to earning power; was applicable to all vocations and not to the character of the work. . . . As contrasted with this statute, the New York Minimum Wage Law provides a definite standard for wages paid. It provides that the worker is to be paid at least the value of the services rendered." The opinion continues: "This is a difference in phraseology and not in principle. The New York act, as above stated, prohibits an oppressive and unreasonable wage, which means *both* less than the fair and reasonable value of the services rendered *and* less than sufficient to meet the minimum cost of living necessary for health. The act of Congress had one standard, the living wage; this State act has added another, reasonable value. The minimum wage must include both. What was vague before has not been made any clearer. One of the elements, therefore, in fixing the fair wage is the very matter which was the basis of the congressional act. Forcing the payment of wages at a reasonable value does not make inapplicable the principle and ruling of the Adkins Case. The distinctions between this case and the Adkins Case are differences in details, methods and time; the exercise of legislative power to fix wages in any employment is the same." . . .

The state court rightly held that the Adkins Case controls this one and requires that relator be discharged on the ground that the legislation under which he was indicted and imprisoned is repugnant to the due process clause of the Fourteenth Amendment.

To distinguish this from the Adkins Case, petitioner refers to changes in conditions that have come since that decision, cites great increase during recent years in the number of women wage earners and invokes the first section of the act, called "Factual background."

The act is not to meet an emergency; it discloses a permanent policy; the increasing number of women workers suggests that more and more they are getting and holding jobs that otherwise would belong to men. The "Factual background" must be read in the light of the circumstances attending its enactment. The New York legislature passed two minimum wage measures and contemporaneously submitted them to the governor. One was approved; it is the act now before us. The other was vetoed and did not become law. They contained the same definitions of oppressive wage and fair wage and in general provided the same machinery and procedure culminating in fixing minimum wages by directory orders. The one vetoed was for an emergency; it extended to men as well as to women employees; it did not provide for the enforcement of wages by mandatory orders.

It is significant that their "factual backgrounds" are much alike. . . . These legislative declarations, in form of findings or recitals of fact, serve well to illustrate why any measure that deprives employers and adult women of freedom to agree upon wages, leaving employers and men employees free so to do, is necessarily arbitrary. Much, if not all that in them is said in justification of the regulations that the act imposes in respect of women's wages apply with equal force in support of the same regulation of men's wages. While men are left free to fix their wages by agreement with employers, it would be fanciful to suppose that the regulation of women's wages would be useful to prevent or lessen the evils listed in the first section of the act. Men in need of work are as likely as women to accept the low wages offered by unscrupulous employers. Men in greater number than women support themselves and dependents and because of need will work for whatever wages they can get and that without regard to the value of the service and even though the pay is less than minima prescribed in accordance with this act. It is plain that, under circumstances such as those portrayed in the "Factual background," for prescribing of minimum wages for women alone would unreasonably restrain them in competition with men and tend arbitrarily to deprive them of employment and a fair chance to find work. . . .

The New York court's decision conforms to ours in the Adkins Case, and the later rulings that we have made on the authority of that case. That decision was deliberately made upon careful consideration of the oral arguments and briefs of the respective parties and also of briefs submitted on behalf of States and others as *amici curiae*. In the Arizona case the attorney general sought to distinguish the District of Columbia act from the legislation then before us and insisted that the latter was a valid exertion of the police power of the State. Counsel for the California commission submitted a brief *amicus curiae* in which he elaborately argued that our decision in the Adkins Case was erroneous and ought to be overruled. In the Arkansas case the state officers, appellants there, by painstaking and thorough brief presented arguments in favor of the same contention. But this court, after the thoughtful attention to all that was suggested against that decision, adhered to it as sound. And in each case, being clearly of opinion that no discussion was required to show that, having regard to the principles applied in the Adkins Case, the state legislation fixing wages for women was repugnant to the due process clause of the Fourteenth Amendment, we so held and upon the authority of that case affirmed *per curiam* the decree enjoining its enforcement. It is equally plain that the judgment in the case now before us must also be affirmed.

Affirmed.

Mr. Chief Justice Hughes, dissenting.

I am unable to concur in the opinion in this case. In view of the difference between the statutes involved, I cannot agree that the case should be regarded as controlled by *Adkins* v. *Children's Hospital*. And I can find nothing in the Federal Constitution which denies to the State the power to protect women from being exploited by over-reaching employers through the refusal of a fair wage as defined in the New York Statute and ascertained in a reasonable manner by competent authority. . . .

That the difference is a material one, I think is shown by the opinion in the Adkins Case. That opinion contained a broad discussion of state power, but it singled out as an adequate ground for the finding of invalidity that the statute gave no regard to the situation of the employer and to the reasonable value of the service for which the wage was paid. . . .

As the New York act is free of that feature, so strongly denounced, the question comes before us in a new aspect. The Court was closely divided in the Adkins Case, and that decision followed an equal division of the Court, after reargument, in *Stettler* v. *O'Hara* with respect to the validity of the minimum wage law of Oregon. Such divisions are at times unavoidable, but they point to the desirability of fresh consideration when there are material differences in the cases presented. The fact that in the Adkins Case there were dissenting opinions maintaining the validity of the federal statute, despite the nature of the standard it set up, brings out in stronger relief the ground which was taken most emphatically by the majority in that case, and that there would have been a majority for the decision in the absence of that ground must be a matter of conjecture. With that ground absent, the Adkins Case ceases to be a precise authority. . . .

When there are conditions which specially touch the health and well-being of women, the State may exert its power in a reasonable manner for their protection, whether or not a similar regulation is, or could be, applied to men. The distinctive nature and function of women—their particular relation to the social welfare—has put them in a separate class. This separation and corresponding distinctions in legislation is one of the outstanding traditions of legal history. The Fourteenth Amendment found the states with that protective power and did not take it away or remove the reasons for its exercise. Changes have been effected within the domain of state policy and upon an appraisal of state interests. We have not yet arrived at a time when we are at liberty to override the judgment of the State and decide that women are not the special subject of exploitation because they are women and as such are not in a relatively defenseless position. . . .

If liberty of contract were viewed from the standpoint of absolute right, there would be as much to be said against a regulation of the hours of labor of women as against the fixing of a minimum wage. Restriction upon hours is a restriction upon the making of contracts and upon earning power. But the right being a qualified one, we must apply in each case the test of reasonableness in the circumstances disclosed. Here, the special conditions calling for the protection of women, and for the protection of society itself, are abundantly shown. The legislation is not less in the interest of the community as a whole than in the interest of the women employees who are paid less than the value of their services. That lack must be made good out of the public purse. Granted that the burden of support of women who do not receive a living wage cannot be transferred to employers who pay the equivalent of the service they obtain, there is no reason why the burden caused by the failure to pay that equivalent should not be placed upon those who create it. The fact that the State cannot secure the benefit to society of a living wage for women employees by any enactment which bears unreasonably upon employers does not preclude the State from seeking its objective by means entirely fair both to employers and the women employed.

In the Statute before us, no unreasonableness appears. The end is legitimate and the means appropriate. I think that the act should be upheld.

I am authorized to state that Mr. Justice Brandeis, Mr. Justice Stone and Mr. Justice Cardozo join in this opinion.

Mr. Justice Stone, Brandeis and Cardozo, J. J., concurring with him, dissenting:

While I agree with all that the Chief Justice has said, I would not make the differences between the present statute and that involved in the Adkins Case the sole basis of decision. I attach little importance to the fact that the earlier statute was aimed only at a starvation wage and that the present one does not prohibit such a wage unless it is also less than the reasonable value of the service. Since neither statute compels employment at any wage, I do not assume that employers in one case, more than in the other, would pay the minimum wage if the service were worth less.

The vague and general pronouncement of the Fourteenth Amendment against deprivation of liberty without due process of law is a limitation of legislative power, not a formula for its exercise. It does not purport to say in what particular manner that power shall be exerted. It makes no fine-spun distinctions between methods which the legislature may and which it may not choose to solve a pressing problem of government. It is plain too, that, unless the language of the amendment and the decisions of this Court are to be ignored, the liberty which the amendment protects is not freedom from restraint of all law or of any law which reasonable men may think an appropriate means for dealing with any of those matters of public concern with which it is the business of government to deal. There is grim irony in speaking of the freedom of contract of those who, because of their economic necessities, give their service for less than is needful to keep body and soul together. But if this is freedom of contract no one has ever denied that it is freedom which may be restrained, notwithstanding the Fourteenth Amendment, by a statute passed in the public interest.

In many cases this Court has sustained the power of legislatures to prohibit or restrict the terms of a contract, including the price term, in order to accomplish what the legislative body may reasonably consider a public purpose. They include cases, which have neither been overruled nor discredited, in which the sole basis of regulation was the fact that circumstances, beyond the control of the parties, had so seriously curtailed the regulative power of competition as to place buyers or sellers at a disadvantage in the bargaining struggle, such that a legislature might reasonably have contemplated serious consequences to the community as a whole and have sought to avoid them by regulation of the terms of the contract. *Munn* v. *Illinois,* 94 U.S. 113. . . .

In the years which have intervened since the Adkins Case we have had opportunity to learn that a wage is not always the resultant of free bargaining between employers and employees; that it may be one forced upon employees by their economic necessities and upon employers by the most ruthless of their competitors. We have had opportunity to perceive more clearly that a wage insufficient to support the worker does not visit its consequences upon him alone; that it may affect profoundly the entire economic structure of society and, in any case, that it casts on every taxpayer, and on government itself, the burden of solving the problems of poverty, subsistence, health and morals of large numbers in the community. Because of their nature and extent these are public problems. A generation ago they were for the individual to solve; today they are the burden of the nation. I can perceive no more objection, on constitutional grounds, to their solution by requiring an industry to bear the subsistence cost of the labor which it employs, than to the imposition upon it of the cost of its industrial accidents. . . .

It is not for the courts to resolve doubts whether the remedy by wage regulation is as efficacious as many believe, or is better than some other, or is better even than the blind operation of uncontrolled economic forces. The legislature must be free to choose unless government is to be rendered impotent. The Fourteenth Amendment has no more embedded in the Constitution our preference for some particular set of economic beliefs, than it has adopted, in the name of liberty, the system of theology which we may happen to approve.

I know of no rule or practice by which the arguments advanced in support of an application for certiorari restrict our choice between conflicting precedents in deciding a question of constitutional law which the petition, if granted, requires us to answer. Here the question which the petition specifically presents is whether the New York statute contravenes the Fourteenth Amendment. In addition, the petition assigns as a reason for granting it that "the construction and application of the Constitution of the United States and a prior decision" of this Court "are necessarily involved," and again, that "the circumstances prevailing under which the New York law was enacted call for a reconsideration of the Adkins Case in the light of the New York act and conditions aimed to be remedied thereby." Unless we are now to construe and apply the Fourteenth Amendment without regard to our decisions since the Adkins Case, we could not rightly avoid its reconsideration even if it were not asked. We should follow our decision in the Nebbia Case and leave the selection and the method of the solution of the problems to which the statute is addressed where it seems to me the Constitution has left them, to the legislative branch of the government. The judgment should be reversed.

WEST COAST HOTEL CO. v. PARRISH

300 U.S. 379, 81 L.Ed. 703 (1937)

Enough was enough! The Court seemed to hem in the federal government by talking about interference with the reserved powers of the state; and likewise to be hemming in the states by denying that the states' reserved power (police power) could be used in dealing with economic crises. The challenges, which had been going on within the Court itself (note how many opinions were 5-4), and had also come from those actively engaged in the political process and from social scientists, now took a new turn. Franklin D. Roosevelt, re-elected to the presidency in 1936, saw this as an overwhelming vote of confidence in his New Deal legislation. In the Electoral College he carried all states but Maine and Vermont, causing his campaign manager to quip: "As Maine goes so goes Vermont." In the meantime, too, the Court had held other New Deal legislation invalid, as, for example, the Municipal Bankruptcy Act (see ASHTON v. CAMERON COUNTY DISTRICT, 298 U.S. 513) which seemed to jeopardize such other aspects of the program as the National Labor Relations Act, the Social Security Act, the Public Utility Holding Company Act—to mention a few Acts about which cases were still pending. Accordingly, on February 5, 1937, Roosevelt addressed to the Congress (H. R. Doc. No. 142, 75th Cong., 1st Session) a message calling for reorganization of the judiciary. Sarcastically referred to as the "Court Packing Plan," its full context is not a vital part of our survey. What is important here is (1) that in this oblique way the administration attempted to focus public attention on the problem as it saw it: viz., it was not the Constitution which was in the way but rather that certain Justices were reading their own economic predilections into the Constitution; (2) that in its essence, since it also applied to such Justices as Brandeis and Holmes, it alienated some of the very people who readily accepted the New Deal philosophy; (3) that it brought up again a problem with which a democracy is constantly concerned—namely, whether a judiciary is to be really independent or whether it can be made into a political football (cf. The Chase Impeachment of 1805); and (4) that though the core of the "Court Packing Plan" failed, it did produce some vital reforms in judicial organization as set forth ultimately in the Judiciary Act of 1937.

During the fray that erupted after the plan was announced, President Roosevelt in one of his famous radio fireside chats (March 9, 1937) said: "We must have men worthy and equipped to carry out impartial justice. But, at the same time, we must have Judges who will bring to the Courts a present-day sense of the Constitution— Judges who will retain in the Courts the judicial functions of a court, and reject the legislative powers which the Courts have today assumed." The case below involved an Act of 1913 passed by the Legislature of Washington, which authorized the fixing of minimum wages for women and minors by an administrative board. Maintaining that such law was in no way different from those declared void in the Adkins and Morehead cases (see pp. 108 and 203), the West Coast Hotel Company appealed from an adverse decision handed down by the Courts of the State of Washington. And since the case was the first to come up in the midst of the "Court Packing" controversy, it is perhaps well to ask who won the "battle," who the "war."

MR. CHIEF JUSTICE HUGHES delivered the opinion of the Court.

This case presents the question of the constitutional validity of the minimum wage law of the state of Washington. . . .

The appellant relies upon the decision of this Court in *Adkins* v. *Children's Hospital* . . . which held invalid the District of Columbia Minimum Wage Act which was attacked under the due process clause of the Fifth Amendment. On the argument at bar, counsel for the appellees attempted to distinguish the Adkins Case upon the ground that the appellee was employed in a hotel and that the business of an innkeeper was affected with a public interest. That effort at distinction is obviously futile, as it appears that in one of the cases ruled by the Adkins opinion the employee was a woman employed as an elevator operator in a hotel. *Adkins* v. *Lyons*, 261 U.S. 525, at p. 542.

The recent case of *Morehead* v. *New York ex rel. Tipaldo*, 298 U.S. 587, came here on certiorari to the New York court which had held the New York minimum wage act for women to be invalid. A minority of this Court thought that the New York statute was distinguishable in a material feature from that involved in the Adkins

Case, and that for that and other reasons the New York statute should be sustained. But the Court of Appeals of New York had said that it found no material difference between the two statutes and this Court held that the "meaning of the statute" as fixed by the decision of the state court "must be accepted here as if the meaning had been specifically expressed in the enactment." . . . That view led to the affirmance by this Court of the judgment in the Morehead Case, as the Court considered that the only question before it was whether the Adkins Case was distinguishable and that reconsideration of that decision had not been sought. . . .

We think that the question which was not deemed to be open in the Morehead Case is open and is necessarily presented here. The Supreme Court of Washington has upheld the minimum wage statute of that state. It has decided that the statute is a reasonable exercise of the police power of the state. In reaching that conclusion, the state court has invoked principles long established by this Court in the application of the Fourteenth Amendment. The State court has refused to regard the decision in the Adkins Case as determinative and has pointed to our decisions both before and since that case as justifying its position. We are of the opinion that this ruling of the state court demands on our part a re-examination of the Adkins Case. The importance of the question, in which many states having similar laws are concerned, the close division by which the decision in the Adkins Case was reached, and the economic conditions which have supervened, and in the light of which the reasonableness of the exercise of the protective power of the state must be considered, make it not only appropriate, but we think imperative, that in deciding the present case the subject should receive fresh consideration. . . .

The principle which must control our decision is not in doubt. The constitutional provision invoked is the due process clause of the Fourteenth Amendment governing the states, as the due process clause invoked in the Adkins Case governed Congress. In each case the violation alleged by those attacking minimum wage regulation for women is deprivation of freedom of contract. What is this freedom? The Constitution does not speak of freedom of contract. It speaks of liberty and prohibits the deprivation of liberty without due process of law. In prohibiting that deprivation the Constitution does not recognize an absolute and uncontrollable liberty. Liberty in each of its phases has its history and connotation. But the liberty safeguarded is liberty in a social organization which requires the protection of law against the evils which menace the health, safety, morals and welfare of the people. Liberty under the Constitution is thus necessarily subject to the restraints of due process, and regulation which is reasonable in relation to its subject and is adopted in the interests of the community is due process. . . .

The minimum wage to be paid under the Washington statute is

fixed after full consideration by representatives of employers, employees and the public. It may be assumed that the minimum wage is fixed in consideration of the services that are performed in the particular occupations under normal conditions. Provision is made for special licenses at less wages in the case of women who are incapable of full service. The statement of Mr. Justice Holmes in the Adkins Case is pertinent: "This statute does not compel anybody to pay anything. It simply forbids employment at rates below those fixed as the minimum requirement of health and right living. It is safe to assume that women will not be employed at even the lowest wages allowed unless they earn them, or unless the employer's business can sustain the burden. In short the law in its character and operation is like hundreds of so-called police laws that have been upheld." And Chief Justice Taft forcibly pointed out the consideration which is basic in a statute of this character: "Legislatures which adopt a requirement of maximum hours or minimum wages may be presumed to believe that when sweating employers are prevented from paying unduly low wages by positive law they will continue their business, abating that part of their profits, which were wrung from the necessities of their employees, and will concede the better terms required by the law, and that while in individual cases, hardship may result, the restriction will enure to the benefit of the general class of employees in whose interest the law is passed and so to that of the community at large." . . .

We think that the views thus expressed are sound and that the decision in the Adkins Case was a departure from the true application of the principles governing the regulation by the state of the relation of employer and employed. . . .

. . . What can be closer to the public interest than the health of women and their protection from unscrupulous and overreaching employers? And if the protection of women is a legitimate end of the exercise of state power, how can it be said that the requirement of the payment of a minimum wage fairly fixed in order to meet the very necessities of existence is not an admissible means to that end? The legislature of the state was clearly entitled to consider the situation of women in employment, the fact that they are in the class receiving the least pay, that their bargaining power is relatively weak, and that they are the ready victims of those who would take advantage of their necessitous circumstances. The legislature was entitled to adopt measures to reduce the evils of the "sweating system," the exploiting of workers at wages so low as to be insufficient to meet the bare cost of living thus making their very helplessness the occasion of a most injurious competition. The legislature had the right to consider that its minimum wage requirements would be an important aid in carrying out its policy of protection. The adoption of similar requirements by many states evidences a deep-seated conviction both as to the presence of the evil and as to the means adapted to check it. Legislative response to that conviction cannot be regarded as arbitrary or capricious and that is all we have to decide. Even if the wisdom of the policy be regarded as debatable and its effects uncertain, still the legislature is entitled to its judgment. . . .

. . . We may take judicial notice of the unparalleled demands for relief which arose during the recent period of depression and still continue to an alarming extent despite the degree of economic recovery which has been achieved. It is unnecessary to cite official statistics to establish what is of common knowledge through the length and breadth of the land. While in the instant case no factual brief has been presented, there is no reason to doubt that the state of Washington has encountered the same social problem that is present elsewhere. The community is not bound to provide what is in effect a subsidy for unconscionable employers. The community may direct its law-making power to correct the abuse which springs from their selfish disregard of the public interest. . . .

Our conclusion is that the case of *Adkins* v. *Children's Hospital* should be, and it is, overruled. The judgment of the Supreme Court of the State of Washington is

Affirmed.

MR. JUSTICE SUTHERLAND, dissenting.

MR. JUSTICE VAN DEVANTER, MR. JUSTICE McREYNOLDS, MR. JUSTICE BUTLER and I think the judgment of the court below should be reversed.

The principles and authorities relied upon to sustain the judgment, were considered in *Adkins* v. *Children's Hospital* and *Morehead* v. *New York ex rel. Tipaldo,* and their lack of application to cases like the one in hand was pointed out. A sufficient answer to all that is now said will be found in the opinions of the court in those cases. Nevertheless, in the circumstances, it seems well to restate our reasons and conclusions.

Under our form of government, where the written Constitution, by its own terms, is the supreme law, some agency, of necessity, must have the power to say the final word as to the validity of a statute assailed as unconstitutional. The Constitution makes it clear that the power has been intrusted to this Court when the question arises in a controversy within its jurisdiction; and so long as the power remains there, its exercise cannot be avoided without betrayal of the trust.

It has been pointed out many times, as in the Adkins Case, that this judicial duty is one of gravity and delicacy; and that rational doubts must be resolved in favor of the constitutionality of the statute. But whose doubts, and by whom resolved? Undoubtedly it is the duty of a member of the court, in the process of reaching a right conclusion, to give due weight to the opposing views of his associates; but in the end, the question which he must answer is not whether such views seem sound to those who entertain them, but whether they convince him that the statute is constitutional or engender in his mind a rational doubt upon that issue. The oath which he takes as a judge is not a composite oath, but an individual one. And in passing upon the validity of a statute, he discharges a duty imposed upon *him*, which cannot be consummated justly by an automatic acceptance of the views of others which have neither convinced, nor created a reasonable doubt in, his mind. If upon a question so important he thus surrender his deliberate judgment, he stands forsworn. He cannot subordinate his convictions to that extent and keep faith with his oath or retain his judicial and moral independence.

The suggestion that the only check upon the exercise of the judicial power, when properly invoked, to declare a constitutional right superior to an unconstitutional statute is the judge's own faculty of self-restraint, is both ill considered and mischievous. Self-restraint belongs in the domain of will and not of judgment. The check upon the judge is that imposed by his oath of office, by the Constitution and by his own conscientious and informed convictions; and since he has the duty to make up his own mind and adjudge accordingly, it is hard to see how there could be any other restraint. . . .

It is urged that the question involved should now receive fresh consideration, among other reasons, because of "the economic conditions which have supervened"; but the meaning of the Constitution does not change with the ebb and flow of economic events. We frequently are told in more general words that the Constitution must be construed in the light of the present. If by that it is meant that the Constitution is made up of living words that apply to every new condition which they include, the statement is quite true. But to say, if that be intended, that the words of the Constitution mean today what they did not mean when written—that is, that they do not apply to a situation now to which they would have applied then—is to rob that instrument of the essential element which continues it in force as the people have made it until they, and not their official agents, have made it otherwise. . . .

The judicial function is that of interpretation; it does not include the power of amendment under the guise of interpretation. To miss the point of difference between the two is to miss all that the phrase "supreme law of the land" stands for and to convert what was intended as inescapable and enduring mandates into mere moral reflections.

If the Constitution, intelligently and reasonably construed in the light of these principles, stands in the way of desirable legislation, the blame must rest upon that instrument, and not upon the court for enforcing it according to its terms. The remedy in that situation—and the only true remedy—is to amend the Constitution. . . .

Coming, then, to a consideration of the Washington statute, it first is to be observed that it is in every substantial respect identical with the statute involved in the Adkins Case. Such vices as existed in the latter are present in the former. And if the Adkins Case was properly decided, as we who join in this opinion think it was, it necessarily follows that the Washington statute is invalid. . . .

NATIONAL LABOR RELATIONS BOARD v. JONES & LAUGHLIN STEEL CORP.

301 U.S. 1, 81 L.Ed. 893 (1937)

Would the new alignment still hold? Mr. Justice Roberts had swung from one side to the other—some called it from conservatism to liberalism; some called it away from the traditionalists to the "present-day sense of the Constitution"; and some simply called it a swing to save the Court as an institution itself. Was this swing "real," or was it for the instant case alone? Moreover, would some distinguishing characteristic rear its ugly head so as to distinguish the minimum wage case based on state legislation from those pending before the Court based on federal legislation? Within two months, again while the controversy in the political arena still raged about "packing" the Court, the National Labor Relations Act, popularly known as the Wagner Act, came before the Court—and with it again a chance for reinterpretation of the commerce clause. In point of fact the Court had from the very beginning (see GIBBONS v. OGDEN, p. 32) permitted Congress great latitude in its exercise of power over commerce. Those instances in which the contrary was true made themselves felt precisely because they were exceptions. And what seemed to be the key in these exceptions was the fact that the Court was befuddled by "direct and indirect" effects upon commerce—a jargon that made the Court look at individual acts (like production of coal in the Carter case, p. 193) as separate and distinct from the over-all business or enterprise. In the case below the N.L.R.B., created by the National Labor Relations Act of 1935, found that the Jones & Laughlin Steel Corporation had engaged in unfair labor practices by discriminating against members of a union (The Amalgamated Association of Iron, Steel and Tin Workers of America) with regard to hire and tenure of employment, and was interfering by coercion and intimidation in union affairs. Ordered to cease and desist, to reinstate certain employees, to make good their loss of pay, etc., by the Board, the Company refused to comply where-

upon the Board petitioned the Circuit Court of Appeals to enforce the order. The Court denied the petition holding that the order (and hence the act on which the order was based) lay beyond the range of federal power. The Supreme Court granted certiorari.

MR. CHIEF JUSTICE HUGHES delivered the opinion of the Court. . . .

Contesting the ruling of the Board, the respondent argues (1) that the Act is in reality a regulation of labor relations and not of interstate commerce; (2) that the Act can have no application to the respondent's relations with its production employees because they are not subject to regulation by the federal government; and (3) that the provisions of the Act violate section 2 of Article III and the Fifth and Seventh Amendments of the Constitution of the United States.

The facts as to the nature and scope of the business of the Jones and Laughlin Steel Corporation have been found by the Labor Board, and, so far as they are essential to the determination of this controversy, they are not in dispute. The Labor Board has found: The corporation . . . is engaged in the business of manufacturing iron and steel in plants situated in Pittsburgh and nearby Aliquippa, Pa. It manufactures and distributes a widely diversified line of steel and pig iron, being the fourth largest producer of steel in the United States. With its subsidiaries—19 in number—it is a completely integrated enterprise, owning and operating ore, coal and limestone properties, lake and river transportation facilities, and terminal railroads located at its manufacturing plants. It owns or controls mines in Michigan and Minnesota. It operates four ore steamships on the Great Lakes, used in the transportation of ore to its factories. It owns coal mines in Pennsylvania. It operates towboats and steam barges used in carrying coal to its factories. It owns limestone properties in various places in Pennsylvania and West Virginia. It owns the Monongahela connecting railroad which connects the plants of the Pittsburgh works and forms an interconnection with the Pennsylvania, New York Central, and Baltimore and Ohio Railroad systems. It owns the Aliquippa and Southern Railroad Company, which connects the Aliquippa works with the Pittsburgh and Lake Erie, part of the New York Central system. Much of its product is shipped to its warehouses in Chicago, Detroit, Cincinnati, and Memphis—to the last two places by means of its own barges and transportation equipment. In Long Island City, New York, and in New Orleans it operates structural steel fabricating shops in connection with the warehousing of semi-finished materials sent from its works. Through one of its wholly owned subsidiaries it owns, leases, and operates stores, warehouses, and yards for the distribution of equipment and supplies for drilling and operating oil and gas wells and for pipe lines, refineries, and pumping stations. It has sales offices in 20 cities in the United States and a wholly owned subsidiary which is devoted exclusively to distributing its product in Canada. Approximately 75% of its product is shipped out of Pennsylvania.

Summarizing these operations, the Labor Board concluded that the works in Pittsburgh and Aliquippa "might be likened to the heart of a self-contained, highly integrated body. They draw in the raw materials from Michigan, Minnesota, West Virginia, Pennsylvania in part through arteries and by means controlled by the respondent; they transform the materials and then pump them out to all parts of the nation through the vast mechanism which the respondent has elaborated."

To carry on the activities of the entire steel industry, 33,000 men mine ore, 44,000 men mine coal, 4,000 men quarry limestone, 16,000 men manufacture coke, 343,000 men manufacture steel, and 83,000 men transport its product. Respondent has about 10,000 employees in its Aliquippa plant, which is located in a community of about 30,000 persons. . . .

First. *The scope of the Act.*—The Act is challenged in its entirety as an attempt to regulate all industry, thus invading the reserved powers of the states over their local concerns. It is asserted that the references in the Act to interstate and foreign commerce are colorable at best; that the Act is not a true regulation of such commerce or of matters which directly affect it but on the contrary has the fundamental object of placing under the compulsory supervision of the federal government all industrial labor relations within the nation. The argument seeks support in the broad words of the preamble (section 1) and in the sweep of the provisions of the Act, and it is further insisted that its legislative history shows an essential universal purpose in the light of which its scope cannot be limited by either construction or by the application of the separability clause.

If this conception of terms, intent and consequent inseparability were sound, the Act would necessarily fall by reason of the limitation upon the federal power which inheres in the constitutional grant, as well as because of the explicit reservation of the Tenth Amendment. The authority of the federal government may not be pushed to such an extreme as to destroy the distinction, which the commerce clause itself establishes, between commerce "among the several States" and the internal concerns of a state. That distinction between what is national and what is local in the activities of commerce is vital to the maintenance of our federal system. . . .

We think it clear that the National Labor Relations Act may be construed so as to operate within the sphere of constitutional authority. The jurisdiction conferred upon the Board, and invoked in this instance, is found in section 10(a), which provides:

"Sec. 10(a). The Board is empowered, as hereinafter provided, to prevent any person from engaging in any unfair labor practice affecting commerce."

The critical words of this provision, prescribing the limits of the Board's authority in dealing with the labor practices, are "affecting commerce." The Act specifically defines the "commerce" to which it refers (section 2[6]):

"The term 'commerce' means trade, traffic, commerce, transportation, or communication among the several states, or between the District of Columbia or any territory of the United States and any state or other territory, or between any foreign country and any state, territory, or the District of Columbia, or within the District of Columbia or any territory, or between points in the same state but through any other state or any territory or the District of Columbia or any foreign country."

There can be no question that the commerce thus contemplated by the Act (aside from that within a territory or the District of Columbia) is interstate and foreign commerce in the constitutional sense. The Act also defines the term "affecting commerce" (section 2[7]):

"The term 'affecting commerce' means in commerce, or burdening or obstructing commerce or the free flow of commerce, or having led or tending to lead to a labor dispute burdening or obstructing commerce or the free flow of commerce."

This definition is one of exclusion as well as inclusion. The grant of authority to the Board does not purport to extend to the relationship between all industrial employees and employers. Its terms do not impose collective bargaining upon all industry regardless of the effects upon interstate or foreign commerce. It purports to reach only what may be deemed to burden or obstruct that commerce and, thus qualified, it must be construed as contemplating the exercise of control within constitutional bounds. It is a familiar principle that acts which directly burden or obstruct interstate or foreign commerce, or its free flow, are within the reach of the congressional power. Acts having that effect are not rendered immune because they grow out of labor disputes. It is the effect upon commerce, not the source of the injury, which is the criterion. Whether or not particular action does affect commerce in such a close and intimate fashion as to be subject to federal control, and hence to lie within the authority conferred upon the Board, is left by the statute to be determined as individual cases arise. We are thus to inquire whether in the instant case the constitutional boundary has been passed.

Second. *The unfair labor practices in question.*—The unfair labor practices found by the Board are those defined in section 8, subdivisions (1) and (3). These provide:

Sec. 8. It shall be an unfair labor practice for an employer—

(1) To interfere with, restrain, or coerce employees in the exercise of the rights guaranteed in section 7. . . .

(3) By discrimination in regard to hire or tenure of employment or any

term or condition of employment to encourage or discourage membership in any labor organizations: . . .

Section 8, subdivision (1), refers to section 7, which is as follows:

Sec. 7. Employees shall have the right to self-organization, to form, join, or assist labor organizations, to bargain collectively through representatives of their own choosing, and to engage in concerted activities, for the purpose of collective bargaining or other mutual aid or protection.

Thus, in its present application, the statute goes no further than to safeguard the right of employees to self-organization and to select representatives of their own choosing for collective bargaining or other mutual protection without restraint or coercion by their employer.

That is a fundamental right. Employees have as clear a right to organize and select their representatives for lawful purposes as the respondent has to organize its business and select its own officers and agents. Discrimination and coercion to prevent the free exercise of the right of employees to self-organization and representation is a proper subject for condemnation by competent legislative authority. Long ago we stated the reason for labor organizations. We said that they were organized out of the necessities of the situation; that a single employee was helpless in dealing with an employer; that he was dependent ordinarily on his daily wage for the maintenance of himself and family; that if the employer refused to pay him the wages that he thought fair, he was nevertheless unable to leave the employ and resist arbitrary and unfair treatment; that union was essential to give laborers opportunity to deal on an equality with their employer. . . . Fully recognizing the legality of collective action on the part of employees in order to safeguard their proper interests, we said that Congress was not required to ignore this right but could safeguard it. Congress could seek to make appropriate collective action of employees an instrument of peace rather than of strife. We said that such collective action, would be a mockery if representation were made futile by interference with freedom of choice. Hence the prohibition by Congress of interference with the selection of representatives for the purpose of negotiation and conference between employers and employees, "instead of being an invasion of the constitutional right of either, was based on the recognition of the rights of both." . . .

Third. *The application of the Act to employees engaged in production.—The principle involved.*—Respondent says that whatever may be said of employees engaged in interstate commerce, the industrial relations and activities in the manufacturing department of respondent's enterprise are not subject to federal regulation. The argument rests upon the proposition that manufacturing in itself is not commerce. . . .

The government distinguishes these cases. The various parts of respondent's enterprise are described as interdependent and as thus involving "a great movement of iron ore, coal and limestone along well-defined paths to the steel mills, thence through them, and thence in the form of steel products into the consuming centers of the country—a definite and well-understood course of business." It is urged that these activities constitute a "stream" or "flow" of commerce, of which the Aliquippa manufacturing plant is the focal point, and that industrial strife at that point would cripple the entire movement. Reference is made to our decision sustaining the Packers and Stock-yards Act. *Stafford* v. *Wallace*, 258 U.S. 495. The Court found that the stockyards were but a "throat" through which the current of commerce flowed and the transactions which there occurred could not be separated from that movement. Hence the sales at the stockyards were not regarded as merely local transactions, for while they created "a local change of title" they did not "stop the flow," but merely changed the private interests in the subject of the current. . . . Applying [this] doctrine . . . the Court sustained the Grain Futures Act of 1922 with respect to transactions on the Chicago Board of Trade, although these transactions were "not in and of themselves interstate commerce." Congress had found that they had become "a constantly recurring burden and obstruction to that commerce." *Board of Trade* v. *Olsen*, 262 U.S. 1, 32.

Respondent contends that the instant case presents material distinctions. Respondent says that the Aliquippa plant is extensive in size and represents a large investment in buildings, machinery and equipment. The raw materials which are brought to the plant are delayed for long periods and after being subjected to manufacturing processes, "are changed substantially as to character, utility and value." The finished products which emerge "are to a large extent manufactured without reference to pre-existing orders and contracts and are entirely different from the raw materials which enter at the other end." Hence respondent argues that "If importation and exportation in interstate commerce do not singly transfer purely local activities into the field of congressional regulation, it should follow that their combination would not alter the local situation."

We do not find it necessary to determine whether these features of defendant's business dispose of the asserted analogy to the "stream of commerce" cases. The instances in which that metaphor has been used are but particular, and not exclusive, illustrations of the protective power which the government invokes in support of the present Act. The congressional authority to protect interstate commerce from burdens and obstructions is not limited to transactions which can be deemed to be an essential part of a "flow" of interstate or foreign commerce. Burdens and obstructions may be due to injurious action springing from other sources. The fundamental principle is that the power to regulate commerce is the power to enact "all appropriate legislation" for "its protection and advancement" . . . ; to adopt measures "to promote its growth and insure its safety" . . . ; "to foster, protect, control and restrain." . . . That power is plenary and may be exerted to protect interstate commerce "no matter what the source of the dangers which threaten it." . . . Although activities may be intrastate in character when separately considered, if they have such a close and substantial relation to interstate commerce that their control is essential or appropriate to protect that commerce from burdens and obstructions, Congress cannot be denied the power to exercise that control. Undoubtedly the scope of this power must be considered in the light of our dual system of government and may not be extended so as to embrace effects upon interstate commerce so indirect and remote that to embrace them, in view of our complex society, would effectually obliterate the distinction between what is national and what is local and create a completely centralized government. The question is necessarily one of degree. . . .

That intrastate activities, by reason of close and intimate relation to interstate commerce, may fall within federal control is demonstrated in the case of carriers who are engaged in both interstate and intrastate transportation. There federal control has been found essential to secure the freedom of interstate traffic from interference or unjust discrimination and to promote the efficiency of the interstate service. Shreveport Case (*Houston, E. and W. T. R. Co.* v. *United States*), 234 U.S. 342. It is manifest that intrastate rates deal *primarily* with a local activity. But in rate-making they bear such a close relation to interstate rates that effective control of the one must embrace some control over the other. Under the Transportation Act, 1920, Congress went so far as to authorize the Interstate Commerce Commission to establish a statewide level of intrastate rates in order to prevent an unjust discrimination against interstate commerce. . . .

The close and intimate effect which brings the subject within the reach of federal power may be due to activities in relation to productive industry although the industry when separately viewed is local. This has been abundantly illustrated in the application of the Federal Anti-Trust Act. In the *Standard Oil Co. Case*, 221 U.S. 1, and *American Tobacco Co. Case*, 221 U.S. 106, that statute was applied to combinations of employers engaged in productive industry. . . .

It is thus apparent that the fact that the employees here concerned were engaged in production is not determinative. The question remains as to the effect upon interstate commerce of the labor practice involved. In the *Schechter Case* we found that the effect there was so remote as to be beyond the federal power. To find "immediacy or directness" there was to find it "almost everywhere," a result inconsistent with the maintenance of our federal system. In the *Carter Case*, 298 U.S. 238, [in which the Bituminous Coal Conservation Act of 1935 was struck down] the Court was of the opinion that the provisions of the statute relating to production were invalid upon several grounds,—that there was improper delegation of legislative power, and that the requirements not only went beyond any sustainable measure of protection of interstate commerce but were also inconsistent with due process. These cases are not controlling here.

Fourth. *Effects of the unfair labor practice in respondent's enterprise.*—Giving full weight to respondent's contention with respect to a break in the complete continuity of the "stream of commerce" by reason of respondent's manufacturing operations, the fact remains that the stoppage of those operations by industrial strife would have a most serious effect upon interstate commerce. In view of respondent's far-flung activities, it is idle to say that the effect would be indirect or remote. It is obvious that it would be immediate and might be catastrophic. We are asked to shut our eyes to the plainest facts of our national life and to deal with the question of direct and indirect effects in an intellectual vacuum. Because there may be but indirect and remote effects upon interstate commerce in connection with a host of local enterprises throughout the country, it does not follow that other industrial activities do not have such a close and intimate relation to interstate commerce as to make the presence of industrial strife a matter of the most urgent national concern. When industries organize themselves in a national scale, making their relation to interstate commerce the dominant factor in their activities, how can it be maintained that their industrial labor relations constitute a forbidden field into which Congress may not enter when it is necessary to protect interstate commerce from the paralyzing consequences of industrial war? We have often said that interstate commerce itself is a practical conception. It is equally true that interferences with that commerce must be appraised by a judgment that does not ignore actual experience.

Experience has abundantly demonstrated that the recognition of the right of employees to self-organization and to have representatives of their own choosing for the purpose of collective bargaining is often an essential condition of industrial peace. Refusal to confer and negotiate has been one of the most prolific causes of strife. This is such an outstanding fact in the history of labor disturbances that it is a proper subject of judicial notice and requires no citation of instances. The opinion in the case of *Virginia Railway Co.* v. *System Federation No. 40* [300 U.S. 515] points out that, in the case of carriers, experience has shown that before the amendment, of 1934, of the Railway Labor Act, "when there was no dispute as to the organizations authorized to represent the employees and when there was a willingness of the employer to meet such representative for a discussion of their grievances, amicable adjustment of differences had generally followed and strikes had been avoided." That, on the other hand, "a prolific source of dispute had been the maintenance by the railroads of company unions and the denial by railway management of the authority of representatives chosen by their employees." The opinion in that case also points to the large measure of success of the labor policy embodied in the Railway Labor Act. But with respect to the appropriateness of the recognition of self-organization and representation in the promotion of peace, the question is not essentially different in the case of employees in industries of such a character that interstate commerce is put in jeopardy from the case of employees of transportation companies. And of what avail is it to protect the facility of transportation, if interstate commerce is throttled with respect to the commodities to be transported!

These questions have frequently engaged the attention of Congress and have been the subject of many inquiries. The steel industry is one of the great basic industries of the United States, with ramifying activities affecting interstate commerce at every point. The government aptly refers to the steel strike of 1919–1920 with its far-reaching consequences. The fact that there appears to have been no major disturbance in that industry in the more recent period did not dispose of the possibilities of future and like dangers to interstate commerce which Congress was entitled to foresee and to exercise its protective power to forestall. It is not necessary again to detail the facts as to respondent's enterprise. Instead of being beyond the pale, we think that it presents in a most striking way the close and intimate relation which a manufacturing industry may have to interstate commerce and we have no doubt that Congress had constitutional authority to safeguard the right of respondent's employees to self-organization and freedom in the choice of representatives for collective bargaining. . . .

MR. JUSTICE MCREYNOLDS delivered the following dissenting opinion.

MR. JUSTICE VAN DEVANTER, MR. JUSTICE SUTHERLAND, MR. JUSTICE BUTLER and I are unable to agree with the decisions just announced [including, . . . the decisions in *National Labor Relations Board* v. *Fruehauf Trailer Co.* and *National Labor Relations Board* v. *Friedman–Harry Marks Clothing Co.*]. . . .

The Court as we think departs from well-established principles followed in *Schechter* v. *The United States*, 295 U.S. 495 (May, 1935) and *Carter* v. *Carter Coal Co.*, 298 U.S. 238 (May, 1936). Upon the authority of those decisions, the Circuit Courts of Appeals of the Fifth, Sixth and Second Circuits in the causes now before us have held the power of Congress under the commerce clause does not extend to relations between employers and their employees engaged in manufacture, and therefore the Act conferred upon the National Labor Relations Board no authority in respect of matters covered by the questioned orders. . . . No decision or judicial opinion to the contrary has been cited, and we find none. Every consideration brought forward to uphold the Act before us was applicable to support the Acts held unconstitutional in causes decided within two years. And the lower courts rightly deemed them controlling. . . .

The three respondents happen to be manufacturing concerns—one large, two relatively small. The Act is now applied to each upon grounds common to all. Obviously what is determined as to these concerns may gravely affect a multitude of employers who engage in a great variety of private enterprises—mercantile, manufacturing, publishing, stockraising, mining, etc. It puts into the hands of a Board power of control over purely local industry beyond anything heretofore deemed permissible. . . .

[The Justice here reprints the decisions of the three Circuit Courts.]

V.

In each cause the Labor Board formulated and then sustained a charge of unfair labor practices towards persons employed only in production. It ordered restoration of discharged employees to former positions with payment for losses sustained. . . .

VII.

The precise question for us to determine is whether in the circumstances disclosed Congress has power to authorize what the Labor Board commanded the respondent to do. . . .

The argument in support of the Board affirms: "Thus the validity of any specific application of the preventive measures of this Act depends upon whether industrial strife resulting from the practices in the particular enterprise under consideration would be of the character which Federal power could control if it occurred. If strife in that enterprise could be controlled, certainly it could be prevented."

Manifestly that view of Congressional power would extend it into almost every field of human industry. . . .

Any effect on interstate commerce by the discharge of employees shown here, would be indirect and remote in the highest degree, as consideration of the facts will show. In No. 419 [*National Labor Relations Board* v. *Jones and Laughlin Steel Corp.*] ten men out of ten thousand were discharged; in the other cases only a few. The immediate effect in the factory may be to create discontent among all those employed and a strike may follow, which, in turn, may result in reducing production, which ultimately may reduce the volume of goods moving in interstate commerce. By this chain of indirect and progressively remote events we finally reach the evil with which it is said the legislation under consideration undertakes to deal. A more remote and indirect interference with interstate commerce or a more definite invasion of the powers reserved to the states is difficult, if not impossible, to imagine.

The Constitution still recognizes the existence of States with indestructible powers; the Tenth Amendment was supposed to put them beyond controversy.

VIII.

That Congress has power by appropriate means, not prohibited by the Constitution, to prevent direct and material interference with the conduct of interstate commerce is settled doctrine. But the interference struck at must be direct and material, not some mere possibility contingent on wholly uncertain events; and there must be no impairment of rights guaranteed. A state by taxation on property may indirectly but seriously affect the cost of transportation; it may not lay a direct tax upon the receipts from interstate transportation. The first is an indirect effect, the other direct. . . .

The things inhibited by the Labor Act relate to the management of a manufacturing plant—something distinct from commerce and subject to the authority of the state. And this may not be abridged because of some vague possibility of distant interference with commerce. . . .

The right to contract is fundamental and includes the privilege of selecting those with whom one is willing to assume contractual relations. This right is unduly abridged by the Act now upheld. A private owner is deprived of power to manage his own property by freely selecting those to whom his manufacturing operations are to be entrusted. We think this cannot lawfully be done in circumstances like those here disclosed.

It seems clear to us that Congress has transcended the powers granted.

STEWARD MACHINE CO. v. DAVIS

301 U.S. 548, 81 L.Ed. 1279 (1937)

Once the dike had been opened it was, of course, difficult to find enough "fingers" to stem the flow. This is not to imply that new administrative measures covering the New Deal were hurried to the Court. Hurried they might have been from the standpoint of drafting, but that they were all part of an over-all scheme to meet the economic crisis of the 1930's and that their existence was already known cannot be denied. One of the vital aspects of this program involved the spending power of Congress and its relationship to the general welfare clause of the Constitution. This had already been given a glancing blow in the A.A.A. case, for there it will be recalled the Court had maintained that while congressional power to tax and spend was "not limited by the direct grants of legislative power found in the Constitution," it was, however, limited in that it must concern itself with "matters of national, as distinguished from local, welfare." And of course, the Court, not Congress, was to be the ultimate determinant of this. In the case below the Court was confronted with the unemployment section of the Social Security Act of 1935 (see Titles III and IX, 49 Stat. at Large 620), which required that employers of eight or more workers pay a federal excise tax based on their annual payroll. The tax-payer was permitted to credit against the federal tax up to 90 per cent of the amount contributed by him to state unemployment funds, provided only that the state law met federal standards. The Steward Machine Company paid the tax, and then sought a refund in the District Court. The adverse judgment of the District Court was sustained by the Circuit Court, but the Supreme Court granted certiorari because of a conflict with a decision in another Circuit. For our purposes this case is important because (1) it sets up the proposition that unemployment is a problem of national concern; (2) it permits the nation and state to co-operate lawfully to meet the problem; (3) it clearly enunciates the doctrine—when read together with the decision in HELVERING v. DAVIS, *301 U.S. 619, decided the same day and dealing with the old-age section of the Act—that what pertains to the general welfare "belongs to Congress [to decide] unless the choice is clearly wrong, a display of arbitrary power, not an exercise of judgment"; and (4) it allows the majority decision of Mr. Justice Cardozo to serve as an excellent résumé of all the shibboleths which have run through so many of these cases.*

MR. JUSTICE CARDOZO delivered the opinion of the Court. . . .

The assault on the statute proceeds on an extended front. Its assailants take the ground that the tax is not an excise; that it is not uniform throughout the United States as excises are required to be; that its exceptions are so many and arbitrary as to violate the Fifth Amendment; that its purpose was not revenue, but an unlawful invasion of the reserved powers of the states; and that the states in submitting to it have yielded to coercion and have abandoned governmental functions which they are not permitted to surrender.

The objections will be considered seriatim with such further explanation as may be necessary to make their meaning clear.

First: The tax, which is described in the statute as an excise, is laid with uniformity throughout the United States as a duty, an impost or an excise upon the relation of employment.

1. We are told that the relation of employment is one so essential to the pursuit of happiness that it may not be burdened with a tax. Appeal is made to history. From the precedents of colonial days we are supplied with illustrations of excises common in the colonies. They are said to have been bound up with the enjoyment of particular commodities. Appeal is also made to principle or the analysis of concepts. An excise, we are told, imports a tax upon a privilege; employment, it is said, is the right, not a privilege, from which it follows that employment is not subject to an excise. Neither the one appeal nor the other leads to the desired goal. . . .

The historical prop failing, the prop or fancied prop of principle remains. We learn that employment for lawful gain is a "natural" or "inherent" or "inalienable" right, and not a "privilege" at all. But natural rights, so called, are as much subject to taxation as rights of less importance. An excise is not limited to vocations or activities that may be prohibited altogether. It is not limited to those that are the outcome of a franchise. It extends to vocations or activities pursued as of common right. What the individual does in the operation of a business is amenable to taxation just as much as what he owns, at all events if the classification is not tyrannical or arbitrary. . . .

The subject matter of taxation open to the power of the Congress is as comprehensive as that open to the power of the states, though the method of apportionment may at times be different. "The Congress shall have power to lay and collect taxes, duties, imposts and excises." Art. 1, Sec. 8. If the tax is a direct one, it shall be apportioned according to the census or enumeration. If it is a duty, impost, or excise, it shall be uniform throughout the United States. Together these classes include every form of tax appropriate to sovereignty. . . . Whether the tax is to be classified as an "excise" is in truth not of critical importance. If not that, it is an "impost." . . . A capitation or other "direct" tax it certainly is not. "Although there have been from time to time intimations that there might be some tax which was not a direct tax nor included under the words 'duties, imposts, and excises,' such a tax for more than one hundred years of national existence has as yet remained undiscovered, notwithstanding the stress of particular circumstances has invited thorough investigation into sources of powers." . . .

2. The tax being an excise, its imposition must conform to the canon of uniformity. There has been no departure from this requirement. According to the settled doctrine the uniformity exacted is geographical, not intrinsic. . . .

Second: The excise is not invalid under the provisions of the Fifth Amendment by force of its exemptions.

The statute does not apply, as we have seen, to employers of less than eight. It does not apply to agricultural labor, or domestic service in a private home or to some other classes of less importance. Petitioner contends that the effect of these restrictions is an arbitrary discrimination vitiating the tax. . . .

The Fifth Amendment unlike the Fourteenth has no equal protection clause. . . . But even the states, though subject to such a clause, are not confined to a formula of rigid uniformity in framing measures of taxation. . . . They may tax some kinds of property at one rate, and others at another, and exempt others altogether. . . .

The classifications and exemptions directed by the statute now in controversy have support in considerations of policy and practical convenience that cannot be condemned as arbitrary. The classifications and exemptions would therefore be upheld if they had been adopted by a state and the provisions of the Fourteenth Amendment were invoked to annul them. . . .

Third: The excise is not void as involving the coercion of the states in contravention to the Tenth Amendment or of restrictions implicit in our federal form of government.

The proceeds of the excise when collected are paid into the Treasury at Washington, and thereafter are subject to appropriation like public moneys generally. *Cincinnati Soap Co.* v. *United States,* 301 U.S. 308. No presumption can be indulged that they will be misapplied or wasted. Even if they were collected in the hope or expectation that some other and collateral good would be furthered as an incident, that without more would not make the act invalid. *Sonzinsky* v. *United States,* 300 U.S. 506. This indeed is hardly questioned. The case for the petitioner is built on the contention that here an ulterior aim is wrought into the very structure of the act, and what is even more important that the aim is not only ulterior, but essentially unlawful. In particular, the 90 per cent credit is relied upon as supporting that conclusion. But before the statute succumbs to an assault upon these lines, two propositions must be made out by the assailant. . . . There must be a showing in the first place that separated from the credit the revenue provisions are incapable of standing by themselves. There must be a showing in the second place that the tax and the credit in combination are weapons of coercion, destroying or impairing the autonomy of the states. The truth of each proposition being essential to the success of the assault, we pass for convenience to a consideration of the second, without pausing to inquire whether there has been a demonstration of the first.

To draw the line intelligently between duress and inducement there is need to remind ourselves of facts as to the problem of unemployment that are now matters of common knowledge. . . .

In the presence of this urgent need for some remedial expedient, the question is to be answered whether the expedient adopted has overleapt the bounds of power. The assailants of the statute say that its dominant end and aim is to drive the state legislatures under the whip of economic pressure into the enactment of unemployment compensation laws at the bidding of the central government. Supporters of the statute say that its operation is not constraint, but the creation of a larger freedom, the states and the nation joining in a coöperative endeavor to avert a common evil. . . .

The Social Security Act is an attempt to find a method by which all these public agencies may work together to a common end. Every dollar of the new taxes will continue in all likelihood to be used and needed by the nation as long as states are unwilling, whether through timidity or for other motives, to do what can be done at home. At least the inference is permissible that Congress so believed, though retaining undiminished freedom to spend the money as it pleased. On the other hand fulfilment of the home duty will be lightened and encouraged by crediting the taxpayer upon his account with the Treasury of the nation to the extent that his contributions under the laws of the locality have simplified or diminished the problem of relief and the probable demand upon the resources of the fisc. Duplicated taxes, or burdens that approach them, are recognized hardships that government, state or national, may properly avoid. . . . If Congress believed that the general welfare would better be promoted by relief through local units than by the system then in vogue, the cooperating localities ought not in all fairness to pay a second time.

Who then is coerced through the operation of this statute? Not the taxpayer. He pays in fulfilment of the mandate of the local legislature. Not the state. Even now she does not offer a suggestion that in passing the unemployment law she was affected by duress. . . . For all that appears she is satisfied with her choice, and would be sorely disappointed if it were now to be annulled. The difficulty with the petitioner's contention is that it confuses motive with coercion. "Every tax is in some measure regulatory. To some extent it interposes an economic impediment to the activity taxed as compared with others not taxed." In like manner every rebate from a tax when conditioned upon conduct is in some measure a temptation. But to hold that motive or temptation is equivalent to coercion is to plunge the law in endless difficulties. The outcome of such a doctrine is the acceptance of a philosophical determinism by which choice becomes impossible. Till now the law has been guided by a robust common sense which assumes the freedom of the will as a working hypothesis in the solution of its problems. The wisdom of the hypothesis has illustration in this case. Nothing in the case suggests the exertion of a power akin to undue influence, if we assume that such a concept can ever be applied with fitness to the relations between state and nation. Even on that assumption the location of the point at which pressure turns into compulsion, and ceases to be inducement, would be a question of degree,—at times, perhaps, of fact. The point had not been reached when Alabama made her choice. We cannot say that she was acting, not of her unfettered will, but under the strain of a persuasion equivalent to undue influence, when she chose to have relief administered under laws of her own making, by agents of her own selection, instead of under federal laws, administered by federal officers, with all the ensuing evils, at least to many minds, of federal patronage and power. There would be a strange irony, indeed, if her choice were now to be annulled on the basis of an assumed duress in the enactment of a statute which her courts have accepted as a true expression of her will. . . . We think the choice must stand. . . .

Fourth: The statute does not call for a surrender by the states of powers essential to their quasi-sovereign existence. . . .

A credit to taxpayers for payments made to a state under a state unemployment law will be manifestly futile in the absence of some assurance that the law leading to the credit is in truth what it professes to be. An unemployment law framed in such a way that the unemployed who look to it will be deprived of reasonable protection is one in name and nothing more. What is basic and essential may be assured by suitable conditions. The terms embodied in these sections are directed to that end. A wide range of judgment is given to the several states as to the particular type of statute to be spread upon their books. For anything to the contrary in the provisions of this act they may use the pooled unemployment form, which is in effect with variations in Alabama, California, Michigan, New York, and elsewhere. They may establish a system of merit ratings applicable at once or to go into effect later on the basis of subsequent experience. . . . They may provide for employee contributions as in Alabama and California, or put the entire burden upon the employer as in New York. They may choose a system of unemployment reserve accounts by which an employer is permitted after his reserve has accumulated to contribute at a reduced rate or even not at all. This is the system which had its origin in Wisconsin. What they may not do, if they would earn the credit, is to depart from those standards which in the judgment of Congress are to be ranked as fundamental. Even if opinion may differ as to the fundamental quality of one or more of the conditions, the difference will not avail to vitiate the statute. In determining essentials Congress must have the benefit of a fair margin of discretion. One cannot say with reason that this margin has been exceeded, or that the basic standards have been determined in any arbitrary fashion. In the event that some particular condition shall be found to be too uncertain to be capable of enforcement, it may be severed from the others, and what is left will still be valid. . . .

There are very good reasons of fiscal and governmental policy why a state should be willing to make the Secretary of the Treasury the custodian of the fund. His possession of the moneys and his control of investments will be an assurance of stability and safety in times of stress and strain. A report of the Ways and Means Committee of the House of Representatives . . . develops the situation clearly. Nor is there risk of loss or waste. The credit of the Treasury is at all times back of the deposit, with the result that the right of withdrawal will be unaffected by the fate of any intermediate investments, just as if a checking account in the usual form had been opened in a bank. . . .

The judgment is *Affirmed.*

Separate opinion of MR. JUSTICE McREYNOLDS [dissenting] . . .

No defense is offered for the legislation under review upon the basis of emergency. The hypothesis is that hereafter it will continuously benefit unemployed members of a class. Forever, so far as we can see, the states are expected to function under federal direction concerning an internal matter. By the sanction of this adventure, the door is open for progressive inauguration of others of like kind under which it can hardly be expected that the states will retain genuine independence of action. And without independent states a Federal Union as contemplated by the Constitution becomes impossible.

At the bar counsel asserted that under the present Act the tax upon residents of Alabama during the first year will total $9,000,000. All would remain in the Federal Treasury but for the adoption by the state of measures agreeable to the National Board. If continued, these will bring relief from the payment of $8,000,000 to the United States.

Ordinarily, I must think, a denial that the challenged action of Congress and what has been done under it amount to coercion and impair freedom of government by the people of the state would be regarded as contrary to practical experience. Unquestionably our federate plan of government confronts an enlarged peril.

Separate opinion of Mr. Justice Sutherland, dissenting. . . .

. . . The effect of the dual distribution of powers is completely to deny to the states whatever is granted exclusively to the nation, and, conversely, to deny to the nation whatever is reserved exclusively to the states. "The determination of the Framers Convention and the ratifying conventions to preserve complete and unimpaired state self-government in all matters not committed to the general government is one of the plainest facts which emerge from the history of their deliberations. And adherence to that determination is incumbent equally upon the federal government and the states. State powers can neither be appropriated on the one hand nor abdicated on the other." *Carter* v. *Carter Coal Co.* . . . The purpose of the Constitution in that regard does not admit of doubt or qualification; and it can be thwarted no more by voluntary surrender from within than by invasion from without.

Nor may the constitutional objection suggested be overcome by the expectation of public benefit resulting from the federal participation authorized by the act. Such expectation, if voiced in support of a proposed constitutional enactment, would be quite proper for the consideration of the legislative body. But, as we said in the Carter case, "nothing is more certain than that beneficent aims, however great or well directed, can never serve in lieu of constitutional power." Moreover, everything which the act seeks to do for the relief of unemployment might have been accomplished, as is done by this same act for the relief of the misfortunes of old age, without obliging the state to surrender, or share with another government, any of its powers.

If we are to survive as the United States, the balance between the powers of the nation and those of the states must be maintained. There is grave danger in permitting it to dip in either direction, danger —if there were no other—in the precedent thereby set for further departures from the equipoise. The threat implicit in the present encroachment upon the administrative functions of the states is that greater encroachments, and encroachments upon other functions, will follow.

For the foregoing reasons, I think the judgment . . . should be reversed.

Mr. Justice Van Devanter joins in this opinion.

Mr. Justice Butler, dissenting. . . .

I am also of the opinion that, in principle and as applied to bring about and to gain control over state unemployment compensation, the statutory scheme is repugnant to the Tenth Amendment: "The powers not delegated to the United States by the Constitution, nor prohibited by it to the States, are reserved to the States respectively, or to the people." The Constitution grants to the United States no power to pay unemployed persons or to require the states to enact laws or to raise or disburse money for that purpose. The provisions in question, if not amounting to coercion in a legal sense, are manifestly designed and intended directly to affect state action in the respects specified. And, if valid as so employed, this "tax and credit" device may be made effective to enable federal authorities to induce, if not indeed to compel, state enactments for any purpose within the realm of state power, and generally to control state administration of state laws. . . .

Federal agencies prepared and took draft bills to state legislatures to enable and induce them to pass laws providing for unemployment compensation in accordance with federal requirements, and thus to obtain relief for the employers from the impending federal exaction. Obviously the Act creates the peril of federal tax not to raise revenue but to persuade. Of course, each state was free to reject any measure so proposed. But, if it failed to adopt a plan acceptable to federal authority, the full burden of the federal tax would be exacted. And, as federal demands similarly conditioned may be increased from time to time as Congress shall determine, possible federal pressure in that field is without limit. Already at least 43 states, yielding to the inducement resulting immediately from the application of the federal tax and credit device, have provided for unemployment compensation in form to merit approval of the Social Security Board. Presumably the remaining states will comply whenever convenient for their legislatures to pass the necessary laws.

The terms of the measure make it clear that the tax and credit device was intended to enable federal officers virtually to control the exertion of powers of the states in a field in which they alone have jurisdiction and from which the United States is by the Constitution excluded.

I am of opinion that the judgment of the Circuit Court of Appeals should be reversed.

UNITED STATES v. DARBY

312 U.S. 100, 85 L.Ed. 6091 (1941)

From a very important point of view these New Deal cases demonstrate, at one and the same time, a unity and a diversity within our Court history. For the problem, on one basic level at least, is no more than that of dual federalism versus national supremacy; of Mr. Chief Justice Taney versus Mr. Chief Justice Marshall; of the Tenth Amendment versus the delegated and enumerated powers of Article I, Section 8. Their unity to the past then becomes clear but their diversity in result is still a vital question concerning us and one that makes its appearance on fronts other than economic. The instant case involves The Fair Labor Standards Act of 1938 (also called the Wages and Hours Act, see 52 Stat. at Large 1060, ch. 676), the last major piece of New Deal legislation. In that measure, Congress made it unlawful to ship in interstate commerce goods produced in violation of the wage and hour standards of the Act, which by its own terms was to be applied only to "employees engaged in commerce or in the production of goods for commerce" and hence was not as broad as the Wagner Act which dealt on a larger canvas with unfair labor practices "affecting commerce." The Darby Lumber Company was indicted under the Act because they paid their employees less than the minimum wage of 25 cents per hour and worked them more than the hours set without paying overtime. The District Court sustained a demurrer and quashed the indictment on the ground that the Act was unconstitutional, and the case comes to the Supreme Court on direct appeal as provided for under Section 238 of the Judicial Code. The impact of this decision on the whole question of the relationship of health, morals, police power, etc., as seen, for example, in HAMMER v. DAGEN-HART *and other cases, is too obvious to warrant discussion—public power should be as broad as necessary to meet urgent public needs. What should perhaps be pointed out in passing is the lack of any dissent which, in turn, in view of what the decision below states explicitly and implies just as forcibly, raises the question as to why this is so.*

MR. JUSTICE STONE delivered the opinion of the Court.

The two principal questions raised by the record in this case are, *first*, whether Congress has constitutional power to prohibit the shipment in interstate commerce of lumber manufactured by employees whose wages are less than a prescribed minimum or whose weekly hours of labor at that wage are greater than a prescribed maximum, and, *second*, whether it has power to prohibit the employment of workmen in the production of goods "for interstate commerce" at other than prescribed wages and hours. A subsidiary question is whether in connection with such prohibitions Congress can require the employer subject to them to keep records showing the hours worked each day and week by each of his employees including those engaged "in the production and manufacture of goods to-wit, lumber, for 'interstate commerce.'" . . .

The demurrer, so far as now relevant to the appeal, challenged the validity of the Fair Labor Standards Act under the Commerce Clause and the Fifth and Tenth Amendments. The district court quashed the indictment in its entirety upon the broad grounds that the Act, which it interpreted as a regulation of manufacture within the states, is unconstitutional. It declared that manufacture is not interstate commerce and that the regulation by the Fair Labor Standards Act of wages and hours of employment of those engaged in the manufacture of goods which it is intended at the time of production "may or will be" after production "sold in interstate commerce in part or in whole" is not within the congressional power to regulate interstate commerce. . . .

The prohibition of shipment of the proscribed goods in interstate commerce. Section 15(a) (1) prohibits, and the indictment charges, the shipment in interstate commerce, of goods produced for interstate commerce by employees whose wages and hours of employment do not conform to the requirements of the Act. Since this section is not violated unless the commodity shipped has been produced under labor conditions prohibited by Sec. 6 and Sec. 7, the only question arising under the commerce clause with respect to such shipments is whether Congress has the constitutional power to prohibit them.

While manufacture is not of itself interstate commerce, the shipment of manufactured goods interstate is such commerce and the prohibition of such shipment by Congress is indubitably a regulation of the commerce. The power to regulate commerce is the power "to prescribe the rule by which commerce is governed." *Gibbons* v. *Ogden*, 9 Wheat. 1, 196. It extends not only to those regulations which aid, foster and protect the commerce, but embraces those which prohibit it. *Lottery Case*, 188 U.S. 321. It is conceded that the power of Congress to prohibit transportation in interstate commerce includes noxious articles, stolen articles, kidnapped persons, and articles such as intoxicating liquor or convict made goods, traffic in which is forbidden or restricted by the laws of the state of destination. *Kentucky Whip and Collar Co.* v. *Illinois Central R. Co.*, 299 U.S. 334.

But it is said that the present prohibition falls within the scope of none of these categories; that while the prohibition is nominally a regulation of the commerce its motive or purpose is regulation of wages and hours of persons engaged in manufacture, the control of which has been reserved to the states and upon which Georgia and some of the states of destination have placed no restriction; that the effect of the present statute is not to exclude the proscribed articles from interstate commerce in aid of state regulation as in

Kentucky Whip and Collar Co. v. *Illinois Central R. Co.*, but instead, under the guise of a regulation of interstate commerce, it undertakes to regulate wages and hours within the state contrary to the policy of the state which has elected to leave them unregulated.

The power of Congress over interstate commerce "is complete in itself, may be exercised to its utmost extent, and acknowledges no limitations other than are prescribed in the Constitution." . . . That power can neither be enlarged nor diminished by the exercise or non-exercise of state power. . . . Congress, following its own conception of public policy concerning the restrictions which may appropriately be imposed on interstate commerce, is free to exclude from the commerce articles whose use in the states for which they are destined it may conceive to be injurious to the public health, morals or welfare, even though the state has not sought to regulate their use. . . .

Such regulation is not a forbidden invasion of state power merely because either its motive or its consequence is to restrict the use of articles of commerce within the states of destination; and is not prohibited unless by other Constitutional provisions. It is no objection to the assertion of the power to regulate interstate commerce that its exercise is attended by the same incidents which attend the exercise of the police power of the states. . . .

The motive and purpose of the present regulation are plainly to make effective the Congressional conception of public policy that interstate commerce should not be made the instrument of competition in the distribution of goods produced under substandard labor conditions, which competition is injurious to the commerce and to the states from and to which the commerce flows. The motive and purpose of a regulation of interstate commerce are matters for the legislative judgment upon the exercise of which the Constitution places no restriction and over which the courts are given no control. . . . "The judicial cannot prescribe to the legislative department of the government limitations upon the exercise of its acknowledged power." *Veazie Bank* v. *Fenno*, 8 Wall. 533. Whatever their motive and purpose, regulations of commerce which do not infringe some constitutional prohibition are within the plenary power conferred on Congress by the Commerce Clause. Subject only to that limitation, presently to be considered, we conclude that the prohibition of the shipment interstate of goods produced under the forbidden substandard labor conditions is within the constitutional authority of Congress.

In the more than a century which has elapsed since the decision of *Gibbons* v. *Ogden*, these principles of constitutional interpretation have been so long and repeatedly recognized by this Court as applicable to the Commerce Clause, that there would be little occasion for repeating them now were it not for the decision of this Court twenty-two years ago in *Hammer* v. *Dagenhart*, 247 U.S. 251. In that case it was held by a bare majority of the Court over the powerful and now classic dissent of Mr. Justice Holmes setting forth the fundamental issues involved, that Congress was without power to exclude the products of child labor from interstate commerce. The reasoning and conclusion of the Court's opinion there cannot be reconciled with the conclusion which we have reached, that the power of Congress under the Commerce Clause is plenary to exclude any article from interstate commerce subject only to the specific prohibitions of the Constitution.

Hammer v. *Dagenhart* has not been followed. The distinction on which the decision was rested that Congressional power to prohibit interstate commerce is limited to articles which in themselves have some harmful or deleterious property—a distinction which was novel when made and unsupported by any provision of the Constitution—has long since been abandoned. The thesis of the opinion that the motive of the prohibition or its effect to control in some measure the use or production within the states of the article thus excluded from the commerce can operate to deprive the regulation of its constitutional authority has long since ceased to have force. And finally we have declared "The authority of the federal government over interstate commerce does not differ in extent or character from that retained by the states over intrastate commerce." *United States* v. *Rock Royal Co-operative*, 307 U.S. 533, 569.

The conclusion is inescapable that *Hammer* v. *Dagenhart* was a departure from the principles which have prevailed in the interpretation of the Commerce Clause both before and since the decision and that such vitality, as a precedent, as it then had has long since been exhausted. It should be and now is overruled.

Validity of the wage and hour requirements. Section 15(a) (2) and Secs. 6 and 7 require employers to conform to the wage and hour provisions with respect to all employees engaged in the production of goods for interstate commerce. As appellee's employees are not alleged to be "engaged in intrastate commerce" the validity of the prohibition turns on the question whether the employment, under other than the prescribed labor standards, of employees engaged in the production of goods for interstate commerce is so related to the commerce and so affects it as to be within the reach of the power of Congress to regulate it. . . .

There remains the question whether such restriction on the production of goods for commerce is a permissible exercise of the commerce power. The power of Congress over interstate commerce is not confined to the regulation of commerce among the states. It extends to those activities intrastate which so affect interstate commerce or the exercise of the power of Congress over it as to make regulation of them appropriate means to the attainment of a legitimate end, the exercise of the granted power of Congress to regulate interstate commerce. . . .

While this Court has many times found state regulation of interstate commerce, when uniformity of its regulation is of national concern, to be incompatible with the Commerce Clause even though Congress has not legislated on the subject, the Court has never implied such restraint on state control over matters intrastate not deemed to be regulations of interstate commerce or its instrumentalities even though they affect the commerce. In the absence of Congressional legislation on the subject state laws which are not regulations of the commerce itself or its instrumentalities are not forbidden even though they affect interstate commerce.

But it does not follow that Congress may not by appropriate legislation regulate intrastate activities where they have a substantial effect on interstate commerce. A recent example is the National Labor Relations Act for the regulation of employer and employee relations in industries in which strikes, induced by unfair labor practices named in the Act, tend to disturb or obstruct interstate commerce. See *National Labor Relations Board* v. *Jones and Laughlin Steel Corp.*, 301 U.S. 1, 38, 40. But long before the adoption of the National Labor Relations Act this Court had many times held that the power of Congress to regulate interstate commerce extends to the regulation through legislative action of activities intrastate which have a substantial effect on the commerce or the exercise of the Congressional power over it.

In such legislation Congress has sometimes left it to the courts to determine whether the intrastate activities have the prohibited effect on the commerce, as in the Sherman Act. It has sometimes left it to an administrative board or agency to determine whether the activities sought to be regulated or prohibited have such effect, as in the case of the Interstate Commerce Act, and the National Labor Relations Act, or whether they come within the statutory definition of the prohibited Act, as in the Federal Trade Commission Act. And sometimes Congress itself has said that a particular activity affects the commerce, as it did in the present Act, the Safety Appliance Act and the Railway Labor Act. In passing on the validity of legislation of the class last mentioned the only function of courts is to determine whether the particular activity regulated or prohibited is within the reach of the federal power.

Congress, having by the present Act adopted the policy of excluding from interstate commerce all goods produced for the commerce which do not conform to the specified labor standards, it may choose the means reasonably adapted to the attainment of the permitted end, even though they involve control of intrastate activities. Such legislation has often been sustained with respect to powers, other than the commerce power granted to the national government, when the means chosen, although not themselves within the granted power, were nevertheless deemed appropriate aids to the accomplishment of some purpose within an admitted power of the national government. A familiar like exercise of power is the regulation of intrastate transactions which are so commingled with or related to interstate commerce that all must be regulated if the interstate commerce is to be effectively controlled. *Shreveport Case*, 234 U.S. 342. Similarly Congress may require inspection and preventive treatment of all cattle in a disease infected area in order to prevent shipment in interstate commerce of some of the cattle without the treatment. It may prohibit the removal, at destination, of labels required by the Pure Food and Drugs Act to be affixed to articles transported in interstate commerce. And we have recently held that Congress in the exercise of its power to require inspection and grading of tobacco shipped in interstate commerce may compel such inspection and grading of all tobacco sold at local auction rooms from which a substantial part but not all of the tobacco sold is shipped in interstate commerce.

We think also that Sec. 15(a) (2), now under consideration, is sustainable independently of Sec. 15(a) (1), which prohibits shipment or transportation of the proscribed goods. As we have said the evils aimed at by the Act are the spread of substandard labor conditions through the use of the facilities of interstate commerce for competition by the goods so produced with those produced under the prescribed or better labor conditions; and the consequent dislocation of the commerce itself caused by the impairment or destruction of local businesses by competition made effective through interstate commerce. The Act is thus directed at the suppression of a method or kind of competition in interstate commerce which it has in effect condemned as "unfair," as the Clayton Act has condemned other "unfair methods of competition" made effective through interstate commerce.

The Sherman Act and the National Labor Relations Act are familiar examples of the exertion of the commerce power to prohibit or control activities wholly intrastate because of their effect on interstate commerce.

The means adopted by Sec. 15(a) (2) for the protection of interstate commerce by the suppression of the production of the condemned goods for interstate commerce is so related to the commerce and so affects it as to be within the reach of the commerce power. Congress, to attain its objective in the suppression of nationwide competition in interstate commerce by goods produced under substandard labor conditions, has made no distinction as to the volume or amount of shipments in the commerce or of production for commerce by any particular shipper or producer. It recognized that in present day industry, competition by a small part may affect the whole and that the total effect of the competition of many small producers may be great. . . .

So far as *Carter* v. *Carter Coal Co.*, 298 U.S. 238, is inconsistent with this conclusion, its doctrine is limited in principle by the decisions under the Sherman Act and the National Labor Relations Act, which we have cited and which we follow.

Our conclusion is unaffected by the Tenth Amendment which provides: "The powers not delegated to the United States by the Constitution, nor prohibited by it to the States, are reserved to the States respectively, or to the people." The amendment states but a truism that all is retained which has not been surrendered. There is nothing in the history of its adoption to suggest that it was more than declaratory of the relationship between the national and state governments as it had been established by the Constitution before the amendment or that its purpose was other than to allay fears that the new national government might seek to exercise powers not granted, and that the states might not be able to exercise fully their reserved powers.

From the beginning and for many years the amendment has been construed as not depriving the national government of authority to resort to all means for the exercise of a granted power which are appropriate and plainly adapted to the permitted end. Whatever doubts may have arisen of the soundness of that conclusion, they have been put at rest by the decisions under the Sherman Act and the National Labor Relations Act which we have cited.

Validity of the requirement of records of wages and hours. Sec. 15(a) (5) and Sec. 11(c). These requirements are incidental to those for the prescribed wages and hours, and hence validity of the former turns on validity of the latter. Since, as we have held, Congress may require production for interstate commerce to conform to those conditions, it may require the employer, as a means of enforcing the valid law, to keep a record showing whether he has in fact complied with it. The requirement for records even of the intrastate transaction is an appropriate means to the legitimate end. . . .

Validity of the wage and hour provisions under the Fifth Amendment. Both provisions are minimum wage requirements compelling the payment of a minimum standard wage with a prescribed increased wage for overtime of "not less than one and one-half times the regular rate" at which the worker is employed. Since our decision in *West Coast Hotel Co.* v. *Parrish,* 300 U.S. 379, it is no longer open to question that the fixing of a minimum wage is within the legislative power and that the bare fact of its exercise is not a denial of due process under the Fifth more than under the Fourteenth Amendment. Nor is it any longer open to question that it is within the legislative power to fix maximum hours. Similarly the statute is not objectionable because applied alike to both men and women. . . .

The Act is sufficiently definite to meet constitutional demands. One who employs persons, without conforming to the prescribed wage and hour conditions, to work on goods which he ships or expects to ship across state lines, is warned that he may be subject to the criminal penalties of the Act. No more is required. . . .

We have considered, but find it unnecessary to discuss other contentions.

Reversed.

YAKUS v. UNITED STATES

321 U.S. 414, 88 L.Ed. 834 (1944)

It is a truism, requiring little or no comment, that economic forces are subject not alone to the so-called "boom and bust" cycle of prosperity and depression, but also to the exigencies connected with what is euphemistically referred to as a "war economy." But to this must also be added new considerations which come into play during a war and which are not in evidence at any other time. These forces, which by the very nature of their being add a complexity to the problems, are, of course, concerned with the need for greater concentration of power in the hands of the executive office for speed of action, and for a procedure of action that would not be disruptive to the vital goal sought to be achieved—to win the war by using economic measures as a part of the strategy involving total mobilization. The case below focuses on these problems by examining the congressional authority given to the Office of Price Administration (OPA) to fix maximum prices under the Emergency Price Control Act of 1942. Under Revised Maximum Price Regulation 169 specific maximum prices for the sale at wholesale of specified cuts of veal and beef were established. Under the Act anyone who thought the price established to be unfair could protest and receive a hearing before the Administrator, whose decision was reviewable by the Emergency Court of Appeals and on certiorari by the Supreme Court. But no temporary injunction could issue against the order until after the Emergency Court of Appeals had heard the case on its merits, and appeals taken by the Administrator would postpone even further the application for an injunction. Moreover, the trial courts, state and federal, were denied the power to examine the validity of any regulation, order, or price schedule, in any criminal prosecutions instituted under the Act. Yakus was convicted of several violations, and without availing himself of the special appeal features of the Act attempted to raise the issue of the constitutionality of the Act. While the extract below deals essentially with the problem of delegation and procedure, it should be borne in mind that the Court upheld the Price Control Act of 1942, and that this case in conjunction with BOWLES v. WILLINGHAM, 321 U.S. 503—which was also decided in 1944 and which upheld rent controls—expresses well the whole attitude of wartime powers in this economic sphere.

Opinion of the Court by MR. CHIEF JUSTICE STONE, announced by MR. JUSTICE ROBERTS. . . .

That Congress has constitutional authority to prescribe commodity prices as a war emergency measure, and that the Act was adopted by Congress in the exercise of that power, are not questioned here, and need not now be considered save as they have a bearing on the procedural features of the Act later to be considered which are challenged on constitutional grounds. . . .

We come to the question whether the provisions of the Act, so construed as to deprive petitioners of opportunity to attack the Regulation in a prosecution for its violation, deprive them of the due process of law guaranteed by the Fifth Amendment. At the trial, petitioners offered to prove that the Regulation would compel them to sell beef at such prices as would render it impossible for wholesalers such as they are, no matter how efficient, to conduct their business other than at a loss. Section 4(d) declares that "Nothing in this Act shall be construed to require any person to sell any commodity. . . ." Petitioners were therefore not required by the Act, nor so far as appears by any other rule of law, to continue selling meat at wholesale if they could not do so without loss. But they argue that to impose on them the choice either of refraining from sales of beef at wholesale or of running the risk of numerous criminal prosecutions and suits for treble damages authorized by Sec. 205(e), without the benefit of any temporary injunction or stay pending determination by the prescribed statutory procedure of the Regulation's validity, is so harsh in its application to them as to deny them due process of law. In addition they urge the inadequacy of the administrative procedure and particularly of the sixty days' period afforded by the Act within which to prepare and lodge a protest with the Administrator.

In considering these asserted hardships, it is appropriate to take into account the purposes of the Act and the circumstances attending its enactment and application as a wartime emergency measure. The Act was adopted January 30, 1942, shortly after our declaration of war against Germany and Japan, when it was common knowledge, as is emphasized by the legislative history of the Act, that there was grave danger of wartime inflation and the disorganization of our economy from excessive price rises. Congress was under pressing necessity of meeting this danger by a practicable and expeditious means which would operate with such promptness, regularity and consistency as would minimize the sudden development of commodity price disparities, accentuated by commodity shortages occasioned by the war. . . .

Congress, in enacting the Emergency Price Control Act, was familiar with the consistent history of delay in utility rate cases. It had in mind the dangers to price control as a preventive of inflation if the validity and effectiveness of prescribed maximum prices were to be subject to the exigencies and delays of litigation originating in eighty-five district courts and continued by separate appeals through eleven separate courts of appeals to this Court, to say nothing of litigation conducted in state courts. . . .

Congress sought to avoid or minimize these difficulties by the establishment of a single procedure for review of the Administrator's regulations, beginning with an appeal to the Administrator's specialized knowledge and experience gained in the administration of the Act, and affording to him an opportunity to modify the regulations and orders complained of before resort to judicial determination of their validity. The organization of such an exclusive procedure especially adapted to the exigencies and requirements of a nationwide scheme of price regulation is, as we have seen, within the constitutional power of Congress to create inferior federal courts and prescribe their jurisdiction. . . .

In the circumstances of this case we find no denial of due process in the statutory prohibition of a temporary stay or injunction. The present statute is not open to the objection that petitioners are compelled to serve the public as in the case of a public utility, or that the only method by which they can test the validity of the regulations promulgated under it is by violating the statute and thus subjecting themselves to the possible imposition of severe and cumulative penalties. . . .

In any event, we are unable to say that the denial of interlocutory relief pending a judicial determination of the validity of the regulation would, in the special circumstances of this case, involve a denial of constitutional right. If the alternatives, as Congress could have concluded, were wartime inflation or the imposition on individuals of the burden of complying with a price regulation while its validity is being determined, Congress could constitutionally make the choice in favor of the protection of the public interest from the dangers of inflation. Compare *Miller* v. *Schoene*, 276 U.S. 272, in which we held that the Fourteenth Amendment did not preclude a state from compelling the uncompensated destruction of private property in order to preserve important public interests from destruction. . . .

Here, in the exercise of the power to protect the national economy from the disruptive influences of inflation in time of war Congress has seen fit to postpone injunctions restraining the operations of price regulations until their lawfulness could be ascertained by an appropriate and expeditious procedure. In so doing it has done only what a court of equity could have done, in the exercise of its discretion to protect the public interest. What the courts could do Congress can do as the guardian of the public interest of the nation in time of war. The legislative formulation of what would otherwise be a rule of judicial discretion is not a denial of due process or a usurpation of judicial functions. . . .

Our decisions leave no doubt that when justified by compelling public interest the legislature may authorize summary action subject to later judicial review of its validity. . . .

. . . Congress, through its power to define the jurisdiction of inferior federal courts and to create such courts for the exercise of the judicial power, could, subject to other constitutional limitations, create the Emergency Court of Appeals, give to it exclusive equity jurisdiction to determine the validity of price regulations prescribed by the Administrator, and foreclose any further or other consideration of the validity of a regulation as a defense to a prosecution for its violation. . . .

Affirmed.

MR. JUSTICE ROBERTS:

I dissent [on the ground that the act unconstitutionally delegates legislative power to the Administrator]. . . .

I am sure that my brethren, no more than I, would say that Congress may set aside the Constitution during war. If not, may it suspend any of its provisions? The question deserves a fair answer. My view is that it may not suspend any of the provisions of the instrument. What any of the branches of government do in war must find warrant in the charter and not in its nullification, either directly or stealthily by evasion and equivocation. But if the court puts its decision on the war power I think it should say so. The citizens of this country will then know that in war the function of legislation may be surrendered to an autocrat whose "judgment" will constitute the law; and that his judgment will be enforced by federal officials pursuant to civil judgments, and criminal punishments will be imposed by courts as matters of routine. . . .

MR. JUSTICE RUTLEDGE, dissenting:

I agree with the Court's conclusions upon the substantive issues. But I am unable to believe that the trial afforded the petitioners conformed to constitutional requirements. The matter is of such importance as requires a statement of the reasons for dissent. . . .

War such as we now fight calls into play the full power of government in extreme emergency. It compels invention of legal, as of martial tools adequate for the times' necessity. Inevitably some will be strange, if also life saving, instruments for a people accustomed to peace and the normal working of constitutional limitations. Citizens must surrender or forego exercising rights which in other times could not be impaired. But not all are lost. War expands the nation's power. But it does not suspend the judicial duty to guard whatever liberties will not imperil the paramount national interest. . . .

The crux of this case comes, as I see it, in the question whether Congress can confer jurisdiction upon federal and state courts in the enforcement proceedings, more particularly the criminal suit, and at the same time deny them "jurisdiction or power to consider the

validity" of the regulations for which enforcement is thus sought. . . .
The prohibition is the statute's most novel feature. In combination
with others it gives the procedure of a culminating summary touch
and presents questions different from those arising from other
features. . . .

It is one thing for Congress to withold jurisdiction. It is entirely
another to confer it and direct that it be exercised in a manner inconsistent with constitutional requirements or, what in some instances
may be the same thing, without regard to them. Once it is held that
Congress can require the courts criminally to enforce unconstitutional
laws or statutes, including regulations, or to do so without regard for
their validity, the way will have been found to circumvent the supreme
law and, what is more, to make the courts parties to doing so. This
Congress cannot do. There are limits to the judicial power. Congress
may impose others. And in some matters Congress or the President
has final say under the Constitution. But whenever the judicial power
is called into play, it is responsible directly to the fundamental law
and no other authority can intervene to force or authorize the
judicial body to disregard it. The problem therefore is not solely one
of individual right or due process of law. It is equally one of the
separation and independence of the powers of government and of
the constitutional integrity of the judicial processes, more especially
in criminal trials. . . .

A procedure so piecemeal, so chopped up, so disruptive of constitutional guarantees in relation to trials for crime, should not and, in my
judgment, cannot be validated, as to such proceedings, under the
Constitution. Even war does not suspend the protections which are
inherently part and parcel of our criminal process. . . .

The procedural pattern is one which may be adapted to the trial of
almost any crime. Once approved, it is bound to spawn progeny. If
in one case Congress can thus withdraw from the criminal court the
power to consider the validity of the regulations on which the charge
is based, it can do so for other cases, unless limitations are pointed
out clearly and specifically. And it can do so for statutes as well. In
short the way will have been found to avoid, if not altogether the
power of the courts to review legislation for consistency with the
Constitution, then in part at least their obligation to observe its commands and more especially the guaranteed protections of persons
charged with crime in the trial of their causes. This is not merely
control or definition of jurisdiction. It is rather unwarranted abridge-
ment of the judicial power in the criminal process, unless at the very
least it is confined specifically to situations where the special proceeding provides a fair and equal substitute for full defense in the criminal
trial or other adequate safeguard is afforded against punishment for
violating an order which itself violates or may violate basic rights. . . .

War requires much of the citizen. He surrenders rights for the time
being to secure their more permanent establishment. Most men do

so freely. According to our plan others must do so also, as far as the nation's safety requires. But the surrender is neither permanent nor total. The great liberties of speech and the press are curtailed but not denied. Religious freedom remains a living thing. With these, in our system, rank the elemental protections thrown about the citizen charged with crime, more especially those forged on history's anvil in great crises. They secure fair play to the guilty and vindication for the innocent. By one means only may they be suspended, even when chaos threatens. Whatever else seeks to dispense with them or materially impair their integrity should fail. Not yet has the war brought extremity that demands or permits them to be put aside. Nor does maintaining price control require this. The effect, though not intended, of the provision which forbids a criminal court to "consider the validity" of the law on which the charge of crime is founded, in my opinion, would be greatly to impair these securities. Hence I cannot assent to that provision as valid. . . .

I am authorized to say that MR. JUSTICE MURPHY joins in this opinion.

UNITED STATES v.
SOUTH-EASTERN UNDERWRITERS ASSOCIATION

322 U.S. 533, 88 L.Ed. 1440 (1944)

In a speech before the New York City Bar Association in 1950, Mr. Justice Douglas maintained that it is "a healthy consequence of our system when stare decisis *must give way before the dynamic component of history" for a judge "cannot . . . let men long dead and unaware of the problems of the age in which he lives do his thinking for him." Yet by the same token* stare decisis *(to abide by or adhere to decided cases) is more than a legal maxim. It is the Gibraltar of the law's fixity, uniformity, continuity, and certainty. This dichotomy has been one of the "leitmotifs" of our constitutional development, but its real role can perhaps best be exemplified in cases dealing with the Sherman Anti-Trust Act and with the problem of insurance. Ask anyone about a business whose*

total assets exceed $37,000,000,000 or the approximate equivalent of the value of all farm lands and buildings in the United States; [whose] annual premium receipts exceed $6,000,000,000, more than the average annual receipts of the United States Government during the last decade; [which] included a labor force of 524,000 experienced workers, almost as many as seek their living in coal mining or automobile manufacturing; [and whose] enterprise directly affects . . . persons in all walks of life [and] touches the home, the family, and the occupation or business of almost every person in the United States. . . . [quoted from a part of the opinion in the case below and omitted therein]

—*ask anyone whether such a business is national in scope and hence subject to federal regulation, and the answer would be apparent. Yet boxed in by a decision in 1869 that the writing of insurance was a local activity, not interstate commerce (see* PAUL v. VIRGINIA, *8 Wall. 168) on the one side, and by a decision of 1895, on the other, that manufacturing precedes commerce and is not a part of it (see* UNITED STATES v. E. C. KNIGHT CO., *p. 123), the problem of controlling or regulating modern-day insurance companies becomes acute. In the case below the United States sought and obtained an indictment against the Underwriters Association on the ground that they violated the Sherman Anti-Trust Act by fixing and maintaining arbitrary and non-competitive premium rates that in effect restrained competition in the southern states. The demurrer of the Underwriters was sustained by the District Court on the ground that "the business of insurance is not commerce either interstate or intrastate," and the United States appealed. What is of equal value to this entire survey of economic life as seen through Supreme Court decisions is not only the fact that the majority were willing to bow to the lessons of experience and better reasoning, but that the minority, while agreeing that insurance as a business had become national in scope, sought to limit their own judicial power by arguing that the Sherman Act was not intended to apply to the business of insurance. While such may be looked upon as a form of modesty it actually raises the question in another form, namely, that of judicial self-restraint. This was stated by Mr. Justice Stone in his dissenting opinion in the Butler (A.A.A.) case, p. 184, when he maintained "Courts are not the only agency of government that must be assumed to have capacity to govern. . . ." If this case does nothing more, it certainly sharpens the focus of the problem as to the proper relation between the Court and the political processes in the regulation of our economic life. And it is perhaps still questionable as to whether the majority or minority view is the "law of the land," for in* RADOVICH v. NATIONAL FOOTBALL LEAGUE, *decided in 1957 (352 U.S. 445), Mr. Justice Clark, speaking for the majority, in maintaining that professional football was subject to the anti-trust laws while professional baseball was not, said in part: "If this ruling is unrealistic, inconsistent, or illogical, it is sufficient to answer that were we considering the question of baseball for the first time upon a clean slate we would have no doubts. . . . We, therefore, conclude that the orderly way to eliminate error or discrimination . . . is by legislation and not by court decision."*

MR. JUSTICE BLACK delivered the opinion of the Court.

For seventy-five years this Court has held, whenever the question has been presented, that the Commerce Clause of the Constitution does not deprive the individual states of power to regulate and tax specific activities of foreign insurance companies which sell policies within their territories. Each state has been held to have this power even though negotiation and execution of the companies' policy contracts involved communications of information and movements of persons, moneys, and papers across state lines. Not one of all these cases, however, has involved an Act of Congress which required the Court to decide the issue of whether the Commerce Clause grants to Congress the power to regulate insurance transactions stretching across state lines. Today for the first time in the history of the Court that issue is squarely presented and must be decided. . . .

The record, then, presents two questions and no others: (1) Was the Sherman Act intended to prohibit conduct of fire insurance companies which restrains or monopolizes the interstate fire insurance trade? (2) If so, do fire insurance transactions which stretch across state lines constitute "Commerce among the several States" so as to make them subject to regulation by Congress under the Commerce Clause? Since it is our conclusion that the Sherman Act was intended to apply to the fire insurance business we shall, for convenience of discussion, first consider the latter question.

Ordinarily courts do not construe words used in the Constitution so as to give them a meaning more narrow than one which they had in the common parlance of the times in which the Constitution was written. To hold that the word "commerce" as used in the Commerce Clause does not include a business such as insurance would do just that. Whatever other meanings "commerce" may have included in 1787, the dictionaries, encyclopedias, and other books of the period show that it included trade: business in which persons bought and sold, bargained and contracted. And this meaning has persisted to modern times. Surely, therefore, a heavy burden is on him who asserts that the plenary power which the Commerce Clause grants to Congress to regulate "Commerce among the several States" does not include the power to regulate trading in insurance to the same extent that it includes power to regulate other trades or businesses conducted across state lines. . . .

A large share of the insurance business is concentrated in a comparatively few companies located, for the most part, in the financial centers of the East. Premiums collected from policyholders in every part of the United States flow into these companies for investment. As policies become payable, checks and drafts flow back to the many states where the policyholders reside. The result is a continuous and indivisible stream of intercourse among the states composed of collections of premiums, payments of policy obligations, and the countless documents and communications which are essential to the negotiation and execution of policy contracts. Individual policyholders living in many different states who own policies in a single company have their separate interests blended in one assembled fund of assets upon which all are equally dependent for payment of their policies. The decisions which that company makes at its home office—the risks it insures, the premiums it charges, the investments it makes, the losses it pays—concern not just the people of the state where the home office happens to be located. They concern people living far beyond the boundaries of that state. . . .

In 1869 this Court held in sustaining a statute of Virginia which regulated foreign insurance companies, that the statute did not offend the Commerce Clause because "issuing a policy of insurance is not a transaction of commerce." *Paul* v. *Virginia*, 8 Wall. 183. Since then, in similar cases, this statement has been repeated, and has been broadened. . . .

In all cases in which the Court has relied upon the proposition that "the business of insurance is not commerce," its attention was focused on the validity of state statutes—the extent to which the Commerce Clause automatically deprived states of the power to regulate the insurance business. Since Congress has at no time attempted to control the insurance business, invalidation of the state statutes would practically have been equivalent to granting insurance companies engaged in interstate activities a blanket license to operate without legal restraint. As early as 1866 the insurance trade, though still in its infancy, was subject to widespread abuses. To meet the imperative need for correction of these abuses the various state legislatures, including that of Virginia, passed regulatory legislation. *Paul* v. *Virginia* upheld one of Virginia's statutes. To uphold insurance laws of other states, including tax laws, *Paul* v. *Virginia*'s generalization and reasoning have been consistently adhered to.

Today, however, we are asked to apply this reasoning, not to uphold another state law, but to strike down an Act of Congress which was intended to regulate certain aspects of the methods by which interstate insurance companies do business; and, in so doing, to narrow the scope of the federal power to regulate the activities of a great business carried on back and forth across state lines. But past decisions of this Court emphasize that legal formulae devised to uphold state power cannot uncritically be accepted as trustworthy guides to determine Congressional power under the Commerce Clause. Furthermore, the reasons given in support of the generalization that "the business of insurance is not commerce" and can never be conducted so as to constitute "Commerce among the States" are inconsistent with many decisions of this Court which have upheld federal statutes regulating interstate commerce under the Commerce Clause. . . .

We may grant that a contract of insurance, considered as a thing apart from negotiation and execution, does not itself constitute interstate commerce. . . . But it does not follow from this that the Court is powerless to examine the entire transaction, of which that contract is but a part, in order to determine whether there may be a chain of events which becomes interstate commerce. Only by treating the Congressional power over commerce among the states as a "technical legal conception" rather than as a "practical one, drawn from the course of business" could such a conclusion be reached. *Swift & Co.* v. *United States*, 196 U.S. 375, 398. In short, a nationwide business is not deprived of its interstate character merely because it is built upon sales contracts which are local in nature. Were the rule otherwise, few businesses could be said to be engaged in interstate commerce.

Another reason advanced to support the result of the cases which follow *Paul* v. *Virginia* has been that, if any aspects of business of insurance be treated as interstate commerce, "then all control over it is taken from the states and the legislative regulations which this Court has heretofore sustained must be declared invalid." Accepted without qualification, that broad statement is inconsistent with many decisions of this Court. It is settled that, for Constitutional purposes, certain activities of a business may be intrastate and therefore subject to state control, while other activities of the same business may be interstate and therefore subject to federal regulation. And there is a wide range of business and other activities which, though subject to federal regulation, are so intimately related to local welfare that, in the absence of Congressional action, they may be regulated or taxed by the states. In marking out these activities the primary test applied by the Court is not the mechanical one of whether the particular activity affected by the state regulation is part of interstate commerce, but rather whether, in each case, the competing demands of the state and national interests involved can be accommodated. And the fact that particular phases of an interstate business or activity have long been regulated or taxed by states has been recognized as a strong reason why, in the continued absence of conflicting Congressional action, the state regulatory and tax laws should be declared valid. . . .

The precise boundary between national and state power over commerce has never yet been, and doubtless never can be, delineated by a single abstract definition. The most widely accepted general description of that part of commerce which is subject to the federal power is that given in 1824 by Chief Justice Marshall in *Gibbons* v. *Ogden*, . . . "Commerce, undoubtedly, is traffic, but it is something more: it is intercourse. It describes the commercial intercourse between nations, and parts of nations, in all its branches. . . ." Commerce is interstate, he said, when it "concerns more States than one." . . . No decision of this Court has ever questioned this as too comprehensive, as a description less comprehensive, the Court has recognized, would deprive the Congress of that full power necessary to enable it to discharge its Constitutional duty to govern commerce among the states.

. . . The power granted Congress is a positive power. It is the power to legislate concerning transactions which, reaching across state boundaries, affect the people of more states than one;—to govern affairs which the individual states, with their limited territorial jurisdictions, are not fully capable of governing. This federal power to determine the rules of intercourse across state lines was essential to weld a loose confederacy into a single, indivisible Nation; its continued existence is equally essential to the welfare of that Nation.

Our basic responsibility in interpreting the Commerce Clause is to make certain that the power to govern intercourse among the states remains where the Constitution placed it. That power, as held by this Court from the beginning, is vested in the Congress, available to be exercised for the national welfare as Congress shall deem necessary. No commercial enterprise of any kind which conducts its activities across state lines has been held to be wholly beyond the regulatory power of Congress under the Commerce Clause. We cannot make an exception of the business of insurance.

We come then to the contention, earnestly pressed upon us by appellees, that Congress did not intend in the Sherman Act to exercise its power over the interstate insurance trade. . . .

Appellees argue that the Congress knew, as doubtless some of its members did, that this Court had prior to 1890 said that insurance was not commerce and was subject to state regulation, and that therefore we should read the Act as though it expressly exempted that business. But neither by reports nor by statements of the bill's sponsors or others was any purpose to exempt insurance companies revealed. And we fail to find in the legislative history of the Act an expression of a clear and unequivocal desire of Congress to legislate only within that area previously declared by this Court to be within the federal power. . . . We have [been] shown not one piece of reliable evidence that the Congress of 1890 intended to freeze the proscription of the Sherman Act within the mold of then current judicial decisions defining the commerce power. On the contrary, all the acceptable evidence points the other way. That Congress wanted to go to the utmost extent of its Constitutional power in restraining trust and monopoly agreements such as the indictment here charges admits of little, if any, doubt. The purpose was to use that power to make of ours, so far as Congress could under our dual system, a competitive business economy. Nor is it sufficient to justify our reading into the Act an exemption for insurance that the Congress of 1890 may have known that states already were regulating the insurance business. The Congress of 1890 also knew that railroads were subject to regulation not only by states but by the federal government itself, but this fact has been held insufficient to bring to the railroad companies the interpretative exemption from the Sherman Act they have sought. *United States* v. *Trans-Missouri Freight Assn.*, 166 U.S. 290, 314–315, 320–325.

Appellees further argue that, quite apart from what the Sherman Act meant in 1890, the succeeding Congresses have accepted and approved the decisions of this Court that the business of insurance is not commerce. They call attention to the fact that at various times since 1890 Congress has refused to enact legislation providing for federal regulation of the insurance business, and that several resolutions proposing to amend the Constitution specifically to authorize federal regulation of insurance have failed of passage. In addition they emphasize that, although the Sherman Act has been amended several times, no amendments have been adopted which specifically bring insurance within the Act's proscription. The Government, for its part, points to evidence that various members of Congress during the period 1900–1914 considered there were "trusts" in the insurance business, and expressed the view that the insurance business should be subject to the anti-trust laws. It also points out that in the Merchant Marine Act of 1920 Congress specifically exempted certain conduct of marine insurance companies from the "anti-trust" laws.

The most that can be said of all this evidence considered together is that it is inconclusive as to any point here relevant. By no means does it show that the Congress of 1890 specifically intended to exempt insurance companies from the all-inclusive scope of the Sherman Act. Nor can we attach significance to the omission of Congress to include in its amendments to the Act an express statement that the Act covered insurance. From the beginning Congress has used language broad enough to include all businesses, and never has amended the Act to define these businesses with particularity. And the fact that several Congresses since 1890 have failed to enact proposed legislation providing for more or less comprehensive federal regulation of insurance does not even remotely suggest that any Congress has held the view that insurance alone, of all businesses, should be permitted to enter into combinations for the purpose of destroying competition by coercive and intimidatory practices.

Reversed.

Mr. Justice Roberts and Mr. Justice Reed took no part in the consideration or decision of this case.

Mr. Chief Justice Stone dissenting: . . .

The numerous and unvarying decisions of this Court that "insurance is not commerce" have never denied that acts of interstate commerce may be incidental to the business of writing and performing contracts of insurance, or that those incidental acts are subject to the commerce power. Our decisions on this subject have uniformly rested on the ground that the formation of an insurance contract, even though it insures against risk of loss to property located in other states or moving in interstate commerce, is not interstate commerce, and that although the incidents of interstate communication and transportation which often attend the formation and performance of an insurance contract are interstate commerce, they do not serve to render the business of insurance itself interstate commerce. . . .

The conclusion that the business of writing insurance is not interstate commerce could not rightly be otherwise unless we were to depart from the universally accepted view that the act of making any contract which does not stipulate for the performance of an act or transaction of interstate commerce is not in itself interstate commerce. And this has been held to be true even though the contract be effected by exchange of communications across state lines. . . .

The conclusion seems inescapable that the formation of insurance contracts, like many others, and the business of so doing, is not, without more, commerce within the protection of the commerce clause of the Constitution and thereby, in large measure, excluded from state control and regulation. . . . This conclusion seems, upon analysis, not only correct on principle and in complete harmony with the uniform rulings by which this Court has held that the formation of all types of contracts which do not stipulate for the performance of acts of interstate commerce, are likewise not interstate commerce, but it has the support of an unbroken line of decisions of this Court beginning with *Paul* v. *Virginia*, seventy-five years ago, and extending down to the present time. . . .

To give blind adherence to a rule or policy that no decision of this Court is to be overruled would be itself to overrule many decisions of the Court which do not accept that view. But the rule of *stare decisis* embodies a wise policy because it is often more important that a rule of law be settled than that it be settled right. This is especially so where, as here, Congress is not without regulatory power. . . . The question then is not whether an earlier decision should be overruled, but whether a particular decision ought to be. And before overruling a precedent in any case it is the duty of the Court to make certain that more harm will not be done in rejecting than in retaining a rule of even dubious validity. . . .

From what has been said it seems plain that our decisions that the business of insurance is not commerce are not unsound in principle, and involve no inconsistency or lack of harmony with accepted doctrine. They place no field of activity beyond the control of both the national and state governments as did *Hammer* v. *Dagenhart* . . . overruled three years ago by a unanimous Court in *United States* v. *Darby*. . . . On the contrary the ruling that insurance is not commerce, and is therefore unaffected by the restrictions which the commerce clause imposes on state legislation, removed the most serious obstacle to regulation of that business by the states. Through their plenary power over domestic and foreign corporations which are not engaged in interstate commerce, the states have developed extensive and effective systems of regulation of the insurance business, often solving regulatory problems of local character with which it would be impractical or difficult for Congress to deal through the exercise of the commerce power. And in view of the broad powers of the federal government to regulate matters which, though not themselves commerce, nevertheless affect interstate commerce, *Wickard* v. *Filburn*, 317 U.S. 111; *Polish Alliance* v. *Labor Board*, 322 U.S. 643, there can be no doubt of the power of Congress if it so desires to regulate many aspects of the insurance business mentioned in this indictment.

But the immediate and only practical effect of the decision now rendered is to withdraw from the states, in large measure, the regulation of insurance and to confer it on the national government, which has adopted no legislative policy and evolved no scheme of regulation with respect to the business of insurance. Congress having taken no action, the present decision substitutes, for the varied and detailed state regulation developed over a period of years, the limited aim and indefinite command of the Sherman Act for the suppression of restraints on competition in the marketing of goods and services in or affecting interstate commerce, to be applied by the courts to the insurance business as best they may. . . .

The judgment should be affirmed.

[MR. JUSTICE FRANKFURTER joined in the dissenting opinion of CHIEF JUSTICE STONE.]

MR. JUSTICE JACKSON, dissenting in part. . . .

The doctrine that insurance business is not commerce always has been criticized as unrealistic, illogical, and inconsistent with other holdings of the Court. I am unable to make any satisfactory distinction between insurance business as now conducted and other transactions that are held to constitute interstate commerce. Were we considering the question for the first time and writing upon a clean slate, I would have no misgivings about holding that insurance business is commerce and where conducted across State lines is interstate commerce and therefore that congressional power to regulate prevails over that of the states. I have little doubt that if the present trend continues federal regulation eventually will supersede that of the states.

The question therefore for me settles down to this: What role ought the judiciary to play in reversing the trend of history and setting the nation's feet on a new path of policy? To answer this I would consider what choices we have in the matter. . . .

Instead of overruling our repeated decisions that insurance is not commerce, the Court could apply to this case the principle that even if it is not commerce the antitrust laws prohibit its manipulation to restrain interstate commerce, just as we hold that the National Labor Relations Act prohibits insurance companies, even if not in commerce, from engaging in unfair labor practices which affect commerce. *Polish Alliance* v. *Labor Board.* This would require the government to show that any acts it sought to punish affect something more than insurance and substantially affect interstate transportation or interstate commerce in some commodity. Whatever problems of reconciliation between state and federal authority this would present—and it would not avoid them all—it would leave the basis of state regulation unimpaired.

The principles of decision that I would apply to this case are neither novel nor complicated and may be shortly put:

1. *As a matter of fact,* modern insurance business, as usually conducted, is commerce; and where it is conducted across state lines, it is in fact interstate commerce.

2. In contemplation of law, however, insurance has acquired an established doctrinal status not based on present day facts. For constitutional purposes a fiction has been established, and long acted upon by the Court, the states, and the Congress, that insurance is not commerce.

3. So long as Congress acquiesces, this Court should adhere to this carefully considered and frequently reiterated rule which sustains the traditional regulation and taxation of insurance companies by the States.

4. Any enactment by Congress either of partial or of comprehensive regulations of the insurance business would come to us with the most forceful presumption of constitutional validity. The fiction that insurance is not commerce could not be sustained against such a presumption, for resort to the facts would support the presumption in favor of the congressional action. The fiction therefore must yield to congressional action and continue only at the sufferance of Congress.

5. Congress also may, without exerting its full regulatory powers over the subject, and without challenging the basis or supplanting the details of state regulation, enact prohibitions of any acts in pursuit of the insurance business which substantially affect or unduly burden or restrain interstate commerce.

6. The antitrust laws should be construed to reach the business of insurance and those who are engaged in it only under the latter congressional power. This does not require a change in the doctrine that insurance is not commerce. The statute as thus construed would authorize prosecution of all combinations in the course of insurance business to commit acts not required or authorized by state law, such as intimidation, disparagement, or coercion, if they unreasonably restrain interstate commerce in commodities or interstate transportation. It would leave state regulation intact. . . .

The orderly way to nationalize insurance supervision, if it be desirable, is not by court decision but through legislation. Judicial decision operates on the states and the industry retroactively. We cannot anticipate, and more than likely we could not agree, what consequences upon tax liabilities, refunds, liabilities under state law to states or to individuals, and even criminal liabilities will follow this decision. Such practical considerations years ago deterred the Court from changing its doctrine as to insurance. Congress, on the other hand, if it thinks the time has come to take insurance regulation into the federal system, may formulate and announce the whole scope and effect of its action in advance, fix a future effective date, and avoid all the confusion, surprise, and injustice which will be caused by the action of the Court.

A judgment as to when the evil of a decisional error exceeds the evil of an innovation must be based on very practical and in part upon policy considerations. When, as in this problem, such practical and political judgments can be made by the political branches of the Government, it is the part of wisdom and self-restraint and good government for courts to leave the initiative to Congress.

Moreover, this is the method of responsible democratic government. To force the hand of Congress is no more the proper function of the judiciary than to tie the hands of Congress. To use my office, at a time like this, and with so little justification in necessity, to dislocate the functions and revenues of the states and to catapult Congress into immediate and undivided responsibility for supervision of the nation's insurance businesses is more than I can reconcile with my view of the function of this Court in our society.

YOUNGSTOWN SHEET & TUBE CO. v. SAWYER

343 U.S. 579, 96 L.Ed. 1153 (1952)

That labor disputes are intimately connected with the economic welfare of a country and that they can, to a large degree, be disruptive of economic values on which prosperity and well-being depend, is not a new concept. Indeed in the period of time at the turn of the century, the phrase "government by injunction" was used by labor to stigmatize government action in support of an economic group. As was seen in the case of IN RE DEBS *(see p. 119), not only did President Cleveland send troops to Chicago to deal with the Pullman strike without any "application" being made by either the Legislature or Executive of the State of Illinois (see Art. IV, Sec. 4 of Constitution), but he ordered his Attorney General to secure a federal court injunction against the strikers despite the lack of any congressional statute authorizing such action. In upholding the exercise of such powers by the President the Court said in part: "Every government, entrusted, by the very terms of its being, with powers and duties to be exercised and discharged for the general welfare, has a right to apply to its own courts for any proper assistance in the exercise of one and the discharge of the other. . . ." In short, the law of self-preservation is not only the first law of nature, it is also a law adhered to by the government and the state as an institution. That the period in which the instant case comes up was one of crisis is a matter of record, for whether one calls the Korean War a war or a police action does not in any way change arose in the steel industry in 1951, President Truman, by executive order (No. 10340) directed his Secretary of Commerce, Sawyer, to the nature of the affair in pragmatic terms. Thus when a labor dispute seize and operate the steel mills. This order was not based on any statutory authority (indeed in the case itself one of the vital questions was whether Congress, in failing to include seizure authority by the President in the Taft-Hartley Labor Act, did not thus limit the inherent powers of the President), but rather was premised on the national emergency that would be created by a threatened strike in an industry so vital to defense production. The Youngstown Steel Company (and others) obtained an injunction from a Federal District Court restraining Secretary of Commerce Sawyer. When the Court of Appeals stayed the injunction the Supreme Court granted certiorari. Aside from the tremendous rapidity with which the Supreme Court acted (the writ was granted on May 3, argument heard on May 12, and the decision handed down on June 2, 1952) and the importance of the issues involved, it should be noted that each of the six justices of the majority delivered a separate opinion, which taken with the dissent of Mr. Chief Justice Vinson means that seven out of nine wrote opinions—a rare thing indeed.*

MR. JUSTICE BLACK delivered the opinion of the Court.

We are asked to decide whether the President was acting within his constitutional power when he issued an order directing the Secretary of Commerce to take possession of and operate most of the Nation's steel mills. The mill owners argue that the President's order amouts to lawmaking, a legislative function which the Constitution has expressly confided to the Congress and not to the President. The Government's position is that the order was made on findings of the President that his action was necessary to avert a national catastrophe which would inevitably result from a stoppage of steel production, and that in meeting this grave emergency the President was acting within the aggregate of his constitutional powers as the Nation's Chief Executive and the Commander in Chief of the Armed Forces of the United States. The issue emerges here from the following series of events:

In the latter part of 1951, a dispute arose between the steel companies and their employees over terms and conditions that should be included in new collective bargaining agreements. Long-continued conferences failed to resolve the dispute. On December 18, 1951, the employees' representative, United Steelworkers of America, C.I.O., gave notice of an intention to strike when the existing bargaining agreements expired on December 31. Thereupon the Federal Mediation and Conciliation Service intervened in an effort to get labor and management to agree. This failing, the President on December 22, 1951, referred the dispute to the Federal Wage Stabilization Board to investigate and make recommendations for fair and equitable terms of settlement. This Board's report resulted in no settlement. On April 4, 1952, the Union gave notice of a nation-wide strike called to begin at 12:01 a.m. April 9. The indispensability of steel as a component of substantially all weapons and other war materials led the President to believe that the proposed work stoppage would immediately jeopardize our national defense and that governmental seizure of the steel mills was necessary in order to assure the continued availability of steel. Reciting these considerations for his action, the President, a few hours before the strike was to begin, issued Executive Order 10340 . . . The order directed the Secretary of Commerce to take possession of most of the steel mills and keep them running. . . .

The President's power, if any, to issue the order must stem either from an act of Congress or from the Constitution itself. There is no statute that expressly authorizes the President to take possession of property as he did here. Nor is there any act of Congress to which our attention has been directed from which such a power can fairly be implied. Indeed, we do not understand the Government to rely on statutory authorization for this seizure. . . .

Moreover, the use of the seizure technique to solve labor disputes in order to prevent work stoppages was not only unauthorized by any congressional enactment; prior to this controversy, Congress had refused to adopt that method of settling labor disputes. When the Taft-Hartley Act was under consideration in 1947, Congress rejected an Amendment which would have authorized such governmental seizures in cases of emergency. . . .

It is clear that if the President had authority to issue the order he did, it must be found in some provision of the Constitution. And it is not claimed that express constitutional language grants this power to the President. The contention is that presidential power should be implied from the aggregate of his powers under the Constitution. Particular reliance is placed on provisions in Article II which say that "the executive Power shall be vested in a President . . ."; that "he shall take Care that the Laws be faithfully executed"; and that he "shall be Commander in Chief of the Army and Navy of the United States."

The order cannot properly be sustained as an exercise of the President's military power as Commander in Chief of the Armed Forces. The Government attempts to do so by citing a number of cases upholding broad powers in military commanders engaged in day-to-day fighting in a theater of war. Such cases need not concern us here. Even though "theater of war" be an expanding concept, we cannot with faithfulness to our constitutional system hold that the Commander in Chief of the Armed Forces has the ultimate power as such to take possession of private property in order to keep labor disputes from stopping production. This is a job for the Nation's lawmakers, not for its military authorities.

Nor can the seizure order be sustained because of the several constitutional provisions that grant executive power to the President. In the framework of our Constitution, the President's power to see that the laws are faithfully executed refutes the idea that he is to be a lawmaker. The Constitution limits his functions in the lawmaking process to the recommending of laws he thinks wise and the vetoing of laws he thinks bad. And the Constitution is neither silent nor equivocal about who shall make laws which the President is to execute. The first section of the first article says that "All legislative Powers herein granted shall be vested in a Congress of the United States. . . ." After granting many powers to the Congress, Article I goes on to provide that Congress may "make all Laws which shall be necessary and proper for carrying into Execution the foregoing Powers and all other Powers vested by this Constitution in the Government of the United States, or in any Department or Officer thereof." . . .

It is said that other Presidents without congressional authority have taken possession of private business enterprises in order to settle labor disputes. But even if this be true, Congress has not thereby lost its exclusive constitutional authority to make laws necessary and proper to carry out the powers vested by the Constitution "in the Government of the United States, or any Department or Officer thereof."

The Founders of this Nation entrusted the law-making power to the Congress alone in both good and bad times. It would do no good to recall the historical events, the fears of power and the hopes for freedom that lay behind their choice. Such a review would but confirm our holding that this seizure order cannot stand.

The judgment of the District Court is *Affirmed.*

MR. JUSTICE FRANKFURTER, concurring.

Although the considerations relevant to the legal enforcement of the principle of separation of powers seem to me more complicated and flexible than may appear from what Mr. Justice Black has written, I join his opinion because I thoroughly agree with the application of the principle to the circumstances of this case. . . .

The issue before us can be met, and therefore should be, without attempting to define the President's powers comprehensively. I shall not attempt to delineate what belongs to him by virtue of his office beyond the power even of Congress to contract; what authority belongs to him until Congress acts; what kind of problems may be dealt with either by the Congress or by the President or by both; . . . what power must be exercised by the Congress and cannot be delegated to the President. It is as unprofitable to lump together in an undiscriminating hotch-potch past presidential actions claimed to be derived from occupancy of the office, as it is to conjure up hypothetical future cases. The judiciary may, as this case proves, have to intervene in determining where authority lies as between the democratic forces in our scheme of government. But in doing so we should be wary and humble. Such is the teaching of the Court's role in the history of the country.

It is in this mood and with this perspective that the issue before the Court must be approached. We must therefore put to one side consideration of what powers the President would have had if there had been no legislation whatever bearing on the authority asserted by the seizure, or if the seizure had been only for a short, explicitly temporary period, to be terminated automatically unless Congressional approval were given. These and other questions, like or unlike, are not now here. I would exceed my authority were I to say anything about them. . . .

In adopting the provisions which it did, by the Labor Management Relations Act of 1947, for dealing with a "national emergency" arising out of a breakdown in peaceful industrial relations, Congress was very familiar with Government seizure as a protective measure. On a balance of considerations Congress chose not to lodge this power in the President. . . .

In any event, nothing can be plainer than that Congress made a conscious choice of policy in a field full of perplexity and peculiarly within legislative responsibility for choice. In formulating legislation for dealing with industrial conflicts, Congress could not more clearly and emphatically have withheld authority than it did in 1947. . . .

. . . But it is now claimed that the President has seizure power by virtue of the Defense Production Act of 1950 and its Amendments. And the claim is based on the occurrence of new events—Korea and the need for stabilization, etc.—although it was well known that seizure power was withheld by the Act of 1947, and although the President, whose specific requests for other authority were in the main granted by Congress, never suggested that in view of the new events he needed the power seizure which Congress in its judgment had decided to withhold from him. . . .

A scheme of government like ours no doubt at times feels the lack of power to act with complete, all-embracing, swiftly moving authority. No doubt a government with distributed authority, subject to be challenged in the courts of law, at least long enough to consider and adjudicate the challenge, labors under restrictions from which other governments are free. It has not been our tradition to envy such governments. In any event our government was designed to have such restrictions. The price was deemed not too high in view of the safeguards which these restrictions afford. . . .

MR. JUSTICE DOUGLAS, concurring.

There can be no doubt that the emergency which caused the President to seize these steel plants was one that bore heavily on the country. But the emergency did not create power; it merely marked an occasion when power should be exercised. And the fact that it was necessary that measures be taken to keep steel in production does not mean that the President, rather than the Congress, had the constitutional authority to act. . . .

. . . The language of the Constitution is not ambiguous or qualified. It places not *some* legislative power in the Congress; Article 1, Sec. 1 says "All legislative Powers herein granted shall be vested in a Congress of the United States, which shall consist of a Senate and House of Representatives."

The legislative nature of the action taken by the President seems to me to be clear. When the United States takes over an industrial plant to settle a labor controversy, it is condemning property. The seizure of the plant is a taking in the constitutional sense. . . . A permanent taking would amount to the nationalization of the industry. A temporary taking falls short of that goal. But though the seizure is only for a week or a month, the condemnation is complete and the United States must pay compensation for the temporary possession. . . .

If we sanctioned the present exercise of power by the President, we would be expanding Article 2 of the Constitution and rewriting it to suit the political conveniences of the present emergency. Article 2 which vests the "executive Power" in the President defines that power with particularity. Article 2, Sec. 2 makes the Chief Executive the Commander in Chief of the Army and Navy. But our history and tradition rebel at the thought that the grant of military power carries with it authority over civilian affairs. Article 2, Sec. 3 provides that the President shall "from time to time give to the Congress Information of the State of the Union, and recommend to their Consideration such Measures as he shall judge necessary and expedient." The power to recommend legislation, granted to the President, serves only to emphasize that it is his function to recommend and that it is the function of the Congress to legislate. Article 2, Sec. 3 also provides that the President "shall take Care that the Laws be faithfully executed." But as Mr. Justice Black and Mr. Justice Frankfurter point out the power to execute the laws starts and ends with the laws Congress has enacted. . . .

Mr. Justice Jackson, concurring in the judgment and opinion of the Court. . . .

1. When the President acts pursuant to an express or implied authorization of Congress, his authority is at its maximum, for it includes all that he possesses in his own right plus all that Congress can delegate. In these circumstances, and in these only, may he be said (for what it may be worth), to personify the federal sovereignty. If his act is held unconstitutional under these circumstances, it usually means that the Federal Government as an undivided whole lacks power. A seizure executed by the President pursuant to an Act of Congress would be supported by the strongest of presumptions and the widest latitude of judicial interpretation, and the burden of persuasion would rest heavily upon anyone who might attack it.

2. When the President acts in absence of either a congressional grant or denial of authority, he can only rely upon his own independent powers, but there is a zone of twilight in which he and Congress may have concurrent authority, or in which its distribution is uncertain. Therefore, congressional inertia, indifference or quiescence may sometimes, at least as a practical matter, enable, if not invite, measures on independent presidential responsibility. In this area, any actual test of power is likely to depend on the imperatives of events and contemporary imponderables rather than on abstract theories of law.

3. When the President takes measures incompatible with the expressed or implied will of Congress, his power is at its lowest ebb, for then he can rely only upon his own constitutional powers minus any constitutional powers of Congress over the matter. Courts can sustain exclusive Presidential control in such a case only by disabling the Congress from acting upon the subject. Presidential claim to a power at once so conclusive and preclusive must be scrutinized with caution, for what is at stake is the equilibrium established by our constitutional system.

Into which of these classifications does this executive seizure of the steel industry fit? It is eliminated from the first by admission, for it is conceded that no congressional authorization exists for this seizure. That takes away also the support of the many precedents and declarations which were made in relation, and must be confined, to this category.

Can it then be defended under flexible tests available to the second category? It seems clearly eliminated from that class because Congress has not left seizure of private property an open field but has covered it by three statutory policies inconsistent with this seizure. In cases where the purpose is to supply needs of the Government itself, two courses are provided: one, seizure of a plant which fails to comply with obligatory orders placed by the Government, another, condemnation of facilities, including temporary use under the power of eminent domain. The third is applicable where it is the general economy of the country that is to be protected rather than exclusive governmental interests. None of these were invoked. In choosing a different and inconsistent way of his own, the President cannot claim that it is necessitated or invited by failure of Congress to legislate upon the occasions, grounds and methods for seizure of industrial properties. . . .

This leaves the current seizure to be justified only by the severe tests under the third grouping, where it can be supported only by any remainder of executive power after subtraction of such powers as Congress may have over the subject. In short, we can sustain the President only by holding that seizure of such strike-bound industries is within his domain and beyond control by Congress. Thus, this Court's first review of such seizures occurs under circumstances which leave Presidential power most vulnerable to attack and in the least favorable of possible constitutional postures. . . .

MR. JUSTICE BURTON, concurring in both the opinion and judgment of the Court. . . .

The controlling fact here is that Congress, within its constitutionally delegated power, has prescribed for the President specific procedures, exclusive of seizure, for his use in meeting the present type of emergency. Congress has reserved to itself the right to determine where and when to authorize the seizure of property in meeting such an emergency. Under these circumstances, the President's order of April 8 invaded the jurisdiction of Congress. It violated the essence of the principle of the separation of governmental powers. Accordingly, the injunction against its effectiveness should be sustained. . . .

MR. JUSTICE CLARK, concurring in the judgment of the Court. . . .

The limits of presidential power are obscure. However, Article II, no less than Article I, is part of "a constitution intended to endure for ages to come, and, consequently, to be adapted to the various crises of human affairs." Some of our Presidents, such as Lincoln, "felt that measures otherwise unconstitutional might become lawful by becoming indispensable to the preservation of the Constitution through the preservation of the nation."

Others, such as Theodore Roosevelt, thought the President to be capable, as a "steward" of the people, of exerting all power save that which is specifically prohibited by the Constitution or the Congress. In my view—taught me not only by the decision of Chief Justice Marshall in *Little* v. *Barreme*, [2 Cranch 170 (1804)] but also by a score of other pronouncements of distinguished members of this bench—the Constitution does grant to the President extensive authority in times of grave and imperative national emergency. In fact, to my thinking, such a grant may well be necessary to the very existence of the Constitution itself. As Lincoln aptly said, "[is] it possible to lose the nation and yet preserve the Constitution?" In describing this authority I care not whether one calls it "residual," "inherent," "moral," "implied," "aggregate," "emergency," or otherwise. I am of the conviction that those who have had the gratifying experience of being the President's lawyer have used one or more of these adjectives only with the utmost of sincerity and the highest of purpose.

I conclude that where Congress has laid down specific procedures to deal with the type of crisis confronting the President, he must follow those procedures in meeting the crisis; but that in the absence of such action by Congress, the President's independent power to act depends upon the gravity of the situation confronting the nation. I cannot sustain the seizure in question because here, as in *Little* v. *Barreme*, Congress had prescribed methods to be followed by the President in meeting the emergency at hand. . . .

. . . The hard fact remains that neither the Defense Production Act nor Taft-Hartley authorized the seizure challenged here, and the Government made no effort to comply with the procedures established by the Selective Service Act of 1948, a statute which expressly authorizes seizures when producers fail to supply necessary defense materiel. . . .

MR. CHIEF JUSTICE VINSON, with whom MR. JUSTICE REED and MR. JUSTICE MINTON join, dissenting. . . .

In passing upon the question of Presidential powers in this case, we must first consider the context in which those powers were exercised.

Those who suggest that this is a case involving extraordinary powers should be mindful that these are extraordinary times. A world not yet recovered from the devastation of World War II has been forced to face the threat of another and more terrifying global conflict. . . .

The steel mills were seized for a public use. The power of eminent domain, invoked in this case, is an essential attribute of sovereignty and has long been recognized as a power of the Federal Government. . . .

Admitting that the Government could seize the mills, plaintiffs claim that the implied power of eminent domain can be exercised only under an Act of Congress; under no circumstances, they say, can that power be exercised by the President unless he can point to an express provision in enabling legislation. This was the view adopted by the District Judge when he granted the preliminary injunction. Without an answer, without hearing evidence, he determined the issue on the basis of his "fixed conclusion . . . that defendant's acts are illegal" because the President's only course in the face of an emergency is to present the matter to Congress and await the final passage of legislation which will enable the Government to cope with threatened disaster.

Under this view, the President is left powerless at the very moment when the need for action may be most pressing and when no one, other than he, is immediately capable of action. Under this view, he is left powerless because a power not expressly given to Congress is nevertheless found to rest exclusively with Congress. . . .

In passing upon the grave constitutional question presented in this case, we must never forget, as Chief Justice Marshall admonished, that the Constitution is "intended to endure for ages to come, and, consequently, to be adapted to the various *crises* of human affairs," and that "its means are adequate to its ends." Cases do arise presenting questions which could not have been foreseen by the Framers. In such cases, the Constitution has been treated as a living document adaptable to new situations. But we are not called upon today to expand the Constitution to meet a new situation. For, in this case, we need only look to history and time-honored principles of constitutional law—principles that have been applied consistently by all branches of the Government throughout our history. It is those who assert the invalidity of the Executive Order who seek to amend the Constitution in this case. . . .

A review of executive action demonstrates that our Presidents have on many occasions exhibited the leadership contemplated by the Framers when they made the President Commander in Chief, and imposed upon him the trust to "take Care that the Laws be faithfully executed." With or without explicit statutory authorization, Presidents have at such times dealt with national emergencies by acting promptly and resolutely to enforce legislative programs, at least to save those programs until Congress could act. Congress and the courts have responded to such executive initiative with consistent approval. . . .

[The Chief Justice here examines executive actions from Washington to Truman dealing with various national emergencies.]

This is but a cursory summary of executive leadership. But it amply demonstrates that Presidents have taken prompt action to enforce the laws and protect the country whether or not Congress happened to provide in advance for the particular method of execution. At the minimum, the executive actions reviewed herein sustain the action of the President in this case. And many of the cited examples of Presidential practice go far beyond the extent of power necessary to sustain the President's order to seize the steel mills. The fact that temporary executive seizures of industrial plants to meet an emergency have not been directly tested in this Court furnishes not the slightest suggestion that such actions have been illegal. Rather, the fact that Congress and the courts have consistently recognized and given their support to such executive action indicates that such a power of seizure has been accepted throughout our history. . . .

As the District Judge stated, this is no time for "timorous" judicial action. But neither is this a time for timorous executive action. Faced with the duty of executing the defense programs which Congress had enacted and the disastrous effects that any stoppage in steel production would have on those programs, the President acted to preserve those programs by seizing the steel mills. There is no question that the possession was other than temporary in character and subject to congressional direction—either approving, disapproving or regulating the manner in which the mills were to be administered and returned to the owners. The President immediately informed Congress of his action and clearly stated his intention to abide by the legislative will. No basis for claims of arbitrary action, unlimited powers or dictatorial usurpation of congressional power appears from the facts of this case. On the contrary, judicial, legislative and executive precedents throughout our history demonstrate that in this case the President acted in full conformity with his duties under the Constitution. Accordingly, we would reverse the order of the District Court.

Epilogue

Blackstone, whose *Commentaries on the Laws of England* (first published in 1765–69) formed a vital part of the legal education in the United States from Colonial times on (even Marshall's meager library contained a copy), had declared that "so great is the regard of the Law for private property, that it will not authorize the least violation of it; no, not even for the common good of the whole community." The relationship and reconciliation of law to property and to the common good *is* a problem that we, as a *nation* and as a *people*, attempted to solve as we moved from the old frontier of Frederick Jackson Turner to the new frontier of President Kennedy. In a way, then, it can be said that the theme of this entire volume has been the fate of Blackstone's statement in America. It is, of course, inevitable that any institution attempting such a reconciliation would, of necessity, perhaps even as a matter of right, create opposition. For it must never be forgotten that institutions do not move or act by themselves. Men are involved; they direct and guide these institutions, and they in turn act not in a vacuum of time, place, or ideology but meet the challenges that confront them with a gift of definition and expression, a mastery of detail, and a subtlety of mind that in no small measure reflect their own ideas and values as the product of the age they represent. And since there is always a gap between that age and the dynamics of the present (be it "left" or "right"), it must be bridged in such a way as to belie the ancient adage that the dead always rule the living.

Yet, despite the fact, as Mr. Justice Brandeis pointed out in his dissent in *Whitney* v. *California* [274 U.S. 357 (1927)], that "those who won our independence by revolution were not cowards [and hence] did not fear political change," it is also true as Mr. Justice Holmes stated in his dissent in *Tyson* v. *Banton* [273 U.S. 418 (1927)] that people and interests are made "uncomfortable by change." And when the stakes are high, as they are when economic power is involved, sophistry and dialectics alone are not adequate to meet the situation. Ideas are not separate from ideals, for both reflect values which can say, as John Jay said, that "the people who own the country ought to govern it," or, as a more recent writer has stated, "that property is a function of inequality"—but in either event they are "weapons" for good or ill; for progress or *status quo*; for the "general will" or for selected private interests; for a class society frightened by the specter of

267

change or for a society welcoming change as a symbol of meeting new problems in a new world.

If what has gone before has whetted one's appetite for more, the selected readings below might indicate a direction to take to discover for oneself the men, the concepts, the age in which all this occurred and which we, as beneficiaries, must somehow re-evaluate—and only by such a re-evaluation can we leave our mark, and hence our legacy, on a problem which those who come after us will also confront.

Suggested Reading

General

Alfange, Dean. *The Supreme Court and the National Will*. New York: Doubleday and Company, Inc., 1937.

Beard, Charles A. *An Economic Interpretation of The Constitution of the United States*. New York: The Macmillan Company, 1913, 1935.

Becker, Carl L. *The Declaration of Independence: A Study in the History of Political Ideas*. New York: Alfred A. Knopf, Inc., 1942.

Boudin, Louis B. *Government by Judiciary*. New York: William Godwin, Inc., 1932.

Brown, Robert E. *Charles Beard and The Constitution: A Critical Analysis of "An Economic Interpretation of the Constitution."* Princeton: Princeton University Press, 1956.

Cardozo, Benjamin N. *The Nature of the Judicial Process*. New Haven: Yale University Press, 1921.

Haines, Charles G., and Sherwood, Foster. *The Role of the Supreme Court in American Government and Politics*. Berkeley: University of California Press, 2 vols.: Vol. 1, 1944; Vol. 2, 1957.

Harris, Robert J. *The Quest for Equality: The Constitution, Congress, and The Supreme Court*. Baton Rouge: Louisiana State University Press, 1960.

Hartz, Louis. *Economic Policy and Democratic Thought*. Cambridge: Harvard University Press, 1948.

Jackson, Robert H. *The Struggle for Judicial Supremacy*. New York: Alfred A. Knopf, Inc., 1941.

McCloskey, Robert G., ed. *Essays in Constitutional Law*. New York: Alfred A. Knopf, Inc., 1957.

McCloskey, Robert G. *The American Supreme Court*. Chicago: University of Chicago Press, 1960.

Mendelson, Wallace. *Capitalism, Democracy, and The Supreme Court*. New York: Appleton-Century-Crofts, Inc., 1960.

Rossiter, Clinton. *Seedtime of the Republic: The Origin of The American Tradition of Political Liberty.* New York: Harcourt, Brace and Co., Inc., 1953.

Rottschaefer, Henry. *The Constitution and Socio-Economic Change.* Ann Arbor: University of Michigan Law School, 1948.

Schmidhauser, John R. *The Supreme Court: Its Politics, Personalities, and Procedures.* New York: Holt, Rinehart and Winston, Inc., 1960.

Schubert, Glendon A. *Constitutional Politics:* The Political Behavior of Supreme Court Justices and the Constitutional Policies that they Make. New York: Holt, Rinehart and Winston, Inc., 1960.

Smith, Howard R. *Democracy and The Public Interest.* Athens, Georgia: University of Georgia Press, 1960.

Swisher, Carl B. *The Supreme Court in Modern Role.* New York: New York University Press, 1958.

The Federalist, edited by Jacob E. Cooke. Middletown, Connecticut: Wesleyan University Press, 1961.

Twiss, Benjamin R. *Lawyers and the Constitution.* Princeton: Princeton University Press, 1942.

Warren, Charles. *The Supreme Court in United States History.* Boston: Little, Brown and Company, 1937.

Westin, Alan F., ed. *The Supreme Court: Views from Inside.* New York: W. W. Norton and Company, Inc., 1961.

Special Studies

Carr, Robert K. *The Supreme Court and Judicial Review.* New York: Rinehart and Company, 1942.

Corwin, Edward S. *The Commerce Power versus States Rights.* Princeton: Princeton University Press, 1936.

Corwin, Edward S. *Court over Constitution:* A Study of Judicial Review as an Instrument of Popular Government. Princeton: Princeton University Press, 1938.

Flack, Horace E. *The Adoption of the 14th Amendment.* Baltimore: The Johns Hopkins University Press, 1908.

Frankfurter, Felix. *The Commerce Clause under Marshall, Taney and Waite.* Chapel Hill, North Carolina: The University of North Carolina Press, 1937.

Gavit, Bernard C. *The Commerce Clause of The United States Constitution.* Bloomington, Indiana: Principia Press, 1932.

James, Joseph B. *The Framing of the Fourteenth Amendment.* Urbana, Illinois: University of Illinois Press, 1957.

Pritchett, C. Herman. *Congress versus the Supreme Court, 1957–1960.* Minneapolis: University of Minnesota Press, 1961.

Ribble, Frederick D. G. *State and National Power Over Commerce.* New York: Columbia University Press, 1937.

Schmidhauser, John R. *The Supreme Court as Final Arbiter in Federal-State Relations 1789–1957.* Chapel Hill, North Carolina: The University of North Carolina Press, 1958.

Wood, Virginia. *Due Process of Law.* Baton Rouge: Louisiana State University Press, 1951.

Wright, Benjamin F., Jr. *The Contract Clause of the Constitution.* Cambridge: Harvard University Press, 1938.

Biographies of Supreme Court Justices

Beveridge, Albert J. *The Life of John Marshall.* Boston: Little, Brown and Company, 1916.

Bowen, Catherine D. *Yankee from Olympus: Justice Holmes and His Family.* Boston: Little, Brown and Company, 1944.

Clark, Floyd B. *The Constitutional Doctrines of Justice Harlan.* Baltimore: The Johns Hopkins Press, 1915.

Curtis, Charles P., Jr. *Lions under The Throne.* Boston: Houghton Mifflin Company, 1947.

Douglas, William O. *We The Judges.* New York: Doubleday and Company, Inc., 1956.

Dunham, Allison, and Kurland, Philip B. *Mr. Justice.* Chicago: University of Chicago Press, 1956.

Ewing, Cortey A. M. *The Judges of the Supreme Court 1789–1937.* Minneapolis: University of Minnesota Press, 1938.

Fairman, Charles. *Mr. Justice Miller and The Supreme Court 1862–1890.* Cambridge: Harvard University Press, 1939.

Frank, John P. *Mr. Justice Black: The Man and His Opinions.* New York: Alfred A. Knopf, Inc., 1949.

Frank, John P. *Marble Palace: The Supreme Court in American Life.* New York: Alfred A. Knopf, Inc., 1958.

Freund, Paul A. *On Understanding The Supreme Court.* Boston: Little, Brown and Company, 1949.

King, Willard L. *Melville Western Fuller, Chief Justice of the United States, 1888–1910.* New York: The Macmillan Company, 1950.

Konefsky, Samuel J. *The Constitutional World of Mr. Justice Frankfurter.* New York: The Macmillan Company, 1949.

Mason, Alpheus T. *Brandeis: A Free Man's Life.* New York: The Viking Press, Inc., 1956.

Mason, Alpheus T. *Harlan Fiske Stone: Pillar of the Law.* New York: The Viking Press, Inc., 1956.

Mason, Alpheus T. *The Supreme Court from Taft to Warren.* Baton Rouge: Louisiana State University Press, 1958.

McCune, Wesley. *The Nine Young Men.* New York: Harper and Brothers, 1947.

McLean, Joseph E. *William Rufus Day.* New York: New York University Press, 1946.

Morgan, Donald G. *Justice William Johnson, The First Dissenter.* Columbia, South Carolina: University of South Carolina Press, 1954.

Paschal, Joel F. *Mr. Justice Sutherland, A Man Against the State.* Princeton: Princeton University Press, 1951.

Pringle, Henry F. *The Life and Times of William Howard Taft.* New York: Farrar and Rinehart, 1939.

Pritchett, C. Herman. *The Roosevelt Court: A Study in Judicial Politics and Values.* New York: The Macmillan Company, 1948.

Pusey, Merlo J. *Charles Evans Hughes.* New York: The Macmillan Company, 1951.

Rodell, Fred. *Nine Men: A Political History of the Supreme Court 1790–1955.* New York: Random House, Inc., 1955.

Swisher, Carl B. *Stephen J. Field: Craftsman of the Law.* Washington, D.C.: Brookings Institution, 1930.

Swisher, Carl B. *Roger B. Taney.* New York: The Macmillan Company, 1936.

Trimble, Bruce R. *Chief Justice Waite.* Princeton: Princeton University Press, 1938.

Weisenburger, Francis P. *The Life of John McLean: A Politician on the United States Supreme Court.* Columbus, Ohio: Ohio State University Press, 1937.

Selected Law Review Articles and Periodicals

Abel, A. S. "The Commerce Clause in The Constitutional Convention and in Contemporary Comment," 25 *Minnesota Law Review,* 432 (1941).

Anderson, William. "The Intention of the Framers: A Note on Constitutional Interpretation," 49 *American Political Science Review,* 340 (1955).

Beard, Charles A. "Supreme Court—Usurper or Guarantee," 27 *Political Science Quarterly,* 1 (1912).

Bikle, H. Wolf. "The Commerce Power and Hammer *v*. Dagenhart," 67 *University of Pennsylvania Law Review*, 21 (1919).

Brown, Roy A. "Due Process of Law, Police Power, and the Supreme Court," 40 *Harvard Law Review*, 943 (1927).

Bunn, Charles. "The Impairment of Contracts: Mortgage and Insurance Moratoria," 1 *University of Chicago Law Review*, 249 (1933).

Cheatham, Elliott E. "Mr. Justice Stone and The Constitution," 36 *California Law Review*, 351 (1936).

Cohen, Harry. "Minimum Wage Legislation and the Adkins Case," 2 *New York University Law Quarterly Review*, 48 (1925).

Collier, Charles S. "Judicial Bootstraps and The General Welfare Clause," 4 *George Washington Law Review*, 211 (1936).

Corwin, Edward S. "Marbury *v*. Madison and the Doctrine of Judicial Review," 12 *Michigan Law Review*, 538 (1914).

Culp, Maurice S. "Methods of Attacking Unconstitutional Legislation," 22 *Virginia Law Review*, 723 (1936).

Cushman, Robert E. "Constitutional Decisions by a Bare Majority of the Court," 19 *Michigan Law Review*, 771 (1921).

Douglas, William O. "Stare Decisis," 49 *California Law Review*, 735 (1949).

Dowling, Noel T. "Interstate Commerce and State Power," 27 *Virginia Law Review*, 1 (1940).

Epstein, Leon. "Economic Predilections of Justice Douglas," 1949 *Wisconsin Law Review*, 531.

Finkelstein, Maurice. "Judicial Self-Limitation," 37 *Harvard Law Review*, 338 (1924); 39 *Harvard Law Review*, 221 (1925).

Frank, John P. "Appointment of Supreme Court Justices," 1941 *Wisconsin Law Review*, 344.

Frankfurter, Felix. "Taney and the Commerce Clause," 49 *Harvard Law Review*, 1286 (1936).

Graham, Howard J. "The Conspiracy Theory of the 14th Amendment," 48 *Yale Law Journal* (1938).

Green, Thomas F., Jr. "Constitutionality of the A.A.A. Processing Tax," 14 *North Carolina Law Review*, 28 (1935).

Hart, Henry M., Jr. "The Gold Clause in United States Bonds," 48 *Harvard Law Review*, 1057 (1935).

Lerner, Max. "The Supreme Court and American Capitalism," 42 *Yale Law Journal*, 668 (1933).

McAllister, Breck P. "Lord Hale and Business Affected With a Public Interest," 43 *Harvard Law Review*, 759 (1930).

Morris, Stanley C. "What Are the Privileges and Immunities of Citizens of the United States?" 28 *West Virginia Law Quarterly*, 38 (1921).

Pound, Roscoe. "Liberty of Contract," 18 *Yale Law Journal*, 454 (1909).

Powell, Thomas Reed. "Child Labor, Congress, and The Constitution," 1 *North Carolina Law Review*, 61 (1922).

Powell, Thomas Reed. "The Judiciality of Minimum Wage Legislation," 37 *Harvard Law Review*, 545 (1924).

Prosser, William L. "The Minnesota Mortgage Moratorium," 7 *Southern California Law Review*, 353 (1934).

Rubinstein, Louis B. "Curbing the Supreme Court—State Experiences and Federal Proposals," 35 *Michigan Law Review*, 762 (1937).

Shelton, Thomas W. "The Police Power versus Property Rights," 7 *Virginia Law Review*, 455 (1921).

Stern, Robert L. "The Commerce Clause and The National Economy 1933–1946," 59 *Harvard Law Review*, 645 (1946).

Stern, Robert L. "The Problems of Yesteryear—Commerce and Due Process," 4 *Vanderbilt Law Review*, 446 (1951).

Warren, Charles. "The New 'Liberty' Under The Fourteenth Amendment," 39 *Harvard Law Review*, 431 (1926).